Contents

PART 1

PARTS, PIECES, AND TOTALS   1

PART 3   PRACTICE MAKES PERFECT   305

Preface

To be effective in the real estate business, one must become comfortable and proficient with a variety of mathematical calculations. As a real estate professional you will need to know how to compute taxes, expenses, income, and the many other figures that are a part of most real estate transactions.

This text was written to assist you in developing a higher level of competence in working with the numbers and calculations used in the real estate business. Whether you are new or experienced in the applied use of mathematics, the information that follows will help you sharpen your skills by explaining the kinds of calculations encountered during typical real estate activities. Read the explanations and directions carefully. Study the examples and work the many practice problems by applying what has been illustrated in the instructional material. With a little patience, concentration, and effort, you will become comfortable with these essential calculations.

Great care has been taken to create a text that is accurate. Because practices are often regional, check the laws and procedures applicable to your area. This is particularly true regarding legal descriptions, ad valorem taxes, transfer taxes, prorations, financing, and settlement procedures.

Special thanks for the development of this 8th edition goes out to contributing author William J. Kukla, ABR, CRS, GRI, SFR, SRES and an associate professor at Collin College in Frisco, Texas, where he instructs real estate math and other subjects. For their additional contributions in making this an accurate and reliable text, the authors and editors would like to thank the following individuals for their advice and suggestions:

C. Wallace Cater, San Jacinto College, Houston, Texas
Thomas C. Engblom, Prairie State College, Crete, Illinois
Ignacio Gonzalez, Mendocino Community College, Ukiah, California
Joseph Irwin, Houston Community College, Houston, Texas
David M. Maull, Long and Foster Institute of Real Estate, Ocean City, Maryland
Mike McBride, Sr., The Real Estate School, Houston, Texas
Kevin S. Morris, San Jacinto College, Houston, Texas
Herb Schroeder, North Harris College, Houston, Texas
Don Shrum, The Real Estate School, Houston, Texas
Ron Smith, San Antonio Board of REALTORS®, San Antonio, Texas
Ralph Tamper, The Real Estate School, Houston, Texas
Donna Townsend, M.A., CETC Unlimited, Inc., Garland, Texas
Darline Waring, Real Estate Educators Association, Summerville, South Carolina

Introduction: How to Use This Book

REFRESHING YOUR MATH SKILLS

This textbook starts at a basic math level. This is done in order to provide a quick review of fundamental concepts and to offer support to students who may experience anxiety in dealing with mathematical concepts. If you feel comfortable with this introductory material, please continue on to the first chapter.

The subject matter has been broken down into a series of numbered exercises. By following the exercises, you can learn the mathematics involved in real estate transactions. Additionally, the text is designed to be augmented by classroom instruction.

The sequence of the exercises is important and designed to help you learn more efficiently. For that reason, you should not skip around in the book.

Almost every exercise presents a learning task that requires some response from you. You should be able to work the exercise or problem and arrive at the correct answer, provided you follow directions precisely, read the material, and work through the book with care.

This kind of book also provides immediate feedback by giving you the answers to the questions asked. These answers have been placed at the end of each chapter. Immediate feedback is an important part of the learning process and will enable you to determine readily how your learning is progressing.

Do not look at the correct answer until after you have solved the problem and recorded your own answer. If you look before answering, you will only impair your own learning. If you make an error, be sure you know why before proceeding to the next exercise.

Finally, this text is designed to be used as a workbook. Work through each problem by writing your computations in the spaces provided. This helps both you and your instructor when discussing the solutions.

Many students using this workbook may find themselves in a math class after several years of doing little math, and it is to this group that this text is primarily addressed. Some students have also built up a fear of math over the years. The exercises in this text will help eliminate those fears and give students sufficient knowledge and self-confidence not only to pass a licensing examination but also to function at a higher level in the field of real estate.

Neatness Counts

One reason many people have trouble with number skills is that they do not practice neatness and legibility in working out problems. For example, it is easier to make a mistake in adding these numbers:

$$
\begin{array}{r}
\$12,345.67 \\
89.10 \\
5,432.08 \\
\underline{76543} \\
\end{array}
$$

than it is to add the same numbers when care has been given to neatness and legibility:

$$
\begin{array}{r}
\$12,345.67 \\
89.10 \\
5,432.08 \\
\underline{76,543.00} \\
\end{array}
$$

It is important to keep decimal points in a straight vertical line and write each digit of each number directly beneath the one above it.

ORDER OF OPERATIONS

Problems that feature multiple operations involve several calculations. Remember, parentheses are used to identify the calculation(s) to be completed first. Also, usually you multiply or divide before adding or subtracting.

EXAMPLE:

$$(5 \times 6) + (3 \times 4) - (6 \times 6) = ?$$

$$5 \times 6 = 30 \quad 3 \times 4 = 12 \quad 6 \times 6 = 36$$

$$30 + 12 - 36 = 6$$

USING UNITS OF MEASUREMENT

Just as you cannot compare apples to oranges, numbers must be of the same kind or in the same form before you perform mathematical functions. To add these unlike things:

$$\frac{1}{2} + \frac{1}{3}$$

or

$$4 \text{ inches} + 5 \text{ feet}$$

or

$$6 \text{ acres} + 7,890 \text{ square feet}$$

You must first put each into similar form, such as:

$$\frac{1}{2} = \frac{3}{6} \text{ and } \frac{1}{3} = \frac{2}{6}$$

$$\frac{3}{6} + \frac{2}{6} = \frac{5}{6}$$

or

$$4 \text{ inches} = \frac{4}{12} \text{ or } \frac{1}{3} \text{ foot}$$

$$\frac{1}{3} \text{ foot} + 5 \text{ feet} = 5\frac{1}{3} \text{ feet}$$

6 acres = 43,560 square feet × 6 = 261,360 square feet

261,360 square feet + 7,890 square feet = 269,250 square feet

E X A M P L E :   Suppose you measure your house for carpet and find that you need 1,125 square feet. However, the carpet store prices its carpeting per square yard. What will it cost if you choose carpet priced at $18 per square yard? First, you must change the units of measurement so they are alike. For simplicity, convert the 1,125 square feet to square yards. There are nine square feet in each square yard, so:

$$\frac{1,125 \text{ square feet}}{9 \text{ square feet/square yard}} = 125 \text{ square yards}$$

Now the units agree, so you can compute the price:

125 square yards × $18/square yard = $2,250

Converting Units of Measurement

Convert inches to feet by dividing inches by 12

E X A M P L E :   9 inches = $\frac{9}{12}$ = 0.75 feet

Convert *yards* to *feet* by multiplying yards by 3.

E X A M P L E :   39 yards × 3 = 117 feet

Convert *fractions* to *decimals* by dividing the top number (numerator) by the bottom number (denominator).

E X A M P L E : $\frac{3}{4}$ = 0.75

Convert *percentages* to *decimals* by moving the decimal point two places to the left and adding zeros as necessary.

E X A M P L E :   22.5% = 0.225
                             80% = 0.80
                             3.4% = 0.034

Convert *square feet* to *square yards* by dividing square feet by 9.

EXAMPLE:
$$\frac{1{,}125 \text{ square feet}}{9} = 125 \text{ square yards}$$

Convert *cubic feet* to *cubic yards* by dividing cubic feet by 27.

EXAMPLE:
$$\frac{486 \text{ cubic feet}}{27} = 18 \text{ cubic yards}$$

BALANCING EQUATIONS

When you progress into simple equations, remember that the "=" (equals) sign means absolutely that. You would not write:

$$1 + 2 = 3 + 4$$

because 3 does *not* equal 7. It is *not* equality or an equation. It is an inequality because it is out of balance. For the equation to balance, the numbers on the left-hand side of the "=" must actually equal the numbers on the right-hand side. This power of the "=" sign cannot be over-stated. While the numbers on either side of the "=" sign must balance, the numbers can be expressed in different formats. Examples will show up at numerous times throughout this text. Balancing numbers on either side of the "=" sign is one of the most useful problem-solving tools in this text and in math generally. If you think of an equation as a child's see-saw, or a balance scale, you recognize that both sides must have the same weight at the same point or the system will tilt and not balance. Therefore, if you wish to consider the preceding example as an equation (where both sides are equal), you must either add something to the left side or subtract something from the right side:

$$1 + 2 = 3 + 4 \qquad \text{No}$$
$$3 = 7 \qquad \text{No}$$

but

$$3 + 4 = 7 \qquad \text{Yes}$$

or

$$3 = 7 - 3 - 1 \qquad \text{Yes}$$

If two numbers are related by addition (+), you can break that relationship by subtraction (−); if they are related by multiplication (×), you can break that relationship by division (÷). To illustrate:

$$5 + 6 = 7 + x$$
$$11 = 7 + x$$

The 7 is joined to x (the unknown number) by addition; therefore, you must use subtraction to balance the equation. In solving this problem, separate the knowns from the unknowns. You know all but the x. Recalling the illustration of the scale, if you subtract 7 from the right-hand side of the equal sign, the equation will be out of balance unless you also subtract 7 from the left-hand side:

$$11 = 7 + x$$
$$\underline{-7 \quad -7} \leftarrow \text{subtracted from both sides}$$
$$4 = 0 + x$$
$$4 = x$$

Sometimes, it is the simplest things that we forget over the years. For instance:

$$(7 - 7) \times 8 = ?$$

Here, you must first perform the operation indicated within the parentheses. In this case, that result is zero. To finish the calculation, zero times any other number is zero.

Also remember that a number divided by itself always equals one. So that:

$$\frac{1}{1} = 1 \text{ or } \frac{486}{486} = 1$$

You can also treat units of measurement or algebraic letters the same way. For example:

$$\frac{\text{feet}}{\text{feet}} = 1$$

$$\frac{\text{acres}}{\text{acres}} = 1$$

$$\frac{x}{x} = 1$$

$$\frac{LW}{LW} = 1$$

Having obtained the answer 1 from any of these operations, if you then multiply that 1 by any other number or unit of measurement or algebraic symbol, the answer is that same number or unit of measurement or algebraic symbol:

$$1 \times 23 = 23$$
$$1 \times \text{foot} = \text{foot}$$
$$1 \times y = y$$
$$1 \times \text{Anything} = \text{Anything}$$

Also, it is important to recall that you cannot divide a number by zero. However, if you divide a number by 1, you have not changed the value of the original number.

Remember:

Always review your work and do a "sanity check" on the answer.

Please do not become anxious or nervous because these rules are treated so sparingly. Remember, this is merely a basic review of things you may already know or had learned in earlier math courses. The purpose of this introduction is to stir your memory, as well as to introduce briefly some of the material to be covered in following chapters.

Finally, in this text, you will encounter two basic types of exercises. These include number problems—which are already set up in the proper format, such as 123 + 456 = ?—and word, or stated, problems. To gain proficiency in solving word problems, which are similar to real-world situations, begin by analyzing each problem. Learn to recognize certain *function indicators*, or key words that indicate whether you should add, subtract, multiply, or divide.

Math Language	
Addition indicators:	plus, more than, sum, increase, and
Subtraction indicators:	minus, less than, decrease, difference, take away
Multiplication indicators:	of, times, factor, product
Division indicators:	quotient, fraction, reciprocal

Units of Measure	
Linear measure	12 inches = 1 foot
	36 inches = 3 feet = 1 yard
	5,280 feet = 1,760 yards = 1 mile
Square measure	144 square inches = 1 square foot
	1,296 square inches = 9 square feet = 1 square yard
	To convert square feet to square yards, divide square feet by 9.
	To convert square yards to square feet, multiply square yards by 9.
Cubic measure	1,728 cubic inches = 1 cubic foot
	46,656 cubic inches = 27 cubic feet = 1 cubic yard
	To convert cubic feet to cubic yards, divide cubic feet by 27.
	To convert cubic yards to cubic feet, multiply cubic yards by 27.
Circular measure	360 degrees = a circle
	60 minutes = 1 degree
	60 seconds = 1 minute
Surveyor's measure	43,560 square feet = 1 acre
	640 acres = 1 square mile = 1 section
	36 sections = a township
	1 township = 36 square miles

Basic Formulas	
For calculating area	Length (in feet) × Width (in feet) = Square feet
	To convert square feet to square yards, divide square feet by 9.
For calculating volume	Length (in feet) × Width (in feet) × Height (in feet) = Cubic feet
	To convert cubic feet to cubic yards, divide cubic feet by 27.
For calculating part, total, or rate* (percent)	Total × Rate (percent) = Part
	Part ÷ Rate (percent) = Total
	Part ÷ Total = Rate (percent)

* Rate may be expressed as a percent or a decimal equivalent. This will be more thoroughly discussed in Chapter 1.

MATH SKILLS ASSESSMENT

When you have solved these problems, check your answers against the answers that follow.

1. 12 feet + 18 inches + 15 yards = ? feet
    a. 45
    b. 58.5
    c. 59
    d. 60

2. [(8 × 9) − (6 × 7) + (4 ÷ 2)] × 2 = ?
    a. 48
    b. 56
    c. 64
    d. 65

3. How many cubic feet are in a carton measuring 6 feet, 8 inches by 3 yards by 4½ inches?
    a. 20.5
    b. 22.5
    c. 23.05
    d. 24.65

4. How many square yards of carpet will be required to cover a living room 18 feet by 20 feet and a dining room 15 feet by 12 feet?
    a. 40
    b. 60
    c. 360
    d. 540

5. What is the total square footage of the following three contiguous tracts of land?

    Tract one is 3 sections. Tract two is 10 acres. Tract three is 130,680 square feet.
    a. 566,388
    b. 696,960
    c. 83,678,760
    d. 84,201,480

6. What is ⅔ plus ½ plus ⅝ plus ¾?
    a. 0.647
    b. ¹¹⁄₁₇
    c. 2½
    d. 2.542

7. How many square feet are in a lot that measures 75 feet across the front and is 150 feet deep?
    a. 150
    b. 450
    c. 1,250
    d. 11,250

8. If a property sold for $250,000, what total commission would the seller pay at 5½ percent?
    a. $12,000
    b. $12,500
    c. $13,750
    d. $15,000

9. A man owns 2 acres of commercially zoned property. If he sells it for $8.25 per square foot, what is the selling price?
    a. $26,626.11
    b. $79,860
    c. $718,740
    d. $6,468,660

10. How many acres are in 653,400 square feet?
    a. 15
    b. 24
    c. 29.6
    d. 150.207

SOLUTIONS: MATH SKILLS ASSESSMENT

1. (b) 18 inches ÷ 12 = 1.5 feet

   15 yards × 3 = 45 feet

   12 feet + 1.5 feet + 45 feet = 58.5 feet

2. (c) (8 × 9 = 72   6 × 7 = 42   4 ÷ 2 = 2)

   (72 − 42 + 2) × 2 = 64

   32 × 2 = 64

3. (b) 8 inches ÷ 12 = 0.667 feet

   0.667 feet + 6 feet = 6.667 feet

   3 yards × 3 = 9 feet

   4.5 inches ÷ 12 = 0.375 feet

   6.667 feet × 9 feet × 0.375 feet = 22.5 cubic feet

4. (b) 18 feet × 20 feet = 360 square feet

   15 feet × 12 feet = 180 square feet

   360 square feet + 180 square feet =

   540 square feet

   540 square feet ÷ 9 = 60 square yards

5. (d) 3 sections × 640 acres × 43,560 square feet = 83,635,200 square feet

   10 acres × 43,560 square feet = 435,600 square feet

   83,635,200 square feet + 435,600 square feet + 130,680 square feet =
   84,201,480 square feet

6. (d) 2 ÷ 3 = 0.667   1 ÷ 2 = 0.5   5 ÷ 8

   = 0.625   3 ÷ 4 = 0.75

   0.667 + 0.50 + 0.625 + 0.75 = 2.542

7. (d) 75 feet × 150 feet = 11,250 square feet

8. (c) 5.5% = 0.055

   0.055 × $250,000 = $13,750

9. (c) 2 acres × 43,560 square feet = 87,120 square feet

   87,120 square feet × $8.25 = $718,740

10. (a) 653,400 square feet ÷ 43,560 square feet = 15 acres

STUDY STRATEGY

It seems appropriate to open our discussion of study strategy with a brief mention of an experience common among students of mathematics: math anxiety. Many people are intimidated by the anticipated difficulties of working math problems, to the point of becoming victims of stress. This book does not provide a psychological analysis of this matter. Rather, the author has set forth some principles that will help students feel more comfortable with math.

Anxiety about one's ability to perform mathematical calculations is very common. Even college mathematics majors often dread math examinations! If this is so, how can this book effectively help people who have no special background in mathematics, who suddenly find that they need some basic math skills to pass a licensing examination or function more competently as a real estate licensee?

In an article "Mastering Math Anxiety," Dr. William L. Boyd of Hardin Simmons University and Elizabeth A. Cox of Howard Payne University offer several ideas:

1. Math anxiety is not an indication of inability. It may be more an indication of excessive concern over possible embarrassment in front of our peers, our instructors, our clients, or our customers.
2. Aptitude in math is not necessarily something we are born with. Our aptitude may reflect our attitude rather than our genes. The old saying, "If you think you can or if you think you can't, you're right," certainly applies in this situation. Through practice and study, we can build our skills and our confidence.
3. Self-image can affect our performance in many areas, including math. Make a determined effort to develop your competency in math. If others expect you to fail, don't fall to the level of their expectations. Rather, rise to the level of your potential through a little extra effort.
4. Learn to congratulate yourself on your successes. When you arrive at a correct solution, make a point of giving yourself the credit for your success.[1]

STRATEGIES THAT WILL BENEFIT YOU

1. Take time to carefully read and understand what is being asked. Consider the information given in the problem and decide how each portion relates to the solution. Careful and thoughtful reading will help you understand the problem.
2. Learn to discard those facts that have no bearing on the solution. You do this automatically in many areas of everyday life. Begin to practice this in math, also, by evaluating each bit of information.
3. Make a special effort to be neat. Sloppy figures carelessly jotted down are an invitation to error.
4. Develop a systematic approach to problem solving. Consider each aspect of the problem in its proper place and do not jump to conclusions. It is better to write down each step in the solution, no matter how trivial it seems, than to rely on performing a calculation "in your head."

---

[1]   William L. Boyd and Elizabeth A. Cox, "Mastering Math Anxiety," Real Estate Today (March/April 1984): 41–43

5. Learn to restate the problem in your own words. By doing this, you can remove many obstacles to a solution. In fact, once you state the problem correctly, you need only perform the mechanics of the arithmetic accurately to arrive at the solution.

6. Form the habit of checking and double-checking your work. It is all too easy to make a mistake out of carelessness. If an error in calculation is not discovered, your solution will be flawed.

7. Request help when you need it. Don't hesitate to ask questions! Others who are puzzled by the same point as you may be reluctant to say so. If you ask the question, you and the entire class benefit.

8. Learn to question the reasonableness of the solution. If the answer you have calculated seems unlikely, perhaps it is. Your common sense can often reveal an error due to carelessness.

9. Become proficient with your calculator. The calculator's accuracy helps ensure your good results. But never rely on the machine to do it all! Learn to make your own estimate and compare this with the results of the calculator. If the calculator's answer does not seem plausible, clear the display and work the problem again, making sure you enter the figures and operations correctly. The calculator does not replace you. But it is a wonderful tool to enhance your professionalism.

Exercises and Examinations

Each chapter concludes with Additional Practice problems, consisting of a series of multiple-choice questions patterned after those found in state licensing examinations. Solutions to the problems appear at the end of each chapter.

At the end of this book, you will find a 50-question Review Exam. Answers to all examination questions are in the Answer Key at the end of the exam. These solutions show the step-by-step mathematics.

Local Practices

Because this textbook is used nationally, some of the situations described may differ from practice in your local area. Therefore, your instructor may wish to skip the portions of the textbook that are not applicable to your area.

CALCULATORS

Calculators can be divided into general types by the form of logic they use. Chain logic and algebraic logic are the most common types. The difference between these two types of logic is illustrated as follows. Consider the calculation:

$$2 + 3 \times 4 = ?$$

If the numbers and arithmetic functions are entered into the chain logic calculator as shown above, the answer will be 20; on the algebraic logic calculator, the answer will be 14. The chain logic sees the data entered in the order that it is keyed in:

$$2 + 3 = 5, \text{then}$$
$$5 \times 4 = 20,$$

whereas the algebraic logic follows the order of multiplication, division, addition, and then subtraction:

$$3 \times 4 = 12, \text{ then}$$
$$12 + 2 = 14.$$

Some chain logic calculators use reverse polish notation, where there is no "=" key. In its place is an "ENTER" key. Use the previous example of:

$$2 + 3 \times 4 = ?$$

Data on most calculators are entered using chain logic, just as the user would write it:

Press	2	
Press	+	
Press	3	
Press	×	
Press	4	Answer
Press =	20	

The reverse polish notation keystrokes, however, are as follows:

2		
enter		
3		
+		
4		Answer
×	20	

Because most calculators use chain logic, the examples in this text are designed to fit that type. However, you should thoroughly study the manual furnished with your calculator for instructions on how to enter data.

Four-Function versus Multifunction Calculators

A basic four-function calculator will certainly be sufficient for this course, but if you plan to purchase a calculator, it is strongly recommended that you spend a few more dollars on one having financial functions, such as the BA II PLUS from Texas Instruments, or the 10B II from HP. This type of calculator can be easily identified by these additional keys:

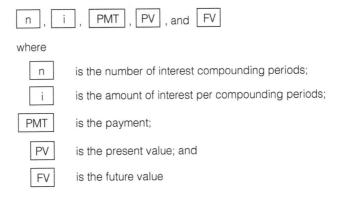

n , i , PMT , PV , and FV

where

n	is the number of interest compounding periods;
i	is the amount of interest per compounding periods;
PMT	is the payment;
PV	is the present value; and
FV	is the future value

When attempting to use these tools, carefully study the owner's manual that comes with the machine to become thoroughly familiar with its features and capabilities. Keep the handy reference card with the machine in case you forget how to perform one of the functions. Be extra careful when entering numbers on the keypad of your calculator. It is not unusual for students to understand the math yet get the wrong answer because of operator error in using the calculator.

Differences in Rounding

Calculators may display six, eight, or ten digits, but regardless of the number, a calculator retains far more numbers than are displayed in a calculation. For example, if a calculator displays six digits, or single numbers, such as 123456, the calculator knows what follows the last digit, or single number, displayed. This last digit depends on whether the calculator *rounds* or *truncates*. Consider an answer of 123456.7. This calculation displayed on a six-digit calculator will be 123457 for a calculator that rounds and 123456 for a calculator that truncates.

Rounds means that if the next digit not displayed is *less than 5*, the last digit to be displayed remains the same. However, if the next digit not displayed is *greater than or equal to 5*, the last digit to be displayed will be *increased* or *rounded up* to the next larger digit.

Truncates means that regardless of the value of the next digit not displayed, the calculator merely cuts off the display, or truncates, when its display capacity is full. Greater calculator accuracy can be obtained if you leave the answer on the display and perform the next calculation by depressing additional keys, rather than if you write down the answer, clear the calculator, and re-enter that number as the first step of the following calculation. Leaving the answer on the display is the default approach and the one that is recommended. Re-entering numbers significantly increases your chances of making unnecessary errors! Your instructor will direct you as to how many digits beyond the decimal point to leave in an answer. It will be important at times to get the exact answer to, let's say, 5 decimal places for a learning moment. Other times having a close answer because of rounding differences will be acceptable. Again, using calculators with similar function capability will allow for identical answers between instructor and student.

PARTS, PIECES, AND TOTALS

CHAPTER

Fractions, Decimals, and Percentages

Most of the math you will encounter in real estate will require you to be comfortable with fractions, decimals, and percentages. When you have completed your work in Chapter 1, you will be able to

- accurately convert percentages and fractions to decimals,

- apply the basic formulas for problem solving for part, total, or rate (percentage), and

- use the following diagram as a tool in solving total, rate, and part problems:

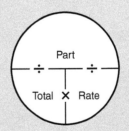

A UNIFORM APPROACH

CALCULATE

At the outset of this chapter, a word about calculators is important. Most calculators have a "%" key, which requires fewer keystrokes to calculate percentages. However, owing to the various ways of entering data on different calculators, this text will use decimals in all problems and solutions.

A *part* of the *total* can be expressed as a

Fraction

E X A M P L E :   25 is ¼ of 100

Decimal

E X A M P L E :   25 is 0.25 of 100

Percentage

E X A M P L E :   25 is 25 percent of 100

To convert a fraction to a decimal, divide the fraction's top number (numerator) by its bottom number (denominator).

E X A M P L E : $\dfrac{7}{8}$

$7 \div 8 = 0.875$

To convert a *percentage* to a *decimal*, move the decimal two places to the left and drop the percent sign. If necessary, add zeros.

E X A M P L E : $75\% = 0.75$
$3.5\% = 0.035$

CONVERTING FRACTIONS TO DECIMALS

Proper Fractions

FRACTION
$\dfrac{1 \leftarrow \text{numerator}}{2 \leftarrow \text{denominator}}$

A proper fraction is one whose numerator is less than its denominator. It is a part of the total, and its value is *always* less than 1.

E X A M P L E : $\dfrac{1}{2}$ $\dfrac{1}{4}$ $\dfrac{1}{5}$ $\dfrac{5}{19}$ $\dfrac{7}{100}$

The *numerator* (top number of a fraction) indicates how many parts there are in the fractional amount.

The *denominator* (bottom number of a fraction) indicates how many parts make up the whole.

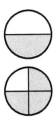

The fraction ½ means 1 part of the total that is made up of 2 equal parts.

The fraction ¾ means 3 parts of the total that is made up of 4 equal parts.

The figure 35 percent means 35 parts out of the 100 parts that make up the total. It can also be written as the fraction ³⁵⁄₁₀₀ or as the decimal 0.35.

1. Convert the following fractions to decimals.

   a. $\dfrac{1}{5}$

   b. $\dfrac{1}{2}$

   c. $\dfrac{5}{100}$

   d. $\dfrac{97}{100}$

NOTE: The answers for chapter problems are located at the end of each chapter.

Improper Fractions

An improper fraction is one whose numerator is equal to or greater than its denominator. The value of an improper fraction is *more* than 1.

E X A M P L E : $\dfrac{5}{4}$ $\dfrac{10}{9}$ $\dfrac{81}{71}$

To change an improper fraction to a whole number, divide the numerator by the denominator. Any part left over will be shown as a decimal.

E X A M P L E :   Change ⅘ to a whole number.

$$\frac{8}{5} = 1.6$$

2. Change the following improper fractions to whole numbers.

a. $\dfrac{5}{4}$

b. $\dfrac{9}{2}$

c. $\dfrac{16}{5}$

d. $\dfrac{26}{9}$

Mixed Numbers

A mixed number (a whole number and a fraction), such as 1¾, can be changed by converting the fraction to a decimal (divide the top number by the bottom number) and adding back the whole number.

E X A M P L E :

1¾

$$3 \div 4 = 0.75$$
$$0.75 + 1 = 1.75$$

3. Change the following mixed numbers to whole numbers plus decimal equivalents.

    a. $2\frac{1}{4}$

    b. $3\frac{2}{3}$

    c. $8\frac{1}{4}$

    d. $1\frac{5}{6}$

4. Convert the following fractions to decimals.

    a. $\frac{8}{5}$

    b. $\frac{9}{10}$

    c. $6\frac{7}{8}$

    d. $\frac{34}{100}$

    e. $\frac{52}{10}$

    f. $\frac{3}{12}$

    g. $\frac{81}{71}$

> **h.** 13⅓
>
> **i.** 9¾
>
> **j.** 108⁶⁄₁₀

PERCENTAGES

Percent (%) means per hundred or per hundred parts.

per means *by the*
cent means *100*

For example, 50 percent means 50 parts out of a total of 100 parts (100 parts equal 1 whole), and 100 percent means all 100 of the 100 total parts, or 1 whole unit. Throughout this book, we shall refer to 100 percent as the total.

50 percent means ⁵⁰⁄₁₀₀, or 0.50, or ½
100 percent means ¹⁰⁰⁄₁₀₀, or 1.00, or 1

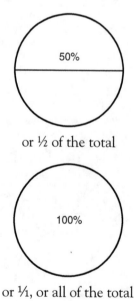

or ½ of the total

or ⅟₁, or all of the total

CONVERTING DECIMALS TO PERCENTAGES

To change a decimal into a percentage, move the decimal point two places to the right and add the "%" sign. Therefore, you can change the number 0.50 to a percentage by moving the decimal point (.) two places or two digits to the right and adding the percent symbol (%). By moving the decimal point two places to the right, you actually multiply 0.50 by 100, to equal 50. When you add the percent symbol, you multiply the 0.50 by 100 according to the definition of percent, so that 0.50 equals 50 percent. Thus, the actual value hasn't changed at all, or you are back where you started.

Any percentage that is less than 100 percent means a part or fraction of 100 percent or the entire unit. For example, because 99 percent means 99 parts out of 100 parts, it is less than the total.

EXAMPLES:
$$0.10 = 10\%$$
$$1.00 = 100\%$$
$$0.98 = 98\%$$
$$0.987 = 98.7\%$$

5. Change the following decimals to percentages.

  a. 0.37

  b. 0.09

  c. 0.080

  d. 0.10000

  e. 0.7095

  f. 0.01010

CONVERTING PERCENTAGES TO DECIMALS

The process of converting percentages to decimals is the reverse of the one you just completed. To change a percentage to a decimal, move the decimal point two places to the left and drop the "%" sign.

All numbers have a decimal point, although it is usually not shown when only zeros follow it.

E X A M P L E S :   99 is really 99.0
                                         6 is really 6.0
                                    $1 is the same as $1.00

So, percentages can be readily converted to decimals.

E X A M P L E S :   99% = 99.0% = 0.990 = 0.99
                                   6% = 6.0% = 0.060 = 0.06
                                   5% = 5.0% = 0.050 = 0.05
                                   70% = 70.0% = 0.700 = 0.70

Note: Adding zeros to the *right* of a decimal point after the last figure does not change the value of the number.

6. Change the following percentages to decimals.

    a. 1 percent

    b. 65 percent

    c. 75.5 percent

    d. 2.1 percent

7. Complete the following chart.

	Simple Fraction	Decimal	Percent
a.			75%
b.	$\frac{1}{10}$		
c.		0.80	
d.	$\frac{1}{8}$		
e.	$\frac{3}{10}$		
f.			67%
g.		0.56	

ADDING DECIMALS

Decimals are added like whole numbers. When you add longhand, decimal points must be lined up under each other, as shown in the examples.

EXAMPLES:

```
   300         0.3          0.891
     5         0.005        0.05
 + 590       + 0.59       + 0.063
   895         0.895        1.004
```

8. Add the following decimals.

a.
```
   0.05
   0.2
 + 0.695
```

b.
```
   0.0983
   0.006
 + 0.32
```

SUBTRACTING DECIMALS

Decimals are subtracted like whole numbers. Again, line up the decimal points.

EXAMPLES:

```
   861         0.861        0.549
 - 190       - 0.190      - 0.32
   671         0.671        0.229
```

9. Practice adding and subtracting the following decimals.

   a. 0.23 + 0.051 + 0.6

   b. 0.941 – 0.6

   c. 0.588 – 0.007

   d. 0.741 + 0.005 + 0.72

MULTIPLYING DECIMALS

Decimal numbers are multiplied like whole numbers. When entering decimal numbers in your calculator, be sure to enter the decimal point in the proper place. A misplaced decimal point will yield an incorrect answer.

10. Practice multiplying the following decimals.

   a. 0.100 × 3

   b. 4.006 × 0.51

   c. 0.035 × 0.012

DIVIDING DECIMALS

You may divide a whole number by a decimal number.

E X A M P L E :   6 ÷ 0.50 = 12

You may divide a decimal number by a whole number.

EXAMPLE: $0.50 \div 6 = 0.083$

11. Practice dividing the following decimals.

    a. $2 \div 0.08$

    b. $0.36 \div 3$

    c. $0.15 \div 5$

PERCENTAGE PROBLEMS

Percentage problems usually involve three elements: the rate (percent), the total, and the part.

EXAMPLE:

5% of 200 is 10
↑   ↑   ↑
rate total part

A problem involving percentages is really a multiplication problem. To solve the problem in the example below, first convert the percentage to a decimal, then multiply.

EXAMPLE:

What is 25 percent of 300?
$25\% = 0.25$
$300 \times 0.25 = 75$

A generalized formula for solving percentage problems follows:

Total × Rate (percent) = Part
(*or*, Rate × Total = Part; the order of multiplication is not important)

To solve a percentage problem, you must know the value of two of the three elements of this formula. The value that you must find is called the *unknown* (most often shown in the formula as *x*).

EXAMPLE: A woman purchased a secondhand Smartphone at 45 percent of the original cost, which was $150. What did she pay for the unit?

Rate × Total = Part
$45\% \times \$150 = Part$
$45 \times \$150 = \$67.50$

12. If a man spent 60 percent of his total savings of $3,000, how much did he spend? What formula will you use to solve the problem?

FORMULAS

When working with problems involving percentages or decimal equivalents, use one of the formulas discussed below.

When you know the total (which always equals 100 percent) and you know the rate (percent) and you are looking for the part, use the following formula:

$$\text{Total} \times \text{Rate (percent)} = \text{Part}$$

When you know the part and the total and you are looking for the rate, use the following formula:

$$\text{Part} \div \text{Total} = \text{Rate}$$

When you know the part and the rate and you are looking for the total, use the following formula:

$$\text{Part} \div \text{Rate} = \text{Total}$$

Many math students have found it helpful to use a circle as an aid in solving for the answer. The part always goes in the top section; the total goes in the lower left section, and the rate (perhaps expressed as a percentage or a decimal equivalent) goes in the lower right section. Enter the two known numbers in their proper places and solve for the unknown by either dividing or multiplying. If your known numbers include one above and one below the horizontal line, divide the top number by the bottom number to solve for the unknown. If your known numbers are side by side, separated by the vertical line, multiply.

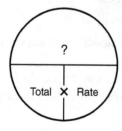

Total × Rate = Part

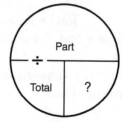

Part ÷ Total = Rate

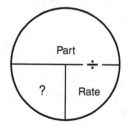

Part ÷ Rate = Total

E X A M P L E :   An acre contains 43,560 square feet. How many square feet are in 40 percent of an acre?

40% = 0.40

43,560 square feet (total) × 0.40 (rate) = 17,424 square feet (part)

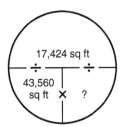

E X A M P L E :   What percentage of an acre does 17,424 square feet represent?

17,424 square feet (part) ÷ 43,560 square feet (total) = 0.40 (rate)

Remember, if you want to express the rate as a percentage, you must move the decimal point two places to the right and add the "%" sign. Therefore, in the above example, 0.40 equals 40 percent.

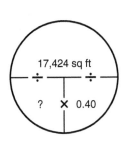

E X A M P L E :   17,424 square feet is 40 percent of an acre. How many square feet are in an acre?

40% = 0.40

17,424 square feet (part) ÷ 0.40 (rate) = 43,560 square feet (total)

Always remember the following information:

- You can find any one of the three elements if you know the other two.
- The long horizontal line separates the circle into division areas.
- The short vertical line separates the circle into multiplication areas.

Knowing this, you can cover the portion of the circle that contains the unknown (or what you are looking for), then perform the indicated multiplication or division.

Applying this to the previous example in which you found 40 percent of 43,560, the part was the unknown. If you cover up the portion of the circle labeled *Part*, you are left with *Total* and *Rate*, separated by a multiplication function.

However, in the example in which you determined 17,424 square feet to be 40 percent of an acre, you looked for the rate. By covering up this part of the circle, you leave *Part* and *Total* separated by a division function.

This shortcut can be used to solve many types of problems, including the following.

E X A M P L E :   If 30 percent of the 1,500 houses in your area have four bedrooms, how many houses have four bedrooms?

We know:

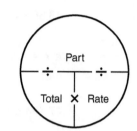

    Rate = 30%, or 0.30
    Total = 1,500

Cover *Part*.

    Total × Rate = ?
    1,500 × 0.30 = 450

13. If 20 percent (or 500) of the houses in your area are less than five years old, how many houses are there in your area?

14. Which of the following values is missing from this problem: 6 is 12 percent of what number?

   a. Total

   b. Part

   c. Rate

   d. None of the above

E X A M P L E :   30 is 50 percent of what number?

The suggested problem-solving sequence is as follows:

Step 1. Read the problem carefully.

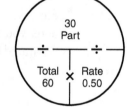

Step 2. Analyze the problem, pick out the important factors, and put those factors into a simplified question.

Step 3. State the formula. $\dfrac{\text{Part}}{\text{Rate}} = \text{Total}$

Step 4. Substitute values. $\dfrac{30}{0.50} = \text{Total}$

Step 5. Solve the problem. $\dfrac{30}{0.50} = 60$

15. 1,500 is 300 percent of what number?

   Step 1. Read the problem.

   Step 2. Analyze the problem.

   Step 3. State the formula.

   Step 4. Substitute values.

   Step 5. Solve the problem.

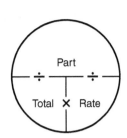

16. Try to solve the following problem without referring back to material in this chapter: $125,000 is 20 percent of what dollar amount?

E X A M P L E :   What percentage of 56 is 14?

Note that the rate element is missing. By covering "Rate" in the circle to the right, you know to divide the part by the total:

$$\frac{\text{Part}}{\text{Total}} = \text{Rate}$$

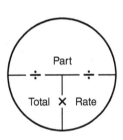

Next, substitute the values from the problem for those elements in the new formula:

$$\frac{14}{56} = \text{Rate}$$

Then divide:

$$\frac{14}{56} = 0.25$$

Finally, convert the decimal to a percentage:

$$0.25 = 25\%$$

E X A M P L E :   What percentage of 87 is 17?

Step 1. Read the problem.

Step 2. Analyze the problem.

Step 3. State the formula. $\dfrac{\text{Part}}{\text{Total}} = \text{Rate}$

Step 4. Substitute values. $\dfrac{17}{87} = \text{Rate}$

Step 5. Solve the problem. $\dfrac{17}{87} = 0.195$

Step 6. Convert the decimal 0.195 = 19.5% to a percentage.

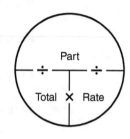

17. What percentage of 95 is 18?

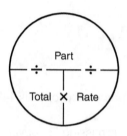

REMEMBER: This diagram will help you remember the formulas for part, total, and rate.

Because *Part* is over *Rate*, make a fraction of these two elements when looking for a *Total*.

$$\frac{\text{Part}}{\text{Rate}} = \text{Total}$$

Because *Part* is over *Total*, make a fraction of these two elements when looking for a *Rate*.

$$\frac{\text{Part}}{\text{Total}} = \text{Rate}$$

Because *Rate* and *Total* are both in the lower part of the diagram, multiply these two elements when looking for a *Part*.

$$\text{Total} \times \text{Rate} = \text{Part}$$

Now try some problems related to the real estate field, using what you've learned about rates (percentages), fractions, and decimals.

18. A lot is assessed at 42 percent of its market value of $150,000. What is its assessed value?

    a. What is the unknown value?

    b. State the formula.

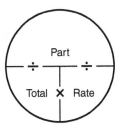

    c. Solve the problem.

19. A bank-owned property sold for $81,000, which was 90 percent of the original price. What was the original list price?

    a. What is the unknown value?

    b. State the formula.

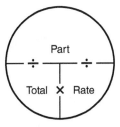

    c. Solve the problem.

20. A property has an assessed value of $115,000. If the assessment is 34 percent of market value, what is the market value?

    a. What is the unknown value?

    b. State the formula.

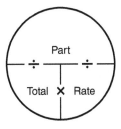

    c. Solve the problem. Round off your answer to the nearest hundred dollars.

PERCENTAGE OF CHANGE

If you hear that houses in your area have increased in value by 3 percent during the past year, and you know that the average price of houses sold last year was $160,000, what portion of the sales price was related to the increased value?

You know the total and rate, so:

$$\$160,000 \times 0.03 = \$4,800$$

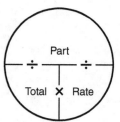

Consider a similar problem from a different starting point: If the average price of one-bedroom condominiums today is $70,000 compared to $60,000 one year ago, what is the percentage of change?

First, find the *amount* of change: $70,000 − $60,000 = $10,000. Next, use the circle aid to find the *rate* of change:

$$\$10,000 \text{ (part)} \div \$60,000 \text{ (total)} = 0.167, \text{ or } 16.7\% \text{ (rate)}$$

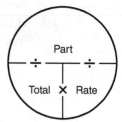

Or remember this general formula:

$$\frac{\text{New value} - \text{Old value}}{\text{Old value}} = \text{Rate (percent) of change}$$

21. If there were 800 foreclosures this year and 700 last year, what is the percentage of change?

Suppose that this year's foreclosures numbered 700 and last year's equaled 800. What is the percentage of change?

New value = 700
Old value = 800
Difference <100> (negative number)
<100> (part) ÷ 800 (total) = <0.125> (rate), or <12.5%>

This means the change occurred in a downward, or negative, direction.

REMEMBER: Fractions, decimals, and percentages are all interrelated.

To convert a *fraction* to a *decimal*, divide the top number by the bottom number.

To convert a *percentage* to a *decimal*, move the decimal two places to the left and drop the "%" sign.

To convert a *decimal* to a *percentage*, move the decimal two places to the right and add the "%" sign.

To solve problems, always *convert fractions* and *percentages* to *decimals*.

Use the circle aid to assist you in solving for an unknown number.

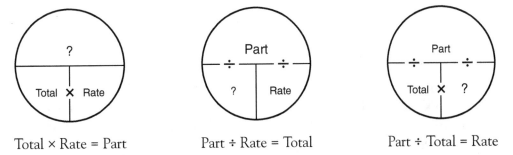

Total × Rate = Part   Part ÷ Rate = Total   Part ÷ Total = Rate

In real estate practice, you will use these formulas in many situations. The following circles show some of the more common ones.

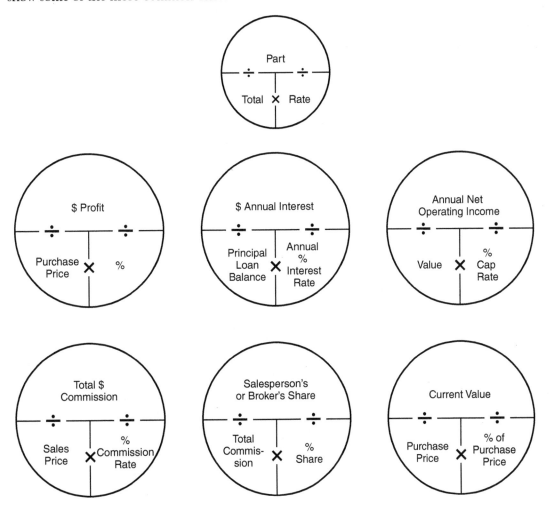

You have now completed Chapter 1. If you feel you understand the material in this chapter, work the Additional Practice problems that follow. After working the problems, you may find that you are unsure about certain points. Review those points before continuing with the next chapter.

ADDITIONAL PRACTICE

When you have finished these problems, check your answers against those at the end of the chapter. If you miss any of the problems, review this chapter before going on to the next chapter.

1. Convert the following to decimals.
   a. 3.875% =
   b. $^{20}\!/_{10}$ =
   c. $^{1}\!/_{6}$ =
   d. 5% =
   e. 348% =

2. A house listed for $155,000 and sold for 90 percent of the list price. What was the sales price of the house?
   a. $139,500
   b. $147,250
   c. $160,500
   d. $170,500

3. A seller sold his house for $240,000, which was 92 percent of the list price. What did the house list for? Round off your answer to the nearest hundred dollars.
   a. $220,800
   b. $226,780
   c. $260,800
   d. $260,900

4. A buyer purchased her home for $250,000. She later sold it for $281,250. What percentage profit did she realize on her investment?
   a. 11.1 percent
   b. 12.5 percent
   c. 14.5 percent
   d. 110 percent

5. A salesperson at ABC Realty sold 86 of the 432 homes sold by her firm last year. What percentage of the sales did she complete?
   a. 19 percent
   b. 19.9 percent
   c. 20 percent
   d. 23.3 percent

6. The assessed value of a residence is 22 percent of the market value of $398,000, which is
   a. $87,300.
   b. $87,485.
   c. $87,560.
   d. $88,500.

7. The office in which you work sold 128 homes last year. You sold 29 of these. Your sales are what percentage of the total sales?
   a. 21.7 percent
   b. 22.7 percent
   c. 44.13 percent
   d. 46.07 percent

8. What percentage of $800 is $420?
   a. 1.9 percent
   b. 5.25 percent
   c. 19 percent
   d. 52.5 percent

9. Mr. Smith received a proceeds check at closing for $67,500. His lot sold for $75,000. What percentage of the sales price did Mr. Smith receive?
   a. 11.1 percent
   b. 90 percent
   c. 94 percent
   d. 99 percent

10. A property is assessed at 53 percent of market value. What is the assessed value of that property if it has a market value of $125,000?
    a. $53,000
    b. $66,250
    c. $191,250
    d. $235,849

11. What percentage of 125,000 is 18,750?
    a. 1.7 percent
    b. 6.67 percent
    c. 15 percent
    d. 85 percent

12. Which of the following formulas is *NOT* correct?
    a. Part × Rate = Total
    b. Rate × Total = Part
    c. Part ÷ Total = Rate
    d. Part ÷ Rate = Total

13. A local company bought a commercial lot for $600,000 and sold it several years later for $1,080,000. The company's percentage of profit is
    a. 44 percent.
    b. 80 percent.
    c. 100 percent.
    d. 180 percent.

14. One-sixth is equal to what percent?
    a. 1.65 percent
    b. 8.25 percent
    c. 12.5 percent
    d. 16.7 percent

15. What is the decimal equivalent of 3¾?
    a. 0.0375
    b. 0.375
    c. 3.75
    d. 37.5

16. You sold 58 of the 256 homes sold by your real estate company last year. What percentage of the homes did others sell in your company?
    a. 53.93 percent
    b. 55.87 percent
    c. 77.3 percent
    d. 78.3 percent

17. What percentage of 250,000 is 37,500?
    a. 1.7 percent
    b. 6.67 percent
    c. 15 percent
    d. 85 percent

18. A 64,000-square-foot hillside lot is to be sub-divided and sold. One-fourth of the lot is too steep to be useful; ³⁄₁₆ of the lot is taken up by a small stream. The remaining area is flat. If ⅛ of the usable area is reserved for roads, how many square feet of usable area are left?
    a. 28,000 square feet
    b. 31,500 square feet
    c. 36,000 square feet
    d. 36,750 square feet

19. A tract of land is divided as follows: ¼ is being developed into building lots; ⁵⁄₁₀ is being cultivated; the remaining portion is 112.5 acres. How many total acres are there in the parcel?
    a. 84 acres
    b. 150 acres
    c. 225 acres
    d. 450 acres

20. You want to build a 2,000-square-foot single-story home on a 7,500 square-foot-lot. A city ordinance permits up to 35 percent of the lot to be covered by structures. Your proposed development will cover approximately how much of the lot?
    a. 18 percent
    b. 27 percent
    c. 37 percent
    d. 40 percent

SOLUTIONS: PROBLEMS IN CHAPTER 1

1. a. $\frac{1}{5} = 0.2$
   b. $\frac{1}{2} = 0.5$
   c. $\frac{5}{100} = 0.05$
   d. $\frac{97}{100} = 0.97$

2. a. $\frac{5}{4} = 1.25$
   b. $\frac{9}{2} = 4.5$
   c. $\frac{16}{5} = 3.2$
   d. $\frac{26}{9} = 2.889$

3. a. $1 \div 4 = 0.25$
      $0.25 + 2 = 2.25$
   b. $2 \div 3 = 0.667$
      $0.667 + 3 = 3.667$
   c. $1 \div 4 = 0.25$
      $0.25 + 8 = 8.25$
   d. $5 \div 6 = 0.833$
      $0.833 + 1 = 1.833$

4. a. $8 \div 5 = 1.6$
   b. $9 \div 10 = 0.9$
   c. $7 \div 8 = 0.875$
      $0.875 + 6 = 6.875$
   d. $34 \div 100 = 0.34$
   e. $52 \div 10 = 5.2$
   f. $3 \div 12 = 0.25$
   g. $81 \div 71 = 1.141$
   h. $13 \div 3 = 4.333$
   i. $3 \div 4 = 0.75$
      $0.75 + 9 = 9.75$
   j. $6 \div 10 = 0.6$
      $0.6 + 108 = 108.6$

5. a. 0.37 = 37%

b. 0.09 = 9%

c. 0.080 = 8%

d. 0.10000 = 10%

e. 0.7095 = 70.95%

f. 0.01010 = 1.01%

6. a. 1% = 0.01

b. 65% = 0.65

c. 75.5% = 0.755

d. 2.1% = 0.021

7.

	Simple Fraction	Decimal	Percent
a.	$\frac{75}{100} = \frac{3}{4}$	0.75	75%
b.	$\frac{1}{10}$	0.10	10%
c.	$\frac{80}{100} = \frac{4}{5}$	0.80	80%
d.	$\frac{1}{8}$	0.125	12.5%
e.	$\frac{3}{10}$	0.30	30%
f.	$\frac{67}{100}$	0.67	67%
g.	$\frac{56}{100} = \frac{14}{25}$	0.56	56%

8. a. 0.05 + 0.2 + 0.695 = 0.945

b. 0.983 + 0.006 + 0.32 = 1.309

9. a. 0.23 + 0.051 + 0.6 = 0.881

b. 0.941 − 0.6 = 0.341

c. 0.588 − 0.007 = 0.581

d. 0.741 + 0.005 + 0.72 = 1.466

10. a. 0.100 × 3 = 0.3

b. 4.006 × 0.51 = 2.04306

c. 0.035 × 0.012 = 0.00042

11. a. 2 ÷ 0.08 = 25

b. 0.36 ÷ 3 = 0.12

c. 0.15 ÷ 5 = 0.03

12.   Total × Rate = Part
$3,000 × 0.60 = $1,800

13.   500 (part) ÷ 0.20 (rate) = 2,500 – houses (total)

14. a. Total. The part is 6 and the rate is 12 percent.
Therefore, 6 divided by 0.12 equals 50

15.   Step 3. Part ÷ Rate = Total
Step 4. 1,500 (part) ÷ 3 (rate) = Total
Step 5. 1,500 (part) ÷ 3 (rate) = 500 (total)

16.   Part ÷ Rate = Total
20% = 0.20
$125,000 ÷ 0.20 = $625,000

17.   Part ÷ Total = Rate
18 ÷ 95 = 0.189473684 or 18.9%

18. a. Part
    b. Total × Rate = Part
    c. $150,000 × 0.42 = $63,000

19. a. Total
    b. Part ÷ Rate = Total
    c. 90% = 0.90
$81,000 ÷ 0.90 = $90,000

20. a. Total
    b. Part ÷ Rate = Total
    c. 34% = 0.34
$115,000 ÷ 0.34 = $338,235.29 or $338,235 (rounded)

21.   800 – 700 = 100
100 ÷ 700 = 0.143 or 14.3%

SOLUTIONS: ADDITIONAL PRACTICE

1. a. 3.875% = 0.03875
    b. $^{20}/_{10}$ = 2
    c. $^{1}/_{6}$ = 0.167
    d. 5% = 0.05
    e. 348% = 3.48

2. (a) 0.9 × $155,000 = $139,500

3. (d) $240,000 ÷ 0.92 = $260,869.57 or $260,900 (rounded)

4. (b) $281,250 – $250,000 = $31,250
        $31,250 ÷ $250,000 = 0.125 or 12.5%

5. (b) 86 ÷ 432 = 0.199074 or 19.9%

6. (c) $398,000 × 0.22 = $87,560

7. (b) 29 ÷ 128 = 0.227 or 22.7%

8. (d) $420 ÷ $800 = 0.525 or 52.5%

9. (b) $67,500 ÷ $75,000 = 0.9 or 90%

10. (b) $125,000 × 0.53 = $66,250

11. (c) 18,750 ÷ 125,000 = 0.15 or 15%

12. (a) Part × Rate = Total

13. (b) $1,080,000 – $600,000 = $480,000
        $480,000 ÷ $600,000 = 0.8 or 80%

14. (d) 1 ÷ 6 = 0.167 or 16.7%

15. (c) 3 ÷ 4 = 0.75
        0.75 + 3 = 3.75

16. (c) $256 - 58 = 198$
$198 \div 256 = 0.773 = 77.3\%$

17. (c) $37{,}500 \div 250{,}000 = 0.15 = 15\%$

18. (b) $1 \div 4 = 0.25$
$3 \div 16 = 0.1875$
$1 \div 8 = 0.125$
$64{,}000 \times 0.25 = 16{,}000$
$64{,}000 \times 0.1875 = 12{,}000$
$64{,}000 - 16{,}000 - 12{,}000 = 36{,}000$
$36{,}000 \times 0.125 = 4{,}500$
$36{,}000 - 4{,}500 = 31{,}500$ square feet

19. (d) $1 \div 4 = 0.25$
$5 \div 10 = 0.5$
$0.25 + 0.5 = 0.75$
$1 - 0.75 = 0.25$
$112.5 \div 0.25 = 450$ acres

20. (b) $2{,}000 \div 7{,}500 = 0.267$ or 27%

2

List Price, Sales Price, and Net Price

In this chapter, you will continue your work with the three basic formulas involving total, rate, and part. You will apply what you learned in the previous chapter to solve for sales price, list price, and net price in various real estate settings. When you have completed your work, you will be able to

■ help a seller price a property to recover the initial investment and achieve the profit margin desired, and

■ mathematically help a seller establish the correct asking price to give the seller the desired net, to cover expenses, and to pay the broker.

Remember and use the equation you learned in the preceding chapter:

$$\text{Total} \times \text{Rate} = \text{Part}$$
$$\text{Part} \div \text{Rate} = \text{Total}$$
$$\text{Part} \div \text{Total} = \text{Rate}$$

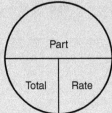

In this chapter—which deals with list price, gross sales price, and net sales price—the three components of this basic formula will generally mean:

Total	Gross selling price (what the buyer pays for the real estate)
Part	Net amount (what the seller receives for the property—gross price minus expenses, commission, etc.)
Rate	100 percent minus deductions (expenses, commission, etc.)

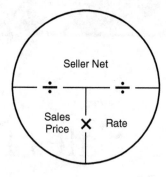

Seller net ÷ Sales Price = Rate
Seller net ÷ Rate = Sales price
Sales price × Rate = Seller net

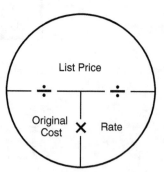

List price ÷ Cost = Rate
List price ÷ Rate = Cost
Cost × Rate = List price

Gross sales price ÷ List price = Rate
Gross sales price ÷ Rate = List price
List price × Rate = Gross sales price

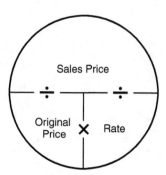

Sales price ÷ Cost = Rate
Sales price ÷ Rate = Cost
Cost × Rate = Sales price

If you have any difficulty understanding the problems in this chapter, review Chapter 1.

1. What are the formulas for solving for total and rate if:

    Total × Rate = Part

    a. _____ ÷ _____ = Total

    b. _____ ÷ _____ = Rate

PROBLEM-SOLVING STRATEGY

This section begins with a look at how to solve word problems. Here is the strategy you should use:

Step 1. Read the problem carefully.

Step 2. Analyze the problem, pick out the important factors, and put those factors into a simplified question, disregarding unimportant factors.

Step 3. Choose the proper formula for the problem.

Step 4. Substitute numbers for the known elements of the formula.

Step 5. Solve the problem.

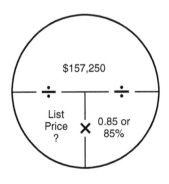

If you use this strategy throughout this chapter, and wherever it applies in this book, you'll have an easier time solving word problems.

E X A M P L E :   Now apply the problem-solving strategy to a typical real estate problem.

Step 1. Read the following problem carefully:

A house sold for $157,250, which was 85 percent of the original list price.
At what price was the house originally listed?

Step 2. Analyze the problem, pick out the important factors, and put those factors into a simplified question.

$157,250 is 85 percent of what amount?

Step 3. Choose the proper formula for the problem.

$$\frac{\text{Part}}{\text{Rate}} = \text{Total}$$

Step 4. Substitute numbers for the known elements of the formula.

$$\frac{\$157,250}{85\%} = \text{Total}$$

Step 5. Solve the problem.

$$\frac{\$157,250}{0.85} = \$185,000$$

2. To prove the answer for the preceding example, ask whether $157,250 is really 85 percent of $185,000 (in other words, what is 85 percent of $185,000?)

   Complete the proof for this problem.

3. Now apply the problem-solving strategy to the following problem:

   The net amount received by the seller for his house after the broker had deducted a sales commission of 6 percent was $55,648. What was the selling price? (Because net sales proceeds and commission rates are known, find the gross sales price.)

   The gross sales price is the total, or 100 percent. If the broker receives 6 percent of the sales price, the seller will net the remainder of 100 percent, which is 94 percent (100% − 6% = 94%).

   a. Analyze and restate the problem.

   b. Choose the proper formula.

   c. Substitute.

   d. Solve.

   Remember, the selling price, or *gross* selling price, is the agreed-on total price to be paid by the purchaser. After the broker deducts the sales commission and expenses from this amount, the seller will be entitled to the net amount of the selling proceeds.

4. Prove your answer for problem 3.

5. Solve the following problem. Work it out step by step, as you've learned:

   Ms. Cornelius paid $75,500 for a lot. She now wants to sell it and net a 20 percent profit after paying the broker's commission. She gave the broker the listing at 5 percent. What would the selling price have to be?

6. Calculate the amount of the broker's commission on the sale of the property described in problem 5, assuming Ms. Cornelius received her required selling price.

7. If you bought a house for $164,000, which was 20 percent less than the list price, what percentage of profit would you net on your investment if you sold the house for 10 percent more than the original list price? What would your profit amount to in dollars?

8. A vacant lot listed for $154,000. The seller received $142,500 net after the broker deducted $7,500 for her 5 percent commission. What was the selling price of this lot?

NET PRICE

Frequently, sellers will tell the broker or salesperson that they want to net a certain amount from the sale of their property. In fact, all sellers have an idea of what they think their property is worth, what they want to net, and/or what they need to net. The broker or salesperson must then estimate the total costs to be paid by the seller and determine whether the resulting list price is within the market value range. The process of taking a new listing will always include a discussion on the numbers!

EXAMPLE: For how much must a debt-free property sell if the owner wants to net $80,000 after paying the broker a 7 percent sales commission and estimated selling expenses equal to 4 percent of the selling price?

First, you must total the expenses:

$$
\begin{array}{ll}
7\% & \text{commission} \\
\underline{+\,4\%} & \text{closing costs} \\
11\% & \text{total sales expenses}
\end{array}
$$

If the seller is to net $80,000, that amount must equal the list price less the sales expenses, or

$$\text{List price} - \text{Sales expenses} = \text{Net}$$

The list price equals 100 percent and the sales expenses equal 11 percent; therefore, the $80,000 net price must equal 89 percent (100% − 11%) of the list price. To express this mathematically:

$$\$80{,}000 = 89\% \text{ of list price}$$

Apply this formula:

$$\frac{\text{Part}}{\text{Rate}} = \text{Total}$$

Substitute numbers:

$$\frac{\$80{,}000}{0.89} = \text{Total}$$

Solve:

$$\frac{\$80{,}000}{0.89} = \$89{,}887.64$$

Proof:

Step 1.	$89,887.64	list price
	× 0.07	commission rate
	$ 6,292.13	commission

Step 2.	$89,887.64	list price
	× 0.04	other closing costs rate
	$ 3,595.51	other closing costs

Step 3.	$6,292.13	commission
	+ 3,595.51	other closing costs
	$ 9,887.64	total sales expenses

Step 4.	$ 89,887.64	list price
	− 9,887.64	total sales expenses
	$ 80,000.00	seller's net

The most common error made in this type of problem is for the salesperson to multiply the seller's net by the total sales expense rate, add this amount to the seller's net, and call this figure the list price. Let's see how this error would affect the calculations for this property:

Step 1.	$80,000	seller's net
	× 0.11	total sales expense rate
	$ 8,800	total sales expenses

Step 2.	$80,000	seller's net
	+ 8,800	total sales expenses
	$88,800	list price

Now, for the proof of error:

Step 1.	$ 88,800	list price
	× 0.11	total sales expense rate
	$ 9,768	total sales expenses

Step 2.	$88,800	list price
	− 9,768	total sales expenses
	$ 79,032	seller's net

Notice that the seller's net indicated in the proof is $79,032—$968 less than the seller wants. Understandably, the seller will be distressed. Who do you suppose the seller might expect to pay for this error?

RATE (PERCENTAGE) OF PROFIT

Another problem frequently encountered in the field is the situation described in the example below.

E X A M P L E :   If a person buys a house for 20 percent less than the list price, then sells it for the original list price, what rate of profit is realized?

First, let's examine two diagrams and visualize them as two rulers, one five inches long and one four inches long:

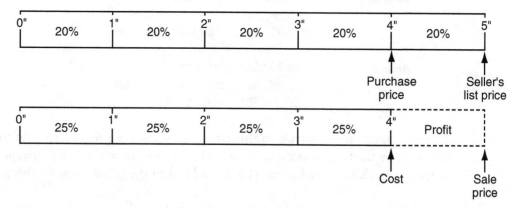

In the five-inch ruler, each of the one-inch increments, or divisions, represents 20 percent of the entire length of five inches to total 100 percent of the list price. Because the buyer paid 20 percent less than the seller's list price, the purchase price can be represented graphically as being at the four-inch mark on the five-inch ruler:

$$100\% - 20\% = 80\%, \text{ or the four-inch mark}$$

The buyer now owns the house, so his 80 percent price now represents 100 percent of his owning price or cost. This can be represented graphically as a four-inch ruler. His percentage of profit upon resale is calculated on his cost or his purchase price. When the house is resold for the original list price, this lengthens the four-inch ruler by an amount sufficient to make the ruler the original length of five inches. Therefore, this graphically displays the original list price:

1. Each inch on the five-inch ruler represents ⅕ (20 percent) of the total length of this ruler, yet
2. Each inch is the same absolute length regardless of which of the two rulers is used, but
3. Each inch on the four-inch ruler represents ¼ (25 percent) of the total length of this ruler.

By examining both diagrams, you can deduce the answer to the problem: 25 percent. In percentages, it depends on where you start, and that starting point is called the total. Therefore, the percentage of profit must be based on what the person paid for the house, not on the list price.

Remember:

Profit is based on the original cost or value.

However, the percentage of reduction must be based on the list price. It all depends on the starting point, the total. If you are still not clear at this point, you may wish to refer back to Chapter 1 and reread "Percentage of Change."

Now, let's suppose that the list price was $100,000 and that the buyer paid 20 percent less and resold at list price. What was the percentage of profit? First, find the buyer's cost, or price:

Step 1. 100% asking price – 20% = 80% purchase price

Step 2. 80% = 0.80

$100,000 (total) × 0.80 = $80,000 purchase price

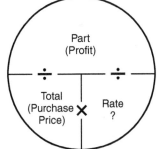

If the property is resold by the new owner at the original asking price, what percentage (rate) of profit would she realize?

Step 3.

$100,000	original asking price
– 80,000	current owner's purchase price
$ 20,000	profit

Step 4.

$\frac{\$20,000}{\$80,000}$ = 0.25 or 25% profit

Remember, the total is always the amount the current owner paid for the property, not what was asked.

9. A first-time buyer bought a house for $150,000 and resold it for $200,000. What rate of profit did she realize?

RATE (PERCENTAGE) OF LOSS

The rate of loss is calculated exactly the same as the profit except that the order of the numbers is reversed. In each case, the rate of profit or loss is figured in relation to the original number or amount.

Rate of loss (depreciation) will be explored in detail in Chapter 3.

ADDITIONAL PRACTICE

When you have finished these problems, check your answers against those at the end of the chapter. If you miss any of the problems, review this chapter before going on to Chapter 3.

1. A small lake cabin in a short sale sold for $62,250, which was 75 percent of the list price. What did the cabin list for?
   a. $74,700
   b. $77,812.50
   c. $81,250
   d. $83,000

2. A seller received a net of $73,320 for her lot after the broker deducted a 6 percent commission. What was the gross sales price of the lot?
   a. $69,654
   b. $77,179
   c. $77,720
   d. $78,000

3. Tom Harrington wishes to sell one of his lots at a 14 percent net profit. He purchased the deep lot for $37,000. What would the sales price have to be to give the Mr. Harrington a 14 percent profit after paying the selling broker a 5 percent commission on the sales price?
   a. $40,936
   b. $44,289
   c. $44,400
   d. $47,360

4. A seller received $321,480 after her broker deducted the agreed-on 6 percent commission. The sales price was
   a. $340,000.
   b. $340,786.
   c. $342,000.
   d. $345,000.

5. When the sale on a country house was closed, the broker withheld the seller's title expense of $250, after deducting his 6.5 percent commission of $5,200, and delivered to the seller a net check for
   a. $71,750.
   b. $74,550.
   c. $75,000.
   d. $84,350.

6. A house sold for $275,500, which was 95 percent of the listing price of
   a. $288,650.
   b. $290,000.
   c. $292,500.
   d. $296,000.

7. The owners want to make a 15 percent profit on the sale of their house after paying a 6 percent broker's fee. Their cost was $400,000. What will their sales price have to be (rounded to the nearest dollar)?
   a. $429,360
   b. $460,000
   c. $489,362
   d. $498,360

8. Indicate the net amount received by the seller from a sale in which the broker received a 6 percent commission of $3,480 and the seller's other expenses were $175 for the title insurance fee and $95 for the transfer tax and recording fee.
   a. $54,250
   b. $54,520
   c. $55,250
   d. $57,730

9. A woman bought a small condo for $188,000 with the intention of remodeling it, then selling it in two years for $250,000. How much can she spend on remodeling if the commission rate is 6 percent of the intended selling price, she has carrying costs of $4,000 and the profit she requires is $22,000?

   a. $19,675
   b. $20,900
   c. $21,000
   d. $24,000

10. A couple bought an 80-acre tract for $1,980 per acre. Taxes, insurance, and other expenses amounted to $12,400 per year. At the end of four years, the property was sold for a net price of 1.75 times its original cost. What was the net profit on the sale of the property?

    a. $32,000
    b. $69,200
    c. $118,800
    d. $227,600

11. Five years ago, an investor bought four lots for $50,000 each. A house was built on one of the lots at a cost of $160,000. The lot with the house recently sold for $255,000, and the remaining vacant lots sold for two times their original cost. The percentage of gross profit was

    a. 42.8 percent.
    b. 57.1 percent.
    c. 75 percent.
    d. 175 percent.

12. If you bought a house for the list price less 20 percent and sold the house for the list price, what percentage of profit would you make?

    a. 20 percent
    b. 25 percent
    c. 80 percent
    d. 125 percent

13. A house listed and sold for $160,000. The seller received $148,800 net after the broker deducted $11,200 for his commission. What rate of commission was the seller charged?

    a. 5 percent
    b. 5.5 percent
    c. 6 percent
    d. 7 percent

14. You bought a distressed bank-owned property for $125,000, which was 20 percent less than the list price, and you sold the house for 10 percent more than the original list price. The list price was

    a. $154,900.
    b. $156,250.
    c. $159,800.
    d. $162,600.

15. You bought a house for 15 percent less than the list price and sold it for the list price one month later. Your percentage of profit was

    a. 15 percent.
    b. 17.6 percent.
    c. 82.4 percent.
    d. 85 percent.

16. A seller wants to net $124,000 after paying the broker a 7 percent brokerage fee and $2,150 in closing costs. At what price must he sell his property (rounded to the nearest dollar)?

    a. $132,766
    b. $134,981
    c. $135,569
    d. $135,645

17. A home was listed for $215,900 and eventually sold for 7 percent less than the list price. What did the seller net after paying the broker a 5.75 percent brokerage fee and $9,300 in closing costs?

    a. $179,073
    b. $179,942
    c. $189,242
    d. $222,487

18. An owner wants to list a property for enough to allow for 5 percent of negotiating room and for paying you a fee of 6 percent. Closing costs usually equal about 3 percent of the sales price. The owner also wants to net 10 percent more than the $183,000 she paid for the property when she purchased it 2½ years ago. At what price should the property be listed? (Round your answer to the nearest dollar.)

   a. $201,300
   b. $221,029
   c. $232,080
   d. $232,851

19. After deducting $5,000 in closing costs and a 5 percent brokerage fee, the seller netted $170,750. What was the selling price?

   a. $179,737
   b. $184,538
   c. $184,737
   d. $185,000

20. A home sold for $108,000, which was 90 percent of the list price. What was the list price?

   a. $97,200
   b. $101,340
   c. $118,800
   d. $120,000

SOLUTIONS: PROBLEMS IN CHAPTER 2

1. a. Part ÷ Rate = Total
    b. Part ÷ Total = Rate

2. $185,000 × 0.85 = $157,250

3. a. $55,648 is 94 percent of what number?
    b. Part ÷ Rate = Total
    c. $55,648 ÷ 0.94 = Total
    d. $55,648 ÷ 0.94 = $59,200

4. $59,200 × 0.94 = $55,648
    or
    $59,200 × 0.06 = $3,552.00
    $59,200 − $3,552 = $55,648

5. $75,500 × 0.2 = $15,100
    $75,500 + $15,100 = $90,600
    100% − 5% = 95% or 0.95
    $90,600 ÷ 0.95 = $95,368.42

6. $95,368.42 × 0.05 = $4,768.42

7. $164,000 ÷ 0.8 = $205,000
    $205,000 × 1.1 = $225,500
    $225,500 − $164,000 = $61,500
    $61,500 ÷ $164,000 = 0.375 or 37.5%

8. $142,500 + $7,500 = $150,000
    or
    $142,500 ÷ 0.95 = $150,000

9. $200,000 − $150,000 = $50,000
    $50,000 ÷ $150,000 = 0.333 or 33.3%

SOLUTIONS: ADDITIONAL PRACTICE

1. (d) $62,250 ÷ 0.75 = $83,000

2. (d) $73,320 ÷ 0.94 = $78,000

3. (c) $37,000 × 1.14 = $42,180
    $42,180 ÷ 0.95 = $44,400

4. (c) $321,480 ÷ 0.94 = $342,000

5. (b) $5,200 ÷ 0.065 = $80,000
    $80,000 − $5,200 − $250 = $74,550

6. (b) $275,500 ÷ 0.95 = $290,000

7. (c) $400,000 × 1.15 = $460,000
    $460,000 ÷ 0.94 = $489,362 (rounded)

8. (a) $3,480 ÷ 0.06 = $58,000
    $58,000 − $3,480 − $175 − $95 = $54,250

9. (c) $250,000 × 0.06 = $15,000
    $250,000 − $188,000 − $22,000 − $15,000 − $4,000 = $21,000

10. (b) 80 acres × $1,980 = $158,400
    $12,400 × 4 = $49,600
    $158,400 × 1.75 = $277,200
    $277,200 − $158,400 − $49,600 = $69,200

11. (c) $50,000 × 4 = $200,000
    $200,000 + $160,000 = $360,000
    $150,000 × 2.5 = $375,000
    $375,000 + $255,000 = $630,000
    $630,000 − $360,000 = $270,000
    $270,000 ÷ $360,000 = 0.75 or 75%

12. (b) 100 − 80 = 20
    20 ÷ 80 = 0.25 or 25%

13. (d) $148,800 ÷ $160,000 = 0.93 or 93%
    100% − 93% = 7%
    or
    $11,200 ÷ $160,000 = 0.07 or 7%

14. (b) $125,000 ÷ 0.8 = $156,250

15. (b) 100 × 0.85 = 85
    100 − 85 = 15
    15 ÷ 85 = 0.17647 or 17.6%

16. (d) 100% − 7% = 93% = 0.93
    $124,000 + $2,150 = $126,150
    $126,150 ÷ 0.93 = $135,645

17. (b) 100% − 7% = 93% = 0.93
    $215,900 × 0.93 = $200,787
    5.75% = 0.0575
    $200,787 × 0.0575 = $11,545.25
    $200,787 − $11,545.25 − $9,300 = $179,942

18. (d) 5% = 0.05
    6% = 0.06
    3% = 0.03
    10% = 0.1
    1 + 0.1 = 1.1
    $183,000 × 1.1 = $201,300
    0.06 + 0.03 = 0.09
    1.00 − 0.09 = 0.91
    $201,300 ÷ 0.91 = $221,208.79
    1 − 0.05 = 0.95
    $221,208.79 ÷ 0.95 = $232,851.359 or $232,851

19. (d) $100\% - 5\% = 95\% = 0.95$

$\$170,750 + \$5,000 = \$175,750$

$\$175,750 \div 0.95 = \$185,000$

20. (d) $90\% = 0.9$

$\$108,000 \div 0.9 = \$120,000$

Appreciation and Depreciation

This chapter covers changes in value of real estate as a result of depreciation or appreciation. Because the use and the definition of depreciation are subject to federal and state laws, Internal Revenue Service (IRS) regulations, and Tax Court rulings, the reader is urged to consult legal counsel regarding any points of law. Any careless discussion of depreciation can lead an unsuspecting seller or buyer into tax consequences that may be unfavorable. The material presented in this chapter is intentionally general in content. This is because of frequent and sometimes major changes in the tax laws. Learn the basic concepts and methods used with appreciation and depreciation so that you can adapt them to whatever tax laws may be in effect. Remember, this is a textbook on real estate math, not a text on taxation.

After working through the material in this chapter, you will be able to

- accurately calculate straight-line appreciation,
- accurately calculate straight-line depreciation, and
- calculate depreciation, using the IRS cost recovery tables for residential and nonresidential properties.

APPRECIATION VERSUS DEPRECIATION

People purchase real estate with the anticipation that it will increase in value over their tenure of ownership. Many investors spend considerable time and energy studying past market performance to arrive at an estimate of the correct rate at which a given property might increase in value over time. *Appreciation*, an increase in value, is generally calculated as a percentage of increase over the original value or purchase price.

E X A M P L E :   A building lot is selling for $100,000. It is anticipated that it will appreciate 10 percent per year over the next five years.

$$5 \text{ years} \times 10\% = 50\% \text{ appreciation}$$

$$100\% \text{ purchase price} + 50\% \text{ appreciation} = 150\% \text{ after 5 years}$$

Another way to look at it is that the lot which was purchased for $100,000 changed by a factor of 1.5 over the next five years.

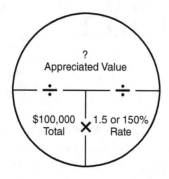
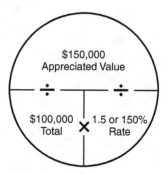

Remember:

The following relationships are very important:

Land
+ Improvement
Real estate or property

(The improvement will be a structure or building.)

Land is generally regarded as an appreciating asset over time because it is indestructible, immovable, and unique. Buildings and improvement, on the other hand, are *wasting assets* that will decrease in value over time. On state licensing exams, you may encounter a problem that will describe a property and give data that indicates that the land increases in value over a given period of time and that the improvements depreciate at a given rate over the same period.

E X A M P L E :   You purchase a property for $125,000. What is the value of that property at the end of eight years if the land appreciates 2.5 percent per year and the improvements depreciate 1.5 percent per year? The value of the land at the time of purchase was 30 percent of the purchase price.

$$30\% = 0.30 \quad 2.5\% = 0.025 \quad 1.5\% = 0.015$$

The land increases in value (appreciates).

$$0.025 \times 8 \text{ years} = 0.20 \text{ or } 20\% \text{ increase}$$

Today the current value of the land is 120 percent (100% + 20% increase = 120%) of its original purchase price.

The building decreases in value (depreciates).

$$0.015 \times 8 \text{ years} = 0.12 \text{ or } 12\% \text{ decrease}$$

Today the current value of the building is 88 percent (100% − 12% decrease = 88%) of its original value.

Remember that 30 percent of the purchase price belongs to the land; the remaining 70 percent of the original value belongs to the improvements.

Land	$125,000 × 0.3 = $37,500
Improvements	$125,000 × 0.7 = $87,500

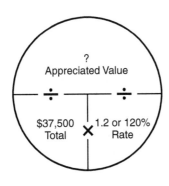 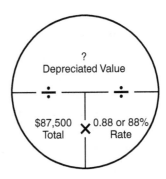

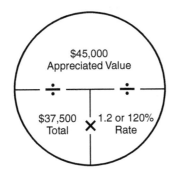 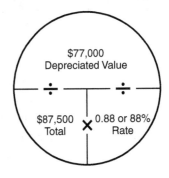

Land:	$37,500 × 1.2 = $ 45,000	Appreciated value
Improvements:	87,500 × 0.88 = $ 77,000	Depreciated value
Current value:	$ 122,000	

As can happen in some cases, the value of the property at the end of eight years is less than the purchase price. Do not assume anything; read the problem carefully! The general rule is that land *appreciates* and improvements *depreciate* over time.

USES OF DEPRECIATION

The term *depreciation* has several shades of meaning, according to its application. Generally, depreciation is used in appraising, tax reporting, and accounting. The real estate salesperson is likely to encounter all of these.

Depreciation in Appraisal

Depreciation is used in the cost approach method for appraising real property. Basically, it measures the amount by which the value of property diminishes owing to physical wasting away. This use of depreciation will not be discussed further here because it is covered more completely in Chapter 11.

Depreciation for Income Tax Purposes

Depreciation may be used as a deduction on federal or state individual or corporate income taxes. As is the case for appraisal, depreciation for tax purposes applies only to buildings and improvements—such as parking lot surfaces, fences, utility lines, and orchards—and *not* to land. Certain qualifying items of personal property used in a trade or business also may be depreciated. Some examples include furniture, equipment, and vehicles. The length or term of depreciation is determined by tax law and IRS regulations.

DEPRECIATION IN ACCOUNTING—BOOKKEEPING FUNCTION

In accounting practices, depreciation may be calculated as a bookkeeping function. It is used in determining the profit and loss of a business establishment. Depreciation is listed as an expense, even though no *actual* expense for that item was incurred. If a business still makes payments on the item being depreciated, those payments and the amount of depreciation have no relationship to one another. The payment depends on the amount and length of a loan or note and its interest rate, while depreciation depends on the economic, or useful, life of the item for bookkeeping purposes.

STRAIGHT-LINE METHOD

Remember:

Straight-line depreciation is the same each year.

The straight-line method of depreciation will be used in the following calculations. This method involves an equal amount of depreciation to be deducted on an annual basis.

NOTE: The term *economic life*, which is used in the following example, refers to that period of time during which the entity can be expected to provide an economic benefit.

EXAMPLE: Under the straight-line method, an air conditioner that cost $10,000 and has an economic life of ten years can be depreciated at $1,000 per year for ten years. By the end of the ten-year period, the entire $10,000 would have been recovered. To determine the annual depreciation amount, divide the initial cost of an item by its economic life or:

Initial cost ÷ Economic life = Annual depreciation amount

Now you try it by working the following exercise.

1. Jeanette bought new display counters and furniture for her craft shop. The entire cost was $4,000. If she depreciates it over a period of seven years, how much depreciation can Jeanette take, or use, each year?

Using the same information, you can prepare a depreciation chart for the seven-year term, showing how the annual depreciation affects the book value of Jeanette's shop furnishings: $4,000 divided by the seven-year period = $571.43 per year straight line

Year	Annual Depreciation	Book Value
New		$4,000.00
1	$571.43	3,428.57
2	$571.43	2,857.14
3	$571.43	2,285.71
4	$571.43	1,714.28
5	$571.43	1,142.85
6	$571.43	571.42
7	$571.42	-0-

EXAMPLE: Susan bought a rental house for $125,000 by paying $25,000 cash and obtaining a mortgage loan for $100,000, to be repaid over a 30-year term. The tax assessor values the lot at $22,500. If Susan depreciates the house over a 27.5-year period, how much depreciation can she take, or use, each year?

First, you must sort out the nonessentials and disregard them. For example, the cash invested, the loan amount, and the length of the loan have no bearing on this problem. Also, remember that the lot, or the land, cannot be depreciated because, theoretically, it does not deteriorate in value. Therefore, the value of the lot must be subtracted from the total cost of the property.

$125,000   total cost of property
– 22,500   value of lot
$102,500   value of building to be depreciated

Next, the depreciation period is 27.5 years, which is not related in any way to the length of the loan. Therefore, the value of the building must be divided by the number of years that the depreciation is to be taken.

$102,500 ÷ 27.5 = $3,727.27 annual depreciation

In the real world of tax laws and regulations, Susan would go to the IRS cost recovery chart (the tax code refers to depreciation as *cost recovery*) for residential investment property and apply the appropriate factor to the original value of the building.

Remember:

Land is not depreciated.

Table 3.1 gives the appropriate factors for calculating depreciation deductions for federal tax purposes. Use the residential chart (27.5 years) for all property used as dwelling units, and use the non-residential chart (39 years) for all other investment property. Apartment buildings are residential properties.

Using the chart the taxpayer will be able to deduct $3,726.90 in years 2–9 ($102,500 × 0.03636 = $3,726.90).

TABLE 3.1

Cost Recovery Chart

IRS Cost Recovery Percentages			
27.5 Straight-Line Residential		**39 Years Straight-Line Nonresidential**	
Year		**Year**	
1	3.485%	1	1.282%
2–9	3.636	2	2.564
10	3.637	3–32	2.564
11–27	Alternates between 3.636 and 3.637	33	2.565
28	1.97	34	2.564
		35	2.565
		36	2.564
		37	2.565
		38	2.564
		39	2.565
		40	1.282

Note: The percentages will vary slightly, depending on the month in which the asset is placed into service.

2. Your local multiple-listing service (MLS) decides to buy its own printing press so that it can produce its own MLS book. If the press costs $40,000 and the MLS plans to depreciate it over ten years, how much depreciation will the MLS have left (the book value) at the end of four years, when it plans to trade for a new laser press?

The following graph shows the relationship of dollars to time in problem 2.

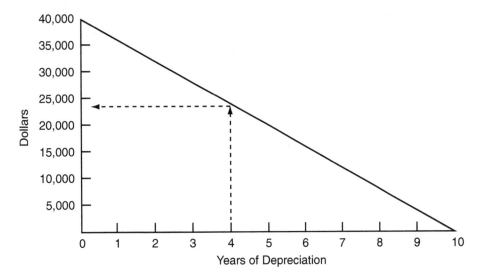

To determine the amount of depreciation left after four years, locate the number 4 on the time line, or horizontal axis, then move straight up until you intersect the diagonal line. At this point, move straight left to the dollar line, or vertical axis. The book value is $24,000.

3. Now you try it. From the graph illustrated, determine how much depreciation will be taken, or used up, at the end of seven years.

Accumulated Depreciation

The initial figure used in problem 3 was $40,000, and $28,000 was used up in seven years. The $28,000 is called *accumulated depreciation*.

$40,000   initial cost
−12,000   depreciation still allowable
$28,000   accumulated depreciation

Application of Depreciation

4. Elaine bought a four-unit apartment house near the local community college. Her cost of the property was $120,000. The lot value was $22,500. She paid $16,000 cash and signed a note to the seller for the balance of $104,000 in seller financing to be paid in monthly installments for 25 years. If Elaine's first-year total operating costs, including taxes and insurance, were $2,000, the total rent income was $15,000, and the total payments on the mortgage loan were $11,340 (of which $985 was for principal), how much taxable income from this property did she have available if she used a 27.5-year depreciation schedule? (This assumes that the tax laws permitted her to use all of the depreciation.) How much depreciation per year is to be taken?

ADDITIONAL PRACTICE

When you have finished these problems, check your answers at the end of the chapter. If you miss any of the problems, review this chapter before going on to Chapter 4.

1. You want to buy a new $48,000 car for use in your real estate business. If you plan to use it 80 percent of the time for business purposes and depreciate it over five years, how much depreciation can you take each year?
    a. $7,200
    b. $7,520
    c. $7,680
    d. $7,720

2. A house and lot are valued at $390,000. If the lot is worth $60,000 and the house is to be depreciated over 30 years, how much total depreciation will be taken in three years?
    a. $11,500
    b. $13,000
    c. $33,000
    d. $34,480

3. You purchased a lot for $35,000 and built a house on it costing $80,000 seven years ago. If the house has depreciated at the rate of 3.636 percent per year straight-line, what is the current value of the house?
    a. $20,361.60
    b. $59,638.40
    c. $94,368.40
    d. $94,638.40

4. If the lot in the above problem appreciated at the rate of 2 percent per year straight-line, what is the current value of the lot?
    a. $4,900
    b. $30,100
    c. $35,700
    d. $39,900

5. What is the current value of the property (house and lot) introduced in problem 3, given the information in problems 3 and 4?
    a. $89,738.40
    b. $94,738.40
    c. $95,338.40
    d. $99,538.40

6. Using a depreciation factor of 2.56 percent per year, what is the depreciated value of an industrial building that has been in service for 17 years if the original cost of the building was $856,000?
    a. $372,360
    b. $482,099
    c. $483,469
    d. $600,564

7. What is the annual amount of depreciation on a $200,000 property if the building accounts for 80 percent of the total property value? The building is eight years old and is to be depreciated over 27.5 years.
    a. $5,818.18
    b. $7,272.73
    c. $46,545.46
    d. $58,181.82

8. A property was purchased four years ago for $220,000. Of the total value, 25 percent is attributed to the land. What is the current value of this property if the land appreciated at 2 percent per year straight-line and the building depreciated at 3.636 percent per year straight-line?
    a. $191,602.40
    b. $196,075.40
    c. $200,402.40
    d. $224,400.40

9. A property was acquired five years ago for $185,000, of which $45,000 was attributed to the land. If during the holding period the land appreciated at 6 percent per year straight-line and the building appreciated at 1.5 percent per year straight-line, what is the current value of the property?
   a. $182,000
   b. $198,500
   c. $201,200
   d. $209,000

10. What is the book value of a three-year-old car if you depreciate it over five years straight-line, you paid $23,500 for it, and you used it for business purposes 80 percent of the time?
   a. $9,400
   b. $11,280
   c. $12,220
   d. $14,100

11. What is the total accumulated depreciation on a four-year-old, $1,200 computer system that is depreciating over five years straight-line?
   a. $955
   b. $960
   c. $975
   d. $1,200

12. Using an annual depreciation rate of 2.778 percent straight-line, calculate the accumulated depreciation on a $450,000, ten-year-old commercial building.
   a. $125,010
   b. $324,990
   c. $405,000
   d. $437,496

13. What is the current book value of a $463,000, six-year-old building that is depreciating at the rate of 3.636 percent per annum straight-line?
   a. $101,017.34
   b. $141,844.68
   c. $321,155.32
   d. $361,991.92

14. If $20,000 cash is paid down on a $125,000 property having a land value of $25,000, how much can be depreciated?
   a. $80,000
   b. $100,000
   c. $105,000
   d. $125,000

15. A business owner bought a new central air-conditioning system for his building. It cost $9,000 and is to be depreciated over nine years. How much depreciation has been taken after three years?
   a. $1,000
   b. $3,000
   c. $6,000
   d. $9,000

16. What did you pay for a storage unit that is worth $155,200 at the end of four years if it has appreciated 2 percent per year?
   a. $142,784
   b. $143,151.54
   c. $143,703.70
   d. $167,616

17. What did you pay for a building that is worth $955,200 at the end of four years if it depreciated 2 percent per year?
   a. $884,444.44
   b. $1,031,616
   c. $1,035,595.10
   d. $1,038,260.80

18. The IRS Cost Recovery Chart for nonresidential shows an annual depreciation rate of 2.564 percent in years 3–32. What is the amount of allowable cost recovery write-off in year 10 of ownership for a building that cost $2,365,000 to build?
   a. $60,638.60
   b. $60,641.03
   c. $606,386
   d. $2,304,361.40

19. The value of the land was $8,000 when you bought a hunting cabin for $87,000 three years ago. What is the value of the land today if the land appreciated at 2 percent per year and the building depreciated at 1 percent per year?

a. $8,480
b. $8,510.64
c. $76,630
d. $76,653.62

20. If the value of your home, *NOT* including the lot, was $175,000 when you purchased it ten years ago, what is its current value if it depreciated at 2.5 percent per year?

a. $43,750
b. $131,250
c. $136,709.72
d. $224,014.79

SOLUTIONS: PROBLEMS IN CHAPTER 3

1. $4,000 ÷ 7 = $571.43

2. $40,000 ÷ 10 = $4,000
   $4,000 × 4 = $16,000
   $40,000 − $16,000 = $24,000

3. Starting at the 7 on the horizontal axis, go up to the depreciation line and over to the left. Only $12,000 remains, so $28,000 depreciation has been used.

4. $120,000 − $22,500 = $97,500
   100% of building value ÷ 27.5 years
   = 3.636 or 0.03636
   $97,500 × 0.03636 = $3,545.10

SOLUTIONS: ADDITIONAL PRACTICE

1. (c) $48,000 × 0.8 = $38,400
   $38,400 ÷ 5 = $7,680

2. (c) $390,000 − $60,000 = $330,000
   $330,000 ÷ 30 = $11,000
   $11,000 × 3 = $33,000

3. (b) 0.03636 × 7 = 0.25452
   $80,000 × 0.25452 = $20,361.60
   $80,000 − $20,361.60 = $59,638.40

4. (d) 0.02 × 7 = 0.14
   $35,000 × 0.14 = $4,900
   $35,000 + $4,900 = $39,900

5. (d) $39,900 + $59,638.40 = $99,538.40

6. (c) 0.0256 × 17 = 0.4352
   $856,000 × 0.4352 = $372,531 (rounded)
   $856,000 − $372,531 = $483,469

7. (a) $200,000 × 0.8 = $160,000
   $160,000 ÷ 27.5 = $5,818.18

8. (c) $220,000 × 0.25 = $55,000
   $220,000 × 0.75 = $165,000
   0.02 × 4 = 0.08
   0.08 × $55,000 = $4,400
   $55,000 + $4,400 = $59,400
   0.14544 × $165,000 = $23,997.60
   $165,000 − $23,997.60 = $141,002.40
   $59,400 + $141,002.40 = $200,402.40

9. (d) $185,000 – $45,000 = $140,000
0.06 × 5 = 0.3
0.3 × $45,000 = $13,500
$45,000 + $13,500 = $58,500
0.015 × 5 = 0.075
0.075 × $140,000 = $10,500
$140,000 + $10,500 = $150,500
$58,500 + $150,500 = $209,000

10. (c) $23,500 × 0.80 = $18,800
$18,800 ÷ 5 = $3,760
$3,760 × 3 = $11,280
$23,500 – $11,280 = $12,220

11. (b) $1,200 ÷ 5 = $240
$240 × 4 = $960

12. (a) 0.02778 × 10 = 0.2778
$450,000 × 0.2778 = $125,010

13. (d) 0.03636 × 6 = 0.21816
$463,000 × 0.21816 = $101,008.08
$463,000 – $101,008.08 = $361,991.92

14. (b) $125,000 – $25,000 = $100,000

15. (b) $9,000 ÷ 9 = $1,000
$1,000 × 3 = $3,000

16. (c) 2% = 0.02
0.02 × 4 = 0.08
0.08 + 1 = 1.08
$155,200 ÷ 1.08 = $143,703.70

17. (d) 2% = 0.02
0.02 × 4 = 0.08
1 – 0.08 = 0.92
$955,200 ÷ 0.92 = $1,038,260.80

18. (a) $2,365,000 \times 0.02564 = \$60,638.60$

19. (a) 2% = $0.02 \times 3 = 0.06$
$0.06 + 1 = 1.06$
$\$8,000 \times 1.06 = \$8,480$

20. (b) 2.5% = 0.025
$0.025 \times 10 = 0.25$
$1 - 0.25 = 0.75$
$\$175,000 \times 0.75 = \$131,250$

Compensation

This chapter will help you apply what you have learned about percentages and decimals to the specific task of calculating real estate commissions. Obviously, this is very important to a real estate agent. Agents usually figure out quickly how to do the math when it comes to their commissions. When you complete your work in Chapter 4, you will be able to

- accurately compute the total commission on a given sales price,
- calculate the listing broker's and salesperson's shares, and
- calculate the sales price when given the commission paid and the commission rate.

METHODS OF COMPENSATION

Traditionally, brokers have been compensated by the sellers who listed their properties for sale with a real estate company whose job was to find a ready, willing, and able buyer to purchase the property at the highest price in the shortest amount of time. As compensation and reward for their successes, the real estate company was paid a percentage of the sales price. A higher sales price equaled a higher fee.

Today, new business models are emerging with new compensation structures. Some salespersons are being paid a salary rather than a percentage of their broker's gross revenue on the sale. Some brokers are charging a flat fee or billing hourly for their company's services. Some are even charging nonrefundable retainer fees before committing their company's resources to market owners' properties.

Buyers' Agents

In recent years, more and more buyers are seeking their own advocates in real estate transactions. They are engaging buyer agents and entering into exclusive representation agreements to have a licensee become their advocate, counselor and/or advisor in a transaction. This new breed of agent can be compensated with a percentage of the sales price at closing, by an agreed-on hourly fee, or with an agreed-on flat fee for services. The buyer may pay the fee directly, or the buyer may structure the transaction so that the fee is paid through the transaction at closing. Often it is charged to the seller's side of the settlement statement.

We will focus on learning to calculate brokerage fees (commissions) as a percentage of the sales price, to be split between the licensees involved in the transactions according to their predetermined splits.

PROBLEM-SOLVING STRATEGY

You will use the same problem-solving strategy presented in Chapter 2, as well as the same basic formulas.

Step 1. Read the problem.

Step 2. Analyze the problem, pick out the important factors, and put those factors into a simplified question, disregarding unimportant factors.

Step 3. Choose the proper formula for the problem.

Step 4. Substitute numbers for the known elements of the formula.

Step 5. Solve the problem.

If you use this strategy throughout this chapter and wherever it applies in this book, you'll have an easier time with word problems. Remember, word problems are simply everyday situations described in writing.

E X A M P L E :   Consider an example that applies the step-by-step strategy to a problem involving a broker's commission.

Step 1. Read the following problem carefully:

A house sold for $163,200. The selling broker received a 7 percent commission on the sale. What amount did the broker receive?

Step 2. Analyze the problem, pick out the important factors, and put those factors into a simplified question.

What is 7 percent of $163,200?

Step 3. Choose the proper formula for the problem from the following:

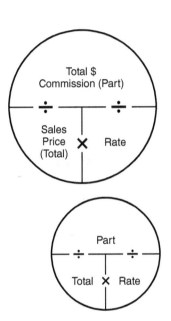

Total × Rate = Part
or
Part ÷ Rate = Total
or
Part ÷ Total = Rate

The correct formula for this problem is

Total × Rate = Part
or
Sales price × Commission rate =
Total commission

Step 4. Substitute numbers for the known elements of the formula.

7% = 0.07
$163,200 (total) × 0.07 (rate) = Part

Step 5. Solve the problem.

$163,200 (total) × 0.07 (rate) = $11,424 (part)

NOTE: The steps and the solution would be the same even if irrelevant factors such as the date of sale, amount of closing costs, and type of financing had been included. Learn to sift out these unimportant factors so you will not be confused by them.

E X A M P L E :   Now apply this strategy to another commission problem. Be careful—this one's a bit different. When you are finished, check your answer below.

Step 1. Read the following problem carefully:

> The selling broker received the entire commission of $1,662 on a real estate transaction. What was the selling price of the property if his rate of commission was 6 percent?

Step 2. Analyze the problem, pick out the important factors, and put those factors into a simplified question.

Step 3. Choose the proper formula for the problem. (If you need to, refer to the formulas shown on the preceding page.)

Step 4. Substitute numbers for the known elements of the formula.

Step 5. Solve the problem.

The answers are as follows:

Step 2. $1,662 is 6 percent of what amount?

Step 3. Part ÷ Rate = Total

Step 4. 6% = 0.06

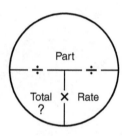

$1,662 (part) ÷ 0.06 (rate) = Total

Step 5. $1,662 (part) ÷ 0.06 (rate) = $27,700 (total)

1. Complete the following formulas. Try not to refer back to material in the book.

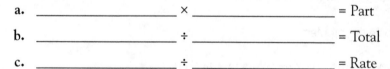

a. _____ × _____ = Part

b. _____ ÷ _____ = Total

c. _____ ÷ _____ = Rate

2. Miss Martin received $9,080 for a parcel of real estate after the broker deducted a 5 percent commission and $40 for advertising expenses. How much did the real estate sell for?

a. Analyze the problem and state it in simplified terms.

b. What value are you looking for (what is the unknown)?

c. What formula will you use?

Let's take a further look at the last problem. First of all, you know that the real estate sold for:

$9,080 + $40 + 5% commission (5 percent of the total)

Therefore, you must add:

$$
\begin{array}{r}
\$9,080 \\
+\quad 40 \\
\hline
\$9,120
\end{array}
$$

Thus, $9,120 plus the 5 percent commission equals the total.

What percentage of the total is $9,120? The total, or the sales price, must equal 100 percent, so:

$$
\begin{array}{r}
100\% \\
-\ 5\% \\
\hline
95\%
\end{array}
$$

Therefore, you can say that $9,120 is 95 percent of the total sales price. Or, in question form:

$9,120 is 95 percent of what amount?

Because you must solve for the total, the correct formula is:

Part ÷ Rate = Total

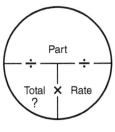

3. Now substitute numbers for the known elements of the formula and solve the problem.

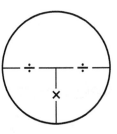

4. Using the figures in problem 3 and the problem-solving strategy, find the amount of the broker's commission.

a. Analyze the problem, pick out the important factors, and put those factors into a simplified question.

b. Choose the proper formula. (Try not to refer back to material in the book.)

c. Substitute numbers for the known elements of the formula.

d. Solve the problem.

5. Apply the problem-solving strategy to the following problem:

A property sold for $75,000. The total commission received by the broker was $4,500. What was the rate of commission?

a. Step 1.

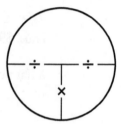

b. Step 2.

c. Step 3.

d. Step 4.

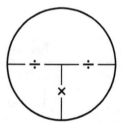

e. Step 5.

SPLITTING COMMISSIONS

Broker and Salesperson

When commissions are divided between a broker and the salesperson, the total commission is calculated first, then the broker's and the salesperson's shares are determined.

Remember, any time a commission is split between a broker and a salesperson, multiple calculations will be involved.

Proceed as follows:

1. Calculate the total commission.

    Sales price (total) × Rate = Total commission (part)

2. Split the total commission between brokers if more
    than one is involved. (This step is deleted on an
    in-house sale.)

3. Split the broker's (company's) share between the bro-
    ker and the salesperson.

    Total commission × Salesperson's share (%) =
    Salesperson's commission

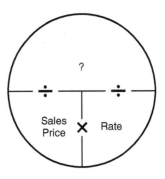

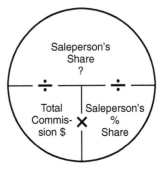

6. The following problem deals with splitting commissions. Apply the problem-solving strat-
    egy and think through the steps as you go along. If you need to, write each step down in
    the space provided.

    Property was sold for $500,800. The salesperson involved in the transaction received
    40 percent of the 6 percent broker's commission. How much money did the salesperson
    receive?

7. Analyze and restate this problem:

    A lakefront lot sold for $455,000 and the total commission was 6 percent of that amount.
    The broker received three-fourths of the commission and the salesperson received one-
    fourth. How much was the salesperson's commission?

8. Here's another type of commission problem. Follow the steps you've learned to solve it.

   What was the selling price of a house if the salesperson received $3,000 as her half of the 6 percent commission charged by the broker?

9. The 6 percent commission charged by a broker for selling a house was divided as follows: The buyer was not represented by another broker, so the listing broker earned the whole 6 percent. Thirty percent of the listing broker's commission goes to the salesperson taking the listing on behalf of the broker, and half of the remainder to the selling salesperson. What was the commission to the selling salesperson if the sales price was $340,000?

10. List the five steps involved in the problem-solving strategy and the three equations you've used in solving commission problems.

    a. Step 1.

    b. Step 2.

    c. Step 3.

    d. Step 4.

    e. Step 5.

More than One Broker: Co-Op Transactions

Frequently, a real estate transaction involves more than one broker. Broker A's salesperson might list the property, and Broker B's salesperson might sell it. The amount of commission that Broker A charges the seller is a matter of negotiation between those two parties, and the division of the commission between the two brokers is subject to negotiation by the two brokers. The manner in which a listing broker shares a portion of the commission with the salesperson is decided by the broker. (*See* Figure 4.1.)

FIGURE 4.1

Flow of Commission Dollars

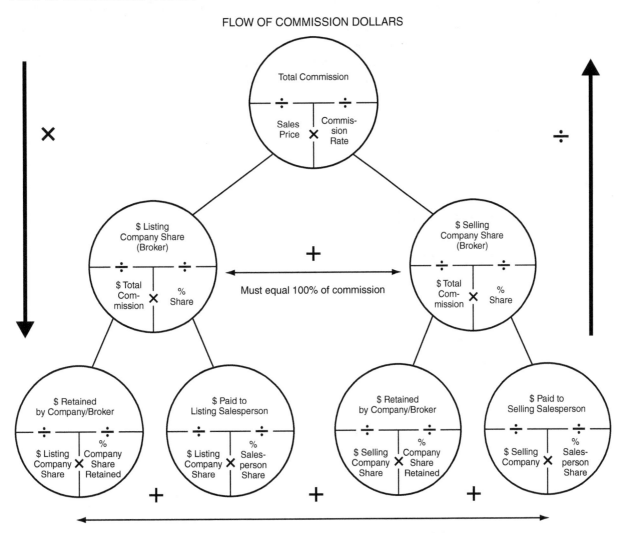

The total of all person's shares must equal 100% of commission.

11. Consider the sale of a $1,000,000 house that involved two brokers. The listing broker negotiated a 6.5 percent commission with the seller, then agreed to pay the selling broker 55 percent of the total commission. The listing salesperson received 25 percent of his broker's commission, and the selling salesperson received 30 percent of his broker's commission. How much did each salesperson receive?

12. A small condominium sold for $85,000 and the commission was 7.25 percent. The broker paid a franchise fee of 5.5 percent of the total commission plus a multiple-listing service transaction fee of ¼ of 1 percent of the total commission. Of the remainder, the agent received 55 percent of the office net commission and paid a $20 computer use fee to the broker on the transaction. How much did the office and the salesperson net?

Charging Graduated Commission Rates

In many markets, brokers charge different rates on different portions of the sales price. When this is done, you simply calculate the commission on each portion and add your answers.

EXAMPLE: A broker charges 6 percent on the first $100,000 of the sales price, 4.5 percent on the next $100,000, and 2 percent on the balance exceeding $200,000. What is the total commission charged on a property selling for $436,500?

$436,500 sales price
−$100,000 × 0.06   = $ 6,000
−$100,000 × 0.045   = $ 4,500
$236,500 ×-0.02   = $ 4,730
                      $15,230 total commission

ADDITIONAL PRACTICE

When you have finished these problems, check your answers against those at the end of the chapter. If you miss any of the problems, review this chapter before going on to Chapter 5.

1. A 6 percent commission was charged by the broker for the sale of a lot that sold for $500,000.

   The commission was divided as follows: 10 percent to the salesperson getting the listing, one-half of the balance to the salesperson making the sale, and the remainder to the broker. What was the amount of commission earned by the salesperson making the sale?
   a. $3,000
   b. $13,500
   c. $14,000
   d. $30,000

2. What was the selling price of a house if the salesperson received $10,000 as her half of the 5 percent commission charged by the broker?
   a. $100,000
   b. $200,000
   c. $400,000
   d. $800,000

3. A house recently sold for $490,000 and the total commission was 6.5 percent of that amount. The broker received three-fourths of that amount, and the salesperson received one-fourth. How much was the broker commission?
   a. $23,887.50
   b. $23,899.50
   c. $24,000
   d. $24,050

4. A sales associate received $7,875 as his half of his broker's 7 percent commission on a sale. The sale price was
   a. $220,000.
   b. $225,000.
   c. $250,000.
   d. $450,000.

5. Two cooperating brokers split equally the 6 percent commission on a sale. Broker A paid her salesperson $8,600 as his 60 percent of broker A's share. The sale price of the property was
   a. $470,000.33
   b. $477,777.76
   c. $478,333.33
   d. $478,339.33

6. A broker paid his salesperson $3,600, the agreed-on three-fifths share of a 6 percent commission. For what amount did the property sell?
   a. $800,000
   b. $100,000
   c. $120,000
   d. $150,000

7. A salesperson received $22,250 as his 50 percent of the commission on a $890,000 sale. The full commission was computed at the rate of
   a. 5 percent.
   b. 5.5 percent.
   c. 6 percent.
   d. 6.5 percent.

8. What was the sales price of a property whose owner paid a $12,000 commission at a 6 percent rate?
   a. $195,000
   b. $199,000
   c. $200,000
   d. $236,000

9. On the sale of a house, the listing broker earns 7 percent of the first $50,000 and 3 percent of any amount exceeding $50,000. What was the selling price of a house if her total commission was $4,475?

a. $32,500
b. $44,750
c. $82,500
d. $89,500

10. A broker was paid a 6 percent commission on the first $100,000 of a house that sold for $150,000. If the total commission was $8,500, what was the percentage of commission paid on the balance?

a. 1.7 percent
b. 2.5 percent
c. 5 percent
d. 5.7 percent

11. A sales associate earns an 8 percent commission on the first $75,000 of sales for the month and 3 percent on all sales exceeding that amount. If he sold one house for $162,100 for the month, how much more would he have earned at a straight 6 percent commission?

a. $810.50
b. $1,113
c. $2,613
d. $9,726

12. The brokerage fee on a house that listed for $490,000 is 6 percent. What is the commission loss to the broker if the actual sales price of the house was 10 percent less than the list price?

a. $2,930
b. $2,940
c. $3,400
d. $3,450

13. The salesperson for ABC Realty sells a house for $484,500. The listing broker receives 50 percent of the 6 percent commission. How much does the salesperson receive if he gets 40 percent of the commission due the selling broker?

a. $5,005
b. $5,814
c. $7,200
d. $7,225

14. A sales associate took a listing for her company that sold for $82,500. A buyer's agent, who works for First Realty, produced the purchasers. The brokers have agreed to divide the 7 percent commission equally, and the agent who took the listing will receive 55 percent of her broker's share, which is

a. $1,229.38.
b. $1,588.13.
c. $2,887.50.
d. $5,775.00.

15. What commission rate was charged if a salesperson received $4,800, which represents 60 percent of the total commission charged to the seller on a $100,000 sales price?

a. 5.75 percent
b. 6 percent
c. 7 percent
d. 8 percent

16. Two brokers split the 6 percent commission equally on the sale of a one-bedroom condominium. What was the sales price of the condominium if the selling salesperson earned a commission of $1,074, which was 40 percent of his broker's share?

a. $44,750
b. $71,600
c. $78,750
d. $89,500

17. You, a broker, have the management contract on a triplex and are to receive 8½ percent of the gross rentals as commission. You collect for one month as follows: $195 for each of two units, $262.50 for the third unit, and $145.53 paid out in repairs. How much was the net amount to the owner?

    a. $55.46
    b. $451.51
    c. $597.04
    d. $652.50

18. A sales associate is working on a 50-50 split with his employing broker. The agent sells a tract of 1,800 acres, bringing in a contract for $1,500 per acre. The listing agreement calls for 10 percent commission on the first $250,000 and 5 percent for everything over that amount. How much will the agent receive?

    a. $22,125
    b. $44,250
    c. $51,625
    d. $73,750

19. A salesperson, is working under an agreement with his broker wherein the broker retains 40 percent of the total commission and the listing and selling salesperson split the remaining 60 percent, with one-fourth going to the listing salesperson and one-half going to the selling salesperson. The sales person lists a piece of land for $325,000 with a 7 percent commission on the first $150,000 of sales price and 10 percent commission on the sales price over $150,000. The land eventually sells at $279,000. How much will the sales person receive?

    a. $2,106
    b. $3,510
    c. $12,900
    d. $14,040

20. A sales associate lists and sells a home for $825,000 at a 7.5 percent commission. How much does she receive after her broker takes 20 percent and a $300 transaction fee?

    a. $39,360
    b. $49,200
    c. $49,260
    d. $49,500

SOLUTIONS: PROBLEMS IN CHAPTER 4

1. a. Total × Rate = Part
   b. Part × Rate = Total
   c. Part × Total = Rate

2. a. $9,080 plus $40 is 95 percent of what amount?
   b. You are looking for the total.
   c. $\dfrac{\text{Part}}{\text{Rate}} = \text{Total}$

3. 95% = 0.95
   $9,120 ÷ 0.95 = $9,600

4. a. What is 5 percent of $9,600?
   b. Rate × Total = Part
   c. 5% × $9,600 = Part
   d. 0.05 × $9,600 = $480

5. Step 1. Read the problem carefully.

   Step 2. Analyze, pick out the important factors, and restate the problem.
   $4,500 is what percentage of $75,000?

   Step 3. Choose the correct formula.

   $$\frac{\text{Part}}{\text{Total}} = \text{Rate}$$

   Step 4. Substitute.

   $$\frac{\$4,500}{\$75,000} = \text{Rate}$$

   Step 5. Solve.

   $$\frac{\$4,500}{\$75,000} = 0.06, \text{ or } 6\%$$

6.   Analysis and restatement: This problem has two parts:

Part 1. What is 6 percent of $500,800?

Part 2. What is 40 percent of that figure?

Formula:

Part 1. Total × Rate = Part

Part 2. Total × Rate = Part

Substitution and solution:

Part 1. 6% × $500,800 = Part

        6% = 0.06

        0.06 × $500,800 = $30,048 total commission

Part 2. 40% × $30,048 = Part

        40% = 0.40

        0.40 × $30,048 = $12,019.20 salesperson's share of the commission

7.   Analysis and restatement: This problem has two parts:

Part 1. What is 6 percent of $455,000?

Part 2. One-fourth = ¼ = 0.25 or 25%

        What is 25 percent of the figure found in Part 1?

Formula:

Part 1. Rate × Total = Part

Part 2. Rate × Total = Part

Substitution and solution:

Part 1. 6% × $455,000 = Part

        6% = 0.06

        0.06 × $455,000 = $27,300 total commission

Part 2. 25% × $27,300 = Part

        25% = 0.25

        0.25 × $27,300 = Part = $6,825 salesperson's commission

8.   Analysis and restatement: $3,000 is one-half of the total commission, so $3,000 plus $3,000 equals $6,000, which is the total commission. $6,000 is 6 percent of what amount?

If you missed this step, correct your solution before you read the rest of the answer.

Formula: Part ÷ Rate = Total

Substitution and solution: $6,000 ÷ 6% = Total

                    6% = 0.06

                    $6,000 ÷ 0.06 = $100,000

9.   Analysis and restatement: This problem has three parts:

Part 1. What is 6 percent of $340,000?

Part 2. What is the listing salesperson's percentage of the total commission?

Part 3. What is the selling salesperson's commission?

Formula:

Part 1. Total × Rate = Part

Part 2. Total × Rate = Part

Part 3. Remaining Total × Rate = Part

Substitution and solution:

Part 1. $340,000 × 6% = Part

   6% = 0.06

   $340,000 × 0.06 = $20,400 total broker's commission

$20,400 = 100 percent of the commission. The salesperson getting the listing receives 30 percent.

Part 2. $20,400 × 30% = Part

   30% = 0.3

   $20,400 × 0.3 = $6,120 listing salesperson's commission

Part 3. $20,400 − $6,120 = $14,280 remaining commission

   Half is 50% = 0.5

   $14,280 × 0.5 = $7,140 selling salesperson's commission

10. a. Read the problem carefully.

  b. Analyze the problem, pick out the important factors, and put those factors into a simplified question.

  c. Choose the proper formula for the problem.

  d. Substitute numbers for the known elements of the formula.

  e. Solve the problem.
     Total × Rate = Part
     Part ÷ Rate = Total
     Part ÷ Total = Rate

11. Step 1. 6.5% = 0.065

$1,000,000 × 0.065 = $65,000 total commission

Step 2. 45% = 0.45

$65,000 × 0.45 = $29,250 to listing broker

Step 3. 55% = 0.55

$65,000 × 0.55 = $35,750 to selling broker

Step 4. 25% = 0.25

$29,250 × 0.25 = $7312.50 to listing salesperson

Step 5. 30% = 0.3

$35,750 × 0.3 = $10,725 to selling salesperson

12. Step 1. 7.25% = 0.0725

$85,000 × 0.0725 = $6,162.50 total commission

Step 2. 5.5% = 0.055

$6,162.50 × 0.055 = $338.94 franchise fee

Step 3. 0.25% = 0.0025

$6,162.50 × 0.0025 = $15.41 MLS fee

Step 4. $6,162.50 – $338.94 – $15.41 = $5,808.15 office net commission

Step 5. 55% = 0.55

$5,808.15 × 0.55 = $3,194.48 salesperson's gross commission

Step 6. $3,194.48 – $20 computer fee = $3,174.48 salesperson's net commission

Step 7. $5,808.15 – $3,174.48 = $2,633.67

SOLUTIONS: ADDITIONAL PRACTICE

1. (b) 6% = 0.06
   $500,000 × 0.06 = $30,000
   100% − 10% = 90% or 0.90
   0.90 × 0.50 = 0.45
   $30,000 × 0.45 = $13,500

2. (c) 50% = 0.5
   $10,000 ÷ 0.5 = $20,000
   5% = 0.05
   $20,000 ÷ 0.05 = $400,000

3. (a) 6.5% = 0.065
   $490,000 × 0.065 = $31,850
   75% = 0.75
   $31,850 × 0.75 = $23,887.50

4. (b) 50% = 0.5
   $7,875 ÷ 0.5 = $15,750
   7% = 0.07
   $15,750 ÷ 0.07 = $225,000

5. (b) 60% = 0.6
   $8,600 ÷ 0.6 = $14,333.333
   50% = 0.5
   $14,333.333 ÷ 0.5 = $28,666.666
   6% = 0.06
   $28,666,666 ÷ 0.06 = $477,777.76

6. (b) three-fifths = 0.6
   $3,600 ÷ 0.6 = $6,000
   $6,000 ÷ 0.06 = $100,000

7. (a) 50% = 0.5
   $22,250 ÷ 0.5 = $44,500
   $44,500 ÷ $890,000 = 0.05 or 5%

8. (c) 6% = 0.06

$12,000 ÷ 0.06 = $200,000

9. (c) 7% = 0.07

$50,000 × 0.07 = $3,500

$4,475 − $3,500 = $975

3% = 0.03

$975 ÷ 0.03 = $32,500

$50,000 + $32,500 = $82,500

10. (c) 6% = 0.06

$100,000 × 0.06 = $6,000

$8,500 − $6,000 = $2,500

$150,000 − $100,000 = $50,000

$2,500 ÷ $50,000 = 0.05 or 5%

11. (b) 8% = 0.08

$75,000 × 0.08 = $6,000

$162,100 − $75,000 = $87,100

3% = 0.03

$87,100 × 0.03 = $2,613

$6,000 + $2,613 = $8,613

6% = 0.06

$162,100 × 0.06 = $9,726

$9,726 − $8,613 = $1,113

12. (b) 10% = 0.1

$490,000 × 0.1 = $49,000

6% = 0.06

$49,000 × 0.06 = $2,940

13. (b) 6% = 0.06

$484,500 × 0.06 = $29,070

50% = 0.5

$29,070 × 0.5 = $14,535

40% = 0.4

$14,535 × 0.4 = $5,814

14. (b) 7% = 0.07

$82,500 × 0.07 = $5,775

50% = 0.5

$5,775 × 0.5 = $2,887.50

55% = 0.55

$2,887.50 × 0.55 = $1,588.13

15. (d) 60% = 0.6

$4,800 ÷ 0.6 = $8,000

$8,000 ÷ $100,000 = 0.08 or 8%

16. (d) 40% = 0.4; 6% = .06

$1,074 ÷ 0.4 = $2,685

$2,685 ÷ 0.5 = $5,370

$5,370 ÷ 0.06 = $89,500

17. (b) 8½% = 8.5% = 0.085

$195 × 2 = $390

$390 + $262.50 = $652.50

$652.50 × 0.085 = $55.46

$652.50 − $55.46 − $145.53 = $451.51

18. (d) 5% = 0.05; 10% = 0.1; 30% = 0.3

$1,800 × $1,500 = $2,700,000

$2,700,000 − $250,000 = $2,450,000

$250,000 × 0.1 = $25,000

$2,450,000 × 0.05 = $122,500

$25,000 + $122,500 = $147,500

$147,500 × 0.5 = $73,750

19. (b) one-fourth = ¼ = 0.25

one-half = ½ = 0.5

7% = 0.07; 10% = 0.1; 40% = 0.4;

60% = 0.6

$279,000 − $150,000 = $129,000

$150,000 × 0.07 = $10,500

$129,000 × 0.1 = $12,900

$10,500 + $12,900 = $23,400

$23,400 × 0.6 = $14,040

$14,040 × 0.25 = $3,510

20. (b) 7.5% = 0.075; 20% = 0.2

1 − 0.2 = 0.8

$825,000 × 0.075 = $61,875

$61,875 × 0.8 = $49,500

$49,500 − $300 = $49,200

CHAPTER

5

Ad Valorem Taxes

It will often be necessary for a real estate salesperson or broker to calculate real estate taxes, so you will need to have a basic understanding of how they are levied.

At the conclusion of your work in this chapter, you will be able to compute annual ad valorem taxes

- based on the market value of property and an assessment ratio,
- based on assessed value, using a tax rate per $100 value,
- given in mills, and
- using an equalization factor.

You also will be able to calculate penalties for delinquent ad valorem taxes.

NOTE: Aspects of the material presented in this chapter may not apply to your state because each state has its own way of calculating ad valorem taxes.

TAXES BASED ON ASSESSED VALUE

Taxes are levied against real estate so that taxpayers will share the cost of various government activities in proportion to the value of their property. Such taxes are known as *ad valorem taxes*. Ad valorem means *according to value*, so an ad valorem tax is a real estate tax based on the value of property.

Valuing and assessing real estate for tax purposes is usually the responsibility of the tax assessor, or in some states, the tax appraisal district, but you will find it helpful to have a basic understanding of how tax is calculated. To figure the amount of tax that will be imposed on a parcel of real estate, you must know two things: the percentage or ratio of assessment to market value used in your area and the tax rate, usually expressed as dollars or cents per hundred or per thousand dollars of assessment.

Suppose, for example, that the assessed value of a particular property is 70 percent of market value, which is estimated at $150,000, and the official tax rate in the city or town is $4 per $100 of assessment. The amount of city tax on the property is computed as follows:

Step 1. Compute the assessed value. In some jurisdictions, this step is not necessary because assessed value and market value are the same. Property may be assessed at 100 percent of market value.

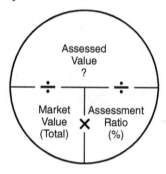

Market value × Assessment ratio = Assessed value

$150,000 × 0.7 = $105,000

Remember:

The tax rate is an annual rate. Therefore, the taxes calculated are yearly taxes.

Step 2. Compute the tax (tax rate expressed in dollars per hundred)

Assessed value ÷ 100 × Tax rate = Annual tax

$105,000 ÷ 100 × $4 = Annual tax

Annual tax = $4,200

E X A M P L E :   Assessed value at 100 percent of market value.

A property in Texas has a market value of $143,500 as defined by the local county appraisal district. Real properties are assessed at 100 percent of market value. What are the annual school taxes if the tax rate is $2.20 per $100 valuation?

Assessed value ÷ 100 × Tax rate = Annual tax

$143,500 ÷ 100 × $2.20 = $3,157

E X A M P L E :   Assessed value as a percentage or ratio of assessment to market value.

A property has a market value of $125,600 in a jurisdiction that assesses property at 53 percent of market value. What is the current year's tax bill to the city if the tax rate is $0.92 per $100 of assessed value?

Market value × Assessment ratio = Assessed value
$125,600 × 0.53 = $66,568 (step 1)

Assessed value ÷ 100 × Tax rate = Annual tax
$66,568 ÷ 100 × $.92 = $612.43 (rounded)

When taxes are based on an assessment equal to 100 percent of market value, eliminate step 1 of this example.

NOTE: Taxes on real estate are determined by state and local laws. The material presented here is in general form. Be sure to inquire about tax procedures in your own locality.

1. A one-bedroom condo has a market value of $80,000. In this area properties are assessed at 70 percent of market value. What is the assessed value?

2. If a lot is assessed at 40 percent of its market value, what would be the assessed value of a parcel worth $247,500?

3. If property is valued at $165,000 and assessed for 60 percent of its value, what is the annual tax if the tax rate is $5.30 per $100 of assessed value?

When the annual taxes are given requiring that you work backwards to determine assessed value or original market value, the question is more challenging. However, fill in what is known and use assessed value or market value as your unknown in this case.

4. If the annual tax on a property comes to $1,467, what is the assessed value of that property, given a tax rate of $1.63 per $100 of assessed value and assuming that this property is assessed at 100 percent of its market value?

5. A house has a market value of $244,200. The assessment ratio is 50 percent of market value and the tax rate is $35 per $1,000 of assessed value. What is the annual tax on the property?

Notice that tax rates may be expressed in any of four ways. The following rates are equivalent:

$3.50 per $100
$35 per $1,000
3.5% (0.035)
35 mills

TAXES GIVEN IN MILLS

The tax rate can be expressed as so many mills on each dollar of assessed value. A mill is one-tenth of one cent. In decimal form, one mill is written as 0.001.

To convert mills to decimal form, divide the number of mills by 1,000.

6. Complete the table below:

$$1 \text{ mill } = \tfrac{1}{10}¢ \ = \$0.001$$

$$10 \text{ mills } = 1¢ \quad = \$0.01$$

$$100 \text{ mills } = 10¢ \quad = \underline{\hspace{2cm}}$$

7. Write 54 mills in decimal form.

Remember:

When calculating taxes, divide the number of mills by 1,000 and multiply by the assessed value to get annual taxes.

EXAMPLE: A property is assessed at $175,500. The tax rate is 23 mills. Compute the annual tax on the property.

$$23 \text{ mills} \div 1,000 = 0.023$$

$$\text{Assessed value} \times \text{Tax rate decimal} = \text{Annual tax}$$

$$\$175,500 \times 0.023 = \$4,036.50$$

8. A property is assessed at $125,600. The tax rate is 48 mills. Compute the annual tax.

9. Taxes are based on an assessment ratio of 53 percent of market value. This year, the school system collects 33 mills per $1 of assessed value. Compute the annual school tax for a property valued at $225,000.

10. Property taxes on a parcel of real estate were $1,641.60. The property was assessed at 20 percent of market value, and the tax rate was 57 mills per $1 of assessed value. What was the market value of the real estate?

TAXES USING AN EQUALIZATION FACTOR

Remember:

To compute the tax rate when it is expressed in mills, divide the number of mills by 1,000 or simply move the decimal point three places to the left.

When a local taxing authority determines certain taxing districts to be undervalued, assessed values are adjusted to make them comparable to those of surrounding areas. The assessed value of a property is multiplied by an equalization factor determined by the assessor's office.

$$\text{Assessed value} \times \text{Equalization factor} = \text{Equalized assessment}$$

The equalized assessment value is then multiplied by the tax rate to compute the amount of the tax bill.

$$\text{Equalized assessment} \times \text{Tax rate} = \text{Annual tax}$$

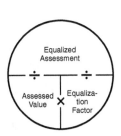

11. If a property is assessed at $82,500, to be adjusted by an equalization factor of 1.3, and the tax rate is $4.35 per $100 of assessed equalized value, how much tax will have to be paid?

PENALTIES FOR DELINQUENT TAXES

Unpaid taxes are subject to penalty charges; for example, 1 percent per month during the delinquency period.

E X A M P L E :   Assume that an owner's annual real estate tax of $7,800 is payable in two equal installments. The due dates are May 1 and September 1. What is the amount of the penalty that will accrue if no tax payments are made until October 30, at which time the full tax is paid? (Assume that delinquent taxes are subject to a penalty of 1 percent per month.)

Step 1. Calculate the installment payments.

$$\$7,800 \div 2 = \$3,900 \text{ per installment}$$

Step 2. Determine the first penalty charge.

$$\$3,900 \times 0.06 \text{ penalty May 1 to October 30} = \$78$$

Step 3. Determine the second penalty charge.

$$\$390 \times 0.02 \text{ penalty September 1 to October 30} = \$7.80$$

Step 4. Add both penalties to arrive at the total.

$$\$234 + \$78 = \$312$$

Delinquent real estate taxes are normally collected when the property is sold at a tax sale or at a private sale. If the delinquent owner is allowed a redemption period by state law, extra penalties are usually added until the time the property is redeemed or a tax deed is issued to the purchaser at the tax or private sale.

12. Real estate taxes in the amount of $1,927 were not paid by a July 1 due date. The property was sold at a tax sale on October 1. The penalty before the tax sale was 1 percent interest per month. The penalty after the tax sale was 12 percent for each six-month period after the sale, without proration. The redemption fee was $5. Find the cost to redeem the property on November 1.

EXEMPTIONS

Some states permit certain exemptions on property taxes. In some cases, this option to grant exemptions extends to lesser taxing entities, such as counties, cities, and school districts. The taxing authority subtracts, or exempts, a prescribed amount of value from the assessed value before applying the other factors.

For example, a state might exempt $10,000 for homestead purposes. If the property composing the homestead is assessed at $160,000, the $10,000 exemption is subtracted and usual factors are applied to the $150,000 valuation.

An exemption might be granted to senior citizens, and again, the amount of the exemption is subtracted from the assessed value. In some cases, exemptions on land used for agricultural purposes are allowed, and the assessed value is based on the productivity value, not the market value of the land. Generally, property owners must make a written application for any type of property tax exemption.

ADDITIONAL PRACTICE

When you have finished these problems, check your answers at the end of the chapter. If you miss any of the problems, review this chapter before going on to Chapter 6.

1. A property has a market value of $676,000. The taxes in the area are levied on 66 percent of market value at a rate of $2.50 per $100 of assessed value. How much tax will be charged for this year?
   a. $10,054
   b. $10,133
   c. $11,154
   d. $11,254

2. A married couple own a lot that is valued at $145,000. The assessed value is 55 percent of market value and the equalization factor to be applied this year is 1.3. The tax rate is 53.5 mills. What will be their tax bill this year?
   a. $3,490.88
   b. $4,266.63
   c. $4,538.14
   d. $5,546.61

3. Based on a tax rate of $2 per $100 of assessed value, the taxes on a property are $2,876. What is the market value of the property assuming an assessment ratio of 100 percent?
   a. $143,500
   b. $143,800
   c. $178,000
   d. $178,900

4. A residential property sold for $375,000. The assessed value for tax purposes is 22 percent of market value. What will be the amount of the tax bill if the tax rate is $6.25 per $100 of assessed value?
   a. $4,325.25
   b. $5,156.25
   c. $5,246.26
   d. $5,435.25

5. A property owner received his tax bill for $12,325. The published tax rate is $2.25 per $100 of assessed value. What is the assessed value of this property? Round to the nearest dollar.
   a. $5,478
   b. $54,780
   c. $123,250
   d. $547,778

6. Your current real estate tax bill is $1,944. The tax rate is $4.50 per $100 of the equalized assessed value. When the equalization factor is 0.80, what is the assessed valuation?
   a. $50,000
   b. $52,000
   c. $54,000
   d. $56,000

7. What is the market value of property rounded to the nearest dollar on which the real estate tax is $1,594.54, when the assessment is 45 percent of market value and the tax rate is 63 mills per dollar?
   a. $52,306
   b. $56,150
   c. $56,242
   d. $56,245

8. Find the tax rate per $100 of assessed value when the tax bill is $9,001.31 and the assessed value is 33 percent of the market value of $475,000.
   a. $0.574
   b. $5.74
   c. $6
   d. $57.42

9. A property owner received a tax bill for $870.54, half of which is payable on June 1 and the other half on October 1. A penalty of 1 percent per month is provided for delinquent taxes. If the owner makes payment in full on October 15, how much will he pay?

a. $883.60
b. $887.95
c. $892.20
d. $896.64

10. A property was assessed for taxes at 50 percent of market value. The tax rate was $3.75 per $100 of assessed value. Five years later, taxes had increased by $300. How much did the property's market value increase?

a. $2,250
b. $8,000
c. $16,000
d. $60,000

11. A house is valued at $175,000 and assessed for 60 percent of its value. If the tax bill is $3,150, what is the rate per $100?

a. $2.90
b. $3
c. $3.50
d. $3.95

12. The tax rate can be expressed as a certain number of mills for each dollar of assessed value. Indicate which of the following decimal equivalents is CORRECT.

a. 23 mills = 0.023
b. 2½ mills = 0.025
c. 2½ mills = 0.225
d. 19 mills = 19

13. A vacant lot has an assessed value of $68,900. The owner is permitted a $10,000 exemption and will owe current annual tax based on $2.28 per $100 of valuation. The annual tax bill will be

a. $1,342.92.
b. $1,570.92.
c. $1,798.92.
d. none of these.

14. What is the annual tax amount due on a property with a market value of $385,600, where an assessment ratio of 48 percent is used and the tax rate is $3.43 per $100 of valuation?

a. $6,348.52
b. $6,533.61
c. $7,009.82
d. $13,226.08

15. A city levies $0.83 per $100 of assessed value. What is the annual tax bill for a property that the appraisal district has assessed at $83,750?

a. $688.13
b. $688.90
c. $695.13
d. $695.83

16. How much annual tax will be paid on a parcel of real estate assessed at $182,500, using an equalization factor of 1.3 and a tax rate of $4.18 per $100 of equalized value?

a. $3,084.25
b. $5,868.08
c. $7,628.50
d. $9,917.05

17. What is the assessed value of a property with a market value of $4,860,300, using an assessment ratio of 0.53?

a. $91,703.77
b. $257,595.90
c. $2,575,959
d. $25,759,590

18. The annual tax bill for the current year is $10,000. The owner is a senior who receives a tax exemption of $30,000. The current tax rate is $4 per $100 of assessed value. What is the market value of this property assuming that the assessment percentage is 100 percent?

a. $250,000
b. $280,000
c. $295,000
d. $305,000

19. A property has market value of $670,000. The assessment ratio used in this county is 82 percent of market value. The tax rate is $2.50 per $100 of assessed value. What are the annual taxes for this property?
   a. $13,735
   b. $13,750
   c. $16,750
   d. $20,426.80

20. A lot is assessed at $55,600. What is the annual tax bill, with taxes assessed at 23 mills?
   a. $12.78
   b. $1,278.80
   c. $12,788
   d. $12,789

SOLUTIONS: PROBLEMS IN CHAPTER 5

1. $80,000 × 0.7 = $56,000

2. $247,500 × 0.4 = $99,000

3. $165,000 × 0.6 = $99,000
   $99,000 ÷ $100 = 990
   990 × $5.30 = $5,247

4. $1,467 ÷ $1.63 = 900
   900 × $100 = $90,000

5. $244,200 × 0.5 = $122,100
   $122,100 ÷ $1,000 = 122.10
   122.1 × $35 = $4,273.50

6. $0.10

7. $0.054

8.   48 ÷ 1,000 = 0.048
   $125,600 × 0.048 = $6,028.80

9.   33 ÷ 1,000 = 0.033
   $225,000 × 0.53 = $119,250
   $119,250 × 0.033 = $3,935.25

10.   57 ÷ 1,000 = 0.057
    $1,641.60 ÷ 0.057 = $28,800
    $28,800 ÷ 0.2 = $144,000

11. $82,500 × 1.3 = $107,250
    $107,250 ÷ $100 = 1,072.5
    1,072.5 × $4.35 = $4,665.38 (rounded)

12. $1927 × 0.03 = $57.81
    $1927 × 0.12 = $231.24
    $1927 + $57.81 + $231.24 + $5 = $2,221.05

SOLUTIONS: ADDITIONAL PRACTICE

1. (c) $676,000 × 0.66 = $446,160
   $446,160 ÷ $100 = 4,461.60
   4,461.6 × $2.50 = $11,154

2. (d) $145,000 × 0.55 = $79,750
   $79,750 × 1.3 = $103,675
   $103,675 × 0.0535 = $5,546.61 (rounded)

3. (b) 2,876 ÷ 0.02 = $143,800

4. (b) 22% = 0.22
   $375,000 × 0.22 = $82,500
   $82,500 ÷ $100 = 825
   825 × $6.25 = $5,156.25

5. (d) $12,325 ÷ $2.25 = $5,477.77777 (round this to the nearest penny)
   $5,477.78 × $100 = $547,778

6. (c) $1,944 ÷ $4.50 = 432
   432 × $100 = $43,200
   $43,200 ÷ 0.8 = $54,000

7. (d) 63 mills ÷ 1,000 = 0.063
   $1,594.54 ÷ 0.063 = $25,310.158
   $25,310.158÷ 0.45 = $56,245 (rounded)

8. (b) $475,000 × 0.33 =$156,750
   $156,750 ÷ 100 = 1,567.5
   $9,001.31 ÷ 1,567.5 = $5.74 (rounded)

9. (d) $870.54 ÷ 2 = $435.27
   $435.27 × 0.01 = $4.35 (rounded)
   $4.35 × 5 = $21.75
   $435.27 + $21.75 = $457.02
   $435.27 + $4.35 = $439.62
   $457.02 + $439.62 = $896.64

10. (c) $300 ÷ $3.75 = 80
80 × $100 = $8,000
$8,000 ÷ 0.5 = $16,000

11. (b) $175,000 × 0.6 = $105,000
$105,000 ÷ $100 = 1,050
$3,150 ÷ 1,050 = $3

12. (a) 23 mills ÷ 1,000 = 0.023

13. (a) $68,900 − $10,000 = $58,900
$58,900 ÷ $100 × $2.28 = $1,342.92

14. (a) $385,600 × 0.48 = $185,088
$185,088 ÷ $100 × $3.43 = $6,348.52 (rounded)

15. (c) $83,750 ÷ $100 × $0.83 = $695.13 (rounded)

16. (d) $182,500 × 1.3 ÷ 100 × $4.18 = $9,917.05

17. (c) $4,860,300 × 0.53 = $2,575,959

18. (b) $10,000 ÷ 4 = $2,500
$2,500 × 100 = $250,000
$250,000 + $30,000 = $280,000

19. (a) $670,000 × 0.82 ÷ 100 × $2.50 = $13,735

20. (b) 23 mills ÷ 1,000 = 0.023
$55,600 × 0.023 = $1,278.80

CHAPTER

6

Property Transfer Taxes

Unlike property taxes, real estate property transfer taxes are state and/or local taxes that are assessed on real property when ownership of the property is transferred between parties. It is assessed only once on the sales transaction instead of on an annual basis like a general property tax. Currently, over two-thirds of the states and the District of Columbia impose a tax on the transfer of real property.

You should be familiar with the amount of transfer tax charged in your state and the current exemptions from the tax. Some states exempt a transfer in which the total consideration is less than some statutory amount or an existing mortgage is assumed by the purchaser. This does not refer to the amount stated in the deed, but to the actual sales price. Many states require a written declaration to be made and signed by one or both parties to a sale in which the selling price is disclosed, together with other facts.

At the conclusion of your work in this brief chapter, you will be able to compute the transfer tax, using the approaches applied by some states. Remember to check the rates for your state if applicable.

TRANSFER TAX RATES

Many states require that a transfer tax be paid when an interest in real estate is sold and conveyed by a deed. Payment of the tax is usually made by purchasing stamps from a state or local official, affixing them to the deed, and having them canceled. Many state transfer taxes were adopted on January 1, 1968, when the federal revenue stamp tax was repealed. Tax rates range from a low of 0.01 percent in Colorado to a high of over 2 percent in Washington, D.C.

Details of the transfer tax differ among states. For example, many states exempt sales in which the consideration is less than $100. Other states tax only the net consideration if the buyer assumes the seller's existing mortgage. The following information should be helpful in working the problems presented in this chapter:

- The transfer tax is applied to the entire sales price.
- It does not matter whether it is an all-cash or a cash/new mortgage transaction. The property tax is still applied to the entire sales price.
- In the rather unusual case today where the seller's current mortgage balance is being assumed by the buyer, the mortgage amount being assumed is subtracted from the sales price before the transfer tax is applied.

A tax rate of $0.50 or $0.55 for each $500 or fractional thereof $500 of the net taxable consideration is common. A percentage of the taxable consideration is another method used.

NOTE: *Or fractional thereof* is an important concept, but it can be confusing. When the amount subject to the transfer tax is divided by the number of taxable increments ($500 for example), the result is then multiplied by the tax rate if it is a whole number. However, if the result is a decimal number (fraction thereof), the number is raised to the next whole number. A number of 501.01 to 501.99 becomes 502. The resultant number is then multiplied by the tax rate.

For example: $23,425 divided into $100 increments = 243.25 taxable increments. In this case, the number is raised to the next whole number or 244. This number is then multiplied by the tax rate to arrive at the property transfer tax.

E X A M P L E :   What value in state transfer stamps must be affixed to a deed when property is sold for $106,000 and the tax rate is $0.50 per $500 or fraction thereof of the selling price?

$$\$106,000 \div \$500 \text{ increments} = 212 \text{ taxable increments}$$

$$212 \times \$0.50 = \$106 \text{ tax}$$

1. A property was sold in a state in which the stamp tax rate is $0.55 for each $500 paid in cash at the time of the transfer. A mortgage balance, if assumed by the buyer, is not a taxable consideration. If the total price of the property was $225,000 and the buyer assumed a $124,000 mortgage, compute the amount of transfer tax paid. (The assumed mortgage is exempt.)

2. Real estate that sold for $377,500 was subject to a transfer tax of $0.50 for each $500 or fraction thereof of the selling price. What amount of tax stamps must be purchased, affixed to the deed, and canceled?

3. A lot was sold for $64,750 and a state transfer tax was required at the rate of $0.26 per $100 or fraction thereof of consideration. How much tax was paid?

4. Real estate was sold for $405,000, with the buyer assuming the seller's mortgage balance of $203,940. The tax rate was 0.005 of the consideration paid in cash at the sale closing. What was the amount of tax if the assumed mortgage was exempt?

Approximate Sales Price

EXAMPLE: In certain states, tax stamps are based on the amount of cash paid at the time of transfer. In this case, the seller's existing mortgage is being assumed by the buyer. Calculate the approximate sales price of the real estate involved in a transaction in which the tax rate was $0.50 for each $500 or fraction thereof, a total of $20.50 in stamps was affixed to the deed, and the buyer assumed the seller's mortgage of $19,812.

Step 1. Calculate the parts.

$$\$20.50 \div \$0.50 = 41$$

Step 2. Determine the cash paid.

$$41 \times \$500 = \$20,500$$

Step 3. Total the cash paid and the mortgage amount.

$$\$20,500 + \$19,812 = \$40,312 \text{ sales price}$$

In most states, only assumed loans are exempt when computing transfer taxes. *New purchase-money loans are not exempt from the amount subject to the transfer tax*, whether the note is to the seller or to a third-party lender.

5. A seller sold his lake property as part of a lender agreed to short sale to a buyer for $145,000. The transaction took place in a state that has a tax rate of $1.75 per $100 or fraction thereof and exempts assumed mortgages. What was the amount of transfer tax on the sale?

6. A man is buying a $400,000 house. He assumed the mortgage, which was for 25 percent of the sales price, and negotiated a second mortgage for 50 percent of the balance, paying the rest in cash. If the transfer tax rate is $0.55 per $500 or fraction thereof and only the assumed mortgage is exempt, what amount of transfer tax stamps must be affixed to the deed?

Remember:

If the problem says "or fraction thereof," always change to the next whole number if it does not come out even.

7. A retired couple have listed their house with Wagner Realty for $320,000. The best offer that they've received is from a couple who are willing to assume the present mortgage of $200,000, pay $25,000 in cash, and obtain a lien mortgage note for $75,000. The transfer tax rate is $0.75 per $500 or fraction thereof and assumed mortgages are exempt. What amount of transfer tax will be charged if the sellers accept this offer?

8. A young couple are purchasing a small condo for $74,000. What amount of transfer tax stamps will have to be affixed to the deed at closing if the state requires $0.50 per $500 or fraction thereof?

ADDITIONAL PRACTICE

When you have finished these problems, check your answers at the end of the chapter. If you miss any of the problems, review this chapter before going on to Chapter 7.

1. A bank foreclosed property sold for $84,000 after being on the market for 6 months at an original list price of $122,000. What amount of transfer tax is due if the tax is based on the sales price at the rate of $0.45 per $500 or fraction thereof?

   a. $28.80
   b. $46.80
   c. $57.60
   d. $75.60

2. The Doyles have a sales contract for their property. The executed sales price per the sales contract is $154,000. What will be the amount of transfer tax if the state requires $0.50 per $500 or fraction thereof and exempts transactions of less than $100 and assumed mortgages?

   a. $40
   b. $60
   c. $120
   d. $154

3. Real estate is being sold for $850,000, with the purchaser assuming the $565,000 unpaid balance of the sellers' existing mortgage. What is the state transfer tax when the rate of tax is $0.50 for each $500 or fraction thereof of the actual consideration less the amount of any assumed mortgage?

   a. $285
   b. $290
   c. $565
   d. $850

4. The sales price of a house is $112,000. The seller is providing owner financing of 50 percent of the sales price over five years at an interest rate of 6 percent. What amount of state transfer tax stamps is required if the state transfer tax is 2 percent of the value of the property?

   a. $520
   b. $1,120
   c. $1,720
   d. $2,240

5. The state transfer tax is $0.30 for each $100 or fraction thereof of the full sales price. The county transfer rate is $0.50 for each $500 or fraction thereof of the sales price less the amount of any assumed mortgage. Compute the total transfer tax required for a sale at $95,000.

   a. $81
   b. $208
   c. $123.50
   d. $380

6. The state transfer tax is $0.50 for each $500 or fraction thereof of the sales price. A report of properties sold lists the addresses and names of grantors and grantees and the amount of transfer tax paid. When an item on the report lists $89.50 as the transfer tax, the sales price of the property is probably

   a. less than $89,000.
   b. $89,500.
   c. greater than $89,500 if the buyer assumed the seller's mortgage.
   d. none of the above.

7. The state transfer tax on deeds is $0.12 for each $100 of sales price; the county tax is $0.30 for each $100 of sales price. The sales price of a residence is $284,000 and is financed by a mortgage loan for 80 percent of the sales price. What amount of transfer tax is due?

   a. $1,000.80
   b. $1,100.80
   c. $1,150.80
   d. $1,192.80

8. A property was sold for $256,000 in a cash transaction. The state levies a transfer tax of $0.43 for each $300 or fraction thereof of the purchase price. What is the amount of the transfer tax?

   a. $366.93
   b. $367.22
   c. $367.65
   d. $478.02

9. A parcel of real estate sold for $264,000, and the buyer assumed a mortgage balance of $64,000. The state in which the transaction took place levies a transfer tax of $0.65 for each $500 or fraction thereof paid at the time of transfer and does not exclude assumed mortgages. What is the amount of transfer tax due?

   a. $252.65
   b. $320.21
   c. $331.20
   d. $343.20

10. A property is sold for $185,500 in cash. The state levies a transfer tax of $0.43 for each $300 of the sales price. What amount of transfer tax is due?

    a. $264.98
    b. $265.88
    c. $267.44
    d. $267.84

11. A home sold for $386,000 in cash. The state levies a transfer tax of $0.55 for each $300 of the sales price, and the county levies $0.25 for each $500 of the sales price. What is the total transfer tax due?

    a. $707.67
    b. $707.87
    c. $900.67
    d. $902.57

12. A property sold for $525,300. The state levies a transfer tax of $0.65 for each $500 or fraction thereof and the county $0.10 for each $500 or fraction thereof paid at the time of transfer. What amount of total transfer tax is due at closing?

    a. $260
    b. $325.06
    c. $746.40
    d. $788.25

SOLUTIONS: PROBLEMS IN CHAPTER SIX

1. $225,000 − $124,000 = $101,000
   $101,000 ÷ $500 = 202
   202 × $0.55 = $111.10

2. $377,500 ÷ $500 = 755
   755 × $0.50 = $377.50

3. $64,750 ÷ $100 = 647.5 or 648
   648 × $0.26 = $168.48

4. $405,000 − $203,940 = $201,060
   $201,060 × 0.005 = $1,005.30

5. $145,000 ÷ $100 = 1,450
   1,450 × $1.75 = $2,537.50

6. $400,000 × 0.25 = $100,000
   $400,000 − $100,000 = $300,000
   $300,000 ÷ $500 = 600
   600 × $0.55 = $330

7. $200,000 + $25,000 + $75,000 = $300,000
   $300,000 − $200,000 = $100,000
   $100,000 ÷ $500 = 200
   200 × $0.75 = $150

8. $74,000 ÷ $500 = 148
   148 × $0.50 = $148 × 0.5 = $74

SOLUTIONS: ADDITIONAL PRACTICE

1. (d) $84,000 ÷ $500 = 168
   168 × $0.45 = $75.60

2. (d) $154,000 ÷ $500 =308
   308 × $0.50 = $154.00

3. (a) $850,000 − $565,000 = $285,000
   $285,000 ÷ $500 = 570
   570 × $0.50 = $285

4. (d) $112,000 × 0.02 = $2,240

5. (d) $95,000 ÷ $100 = 950
   950 × $0.30 = $285
   $95,000 ÷ $500 = 190
   190 × $0.50 = $95
   $285 + $95 = $380

6. (b) $89.50 ÷ 0.50 = $179
   $179 × $500 = $89,500

7. (d) $284,000 ÷ $100 = 2,840
   2,840 × $0.12 = $340.80
   2,840 × $0.30 = $852
   $340.80 + $852 = $1,192.80

8. (b) $256,000 ÷ $300 = 853.333
   854 × $0.43 = $367.22

9. (d) $264,000 ÷ $500 = 528
   528 × $0.65 = $343.20

10. (b) $185,500 ÷ $300 = 628.33333
    628.33333 × $0.43 = $265.88

11. (c) $386,000 ÷ $300 = 1,286.67

   1,286.67 × $0.55 = $707.67 (state)

   $386,000 ÷ $500 = 772

   772 × $0.25 = $193 (county)

   $707.67 + $193 = $900.67

12. (d) $525,300 ÷ $500 = 1,050.60 (must round up to 1,051)

   1,051 × $0.65 = $683.15

   1,051 × $0.10 = $105.10

   $683.15 + $105.10 = $788.25

CHAPTER

Legal Descriptions

Property must be legally described and identified before a legal transfer of ownership can be made. Legal descriptions in many states are based on the rectangular survey system. In this chapter, we will cover the mathematical computations involved in property descriptions using the rectangular survey system. Most subdivisions have lot-and-block property descriptions, such as "Lot 12, Block 34, Green Garden Subdivision to the city of Able, County of Baker, State of Texas." This form of legal description will not be discussed because no mathematical computations are involved. Occasionally, you may encounter a metes-and-bounds description. This chapter will introduce this method because it is important that you be able to convert such a description into a sketch (which may be drawn exactly to scale) of the shape of the subject property.

At the conclusion of your work in this chapter, you will be able to

- accurately determine the number of acres in a tract of land described using the rectangular survey system, and

- sketch a tract of land described by the metes-and-bounds system.

RECTANGULAR SURVEY SYSTEM

The rectangular survey system was enacted by the U.S. Congress in 1785 to standardize the description of land acquired by the Federal government.

The basic unit of measurement in the *rectangular survey system method* is the *township*—an area 6 miles square (36 square miles).

A township is divided into 36 *sections*, each one mile square (one square mile), and identified by numbers, always in the sequence shown in Figure 7.1. Section 1 is always at the northeast corner of the township.

FIGURE 7.1

Rectangular Survey System

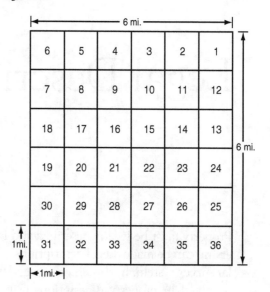

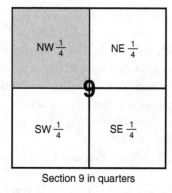

Section 9 in quarters

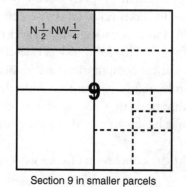

Section 9 in smaller parcels

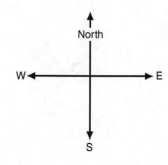

Each section, in turn, can be divided into halves, quarters, and smaller subdivisions.

A section of land contains 640 acres and is 1 mile square, or 5,280 feet by 5,280 feet. A township contains 36 sections and a total of 23,040 acres. The diagram at the left, above, shows a section divided into quarters. The shaded part is described as the NW¼ (*northwest quarter*) of section 9. To find the number of acres in the shaded quarter, convert the fractions to a decimal and multiply 640 by the decimal.

$$\frac{1}{4} = 0.25$$
$$640 \times 0.25 = 160 \text{ acres}$$

The shaded area in the middle diagram, above, is described as the N½ of the NW¼ of section 9. (The location described is found by reading the parts of the description backward. In this case, the NW¼ of section 9 is found, then the N½ of that NW¼.) The acres can be computed by either of two methods.

You can find the acreage of any part of a section by multiplying 640 (acres) by the fraction(s) *converted to a decimal* in the description.

$$½ = 0.5 \qquad ¼ = 0.25$$
$$640 \times 0.5 \times 0.25 = 80 \text{ acres}$$

NOTE: A second, and usually faster, approach may be used whenever all numerators are one: Multiply the denominators, then divide 640 by the result.

Using the example above:

$$½ \ ¼ = 2 \times 4 = 8$$
$$640 \div 8 = 80 \text{ acres}$$

As a variation on the above approach, to calculate the number of acres divide 640 by the denominators in the legal description.

EXAMPLE: N½ of the SW¼ of the NE¼ of section 17

↓   ↓   ↓

640 ÷ 2   ÷ 4   ÷ 4 = 20 acres

Pay careful attention to the words *of* and *and*. Each time you read of (such as SW¼ *of* section 3), multiply by the fraction shown. However, each time you read *and*, start a new calculation and add the result to prior results.

You will find that sketching out the description can give a quick visual confirmation of the acreage involved.

1. Determine the number of acres contained in the shaded area of the diagram at the right. The description of the parcel is as follows: SE¼ of the SE¼ of section 10.

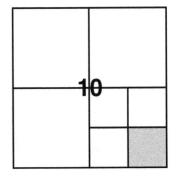

2. Find the number of acres contained in the shaded area of the diagram at the right. The property is described as follows: NW¼ of the SW¼ of the NE¼ of section 12.

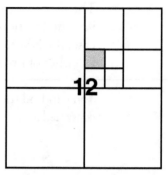

3. The diagram at the right shows a section of land. Determine the number of acres in each of the lettered areas.

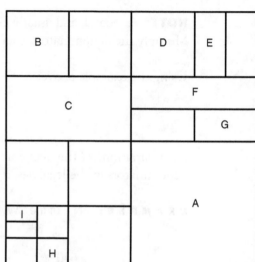

   a. SE¼

   b. W½ of the N½ of the NW¼ (or NW¼ of the NW¼)

   c. S½ of the NW¼

   d. NW¼ of the NE¼

   e. W½ of the NE¼ of the NE¼

   f. N½ of the S½ of the NE¼

   g. E½ of the S½ of the S½ of the NE¼ (or S½ of the SE¼ of the NE¼)

   h. SE¼ of the SW¼ of the SW¼

   i. N½ of the NW¼ of the SW¼ of the SW¼

4. How many acres does the shaded area in the diagram at the right contain?

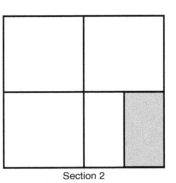

Section 2

5. Locate and shade in the NE¼ of the NW¼ of section 3, shown at the right. How many acres does the parcel contain?

Section 3

Remember:

To determine the numbers of acres involved in a specified part of a section, multiply the denominators and then divide the total into 640.

6. Locate and shade in the S½ of the S½ of the S½ of section 4, shown at the right. How many acres does the parcel contain?

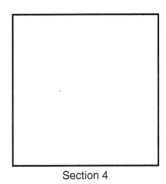

Section 4

7. A woman owns the SW¼ of the SW¼ of a section of unimproved land. If similar land in the area is selling for $1,240 per acre, how much is her property worth?

8. The Valley Development Corporation bought a piece of land described as the W½ of the S½ of the S½ of the NE¼ of section 24. If a total of $120,000 was paid for the land, how much did it cost per acre?

9. A retired farmer still owned the NE¼ of a section. He sold the S½ of the NE¼. How many acres does he still own?

10. A man sold the NW¼ of the NE¼ for $144,000. Based on this price per acre, how much would you pay for the E½ of the NE¼ of the NE¼?

11. Tucker and Lawson formed a corporation. Each conveyed real estate in return for shares of stock in the company, as indicated below:

    Tucker: N½ of the NW¼ of the SW¼ of the SW¼ and the SE¼ of the SW¼ of the SW¼ of section 2

    Lawson: SW¼ of the NW¼ of the SE¼ of the NW¼ of section 3 and the W½ of the SW¼ of section 4

    The corporation issued 500 shares of stock for each acre received.

    a. How many shares did Tucker receive?

    b. How many shares did Lawson receive?

METES-AND-BOUNDS DESCRIPTIONS

Another system of describing real estate is known as *metes and bounds*. This system relies on the metes (measures of distances) and bounds (directions or courses) as described by the surveyor in his or her field notes. Surveying is an exacting profession requiring licensure by most states. Real estate licensees should never attempt to prepare a metes-and-bounds legal description. For example, if the survey does not close (the point of ending is not the same as the point of beginning), the survey is defective. If the legal description is defective, the sales contract may not be enforceable.

Most real estate licensees will rarely need to construct a plat or scaled sketch from a set of field notes. However, if the need does arise, it is important to know how to do it.

FIGURE 7.2

Compass Circle

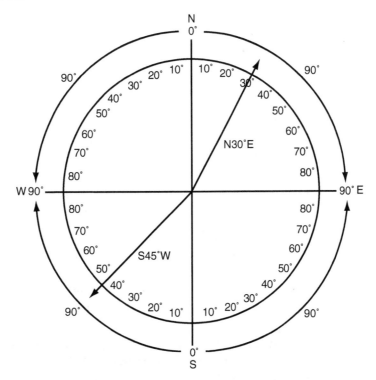

First, we need to recognize that the directions stated in a metes-and-bounds description are the compass directions for all boundary lines. We might say that something lies *northwest* of a certain place or we might say that it lies *westnorth*. Although both words point us in the same direction, through accepted convention, we say *northwest*, *southeast*, and so on. We recite the north or south direction *first*, followed by the direction of declination from north or south. So it is with metes-and-bounds descriptions. For example, the surveyor's call "N30E" means that the direction of the subject line is 30 degrees east of due north. In other words, we look due north and then we pivot 30 degrees to the right and look again. If we now look due east and then we pivot 60 degrees to the left, we are looking in the same direction as before. This is because the compass is divided into 360 degrees, then further subdivided into minutes and seconds. Each degree is divided into 60 minutes (denoted by the symbol ') and each minute is divided into 60 seconds (").

In Figure 7.1, we see that, by convention, due north is toward the top of the page, east is to the right, south is toward the bottom and west is to the left. The circle is divided into four quadrants, as shown, so that our example of the call "N30E" lies in the northeast or upper right quadrant. In like manner, the call "S45W" lies in the southwest or lower left quadrant. Due north and due south are each 0 degrees; due east and due west, 90 degrees.

In preparing a metes-and-bounds description, we must now add the *distances* to our call, which so far contains only directions. In surveyor's shorthand, this is done by adding the distance or length of the line after the direction, so that a boundary line 1,000 feet long running in a northeasterly direction might appear as "N30°E 1,000 feet"—or "N30°30'30"E 1,000 feet," if the line is not exactly 30 degrees east of north. Such a line would lie in a direction 30 degrees, 30 minutes, and 30 seconds east of north.

Let's examine a set of metes-and-bounds field notes. If the property is described as

"Beginning at the southwest corner of the Robert B. Hart Survey, Tarrant County, Texas,

Remember:

1 township =
36 sections =
23,040 acres

1 section =
640 acres

> THENCE N0°E 2,640 feet;
> THENCE N90°E 5,280 feet;
> THENCE S0°W 2,640 feet;
> THENCE S90°W 5,280 feet to the point of beginning,"

we have a rectangular tract of land whose dimensions are 2,640 feet in the north-south direction and 5,280 feet in the east-west direction. This amounts to 320 acres, or one-half of a section (2,640 × 5,280 = 13,939,200; 13,939,200 ÷ 43,560 = 320).

To convert the metes-and-bounds description to a sketch or scaled drawing, we must use a protractor to measure the directions or angles and a scale or ruler to measure the distances.

1. Place the center of the protractor (most protractors have a small hole at this point) directly over the point on the paper from which the indicated direction is to be measured.
2. Carefully align the protractor so that its straight bottom is exactly horizontal to the paper's edge. This means that the straight portion is lined up in the east-west direction on your paper.
3. Notice the direction from north of the metes-and-bounds call.
4. On the curved outer scale of the protractor, locate the number of degrees from north indicated by the call (in our example, it was 0 degrees).
5. Place a dot on the paper at 0 on the protractor.
6. Remove the protractor and, with a suitable scale, draw a line from the beginning point through the dot just made. The length of this line represents the distance shown in the call (in our example, it was 2,640 feet).
7. The protractor to the end of this line and position it so that its center (or the small hole) is directly over the end of the line just drawn.
8. Repeat the above steps until you arrive at the point of beginning. If you successfully arrive at this point, your survey is said to close. If it does not close, either the field notes are defective or (more likely) you have erred in constructing the scaled sketch.

Draw your sketch of the above example here:

Your sketch should look like this:

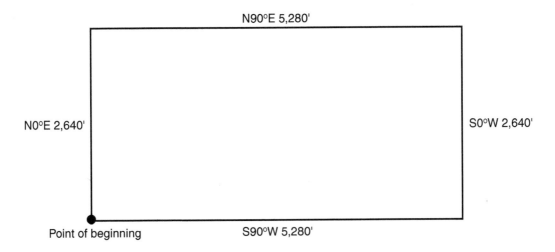

N90°E 5,280'

N0°E 2,640'

S0°W 2,640'

Point of beginning

S90°W 5,280'

Let's try another one:

Beginning at the northeast corner of the William H. Long Survey, Coleman County, Texas,

THENCE S45°W 1,000 feet;
THENCE S90°W 2,000 feet;
THENCE N45°E 1,000 feet;
THENCE N90°E 2,000 feet to the point of beginning.

Your sketch should be in the shape of a parallelogram 2,000 feet in the east-west direction and 1,000 feet in the diagonal direction, which should be inclined below and to the left of the starting point. Draw your sketch here:

Your sketch should look like this:

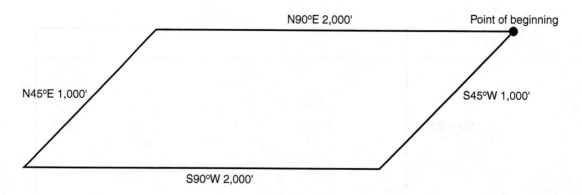

N90ºE 2,000'

Point of beginning

N45ºE 1,000'

S45ºW 1,000'

S90ºW 2,000'

ADDITIONAL PRACTICE

When you have finished these problems, check your answers at the end of the chapter. If you miss any of the problems, review this chapter before going on to Chapter 8.

1. The S½ of the SW¼ of the NW¼ of section 4 was sold for $1,150 per acre. How much did the parcel sell for?
   a. $21,500
   b. $23,000
   c. $26,000
   d. $29,000

2. If the S½ of the NW¼ of the NE¼ of the SW¼ of section 24 sold for $13,250 per acre, what was the total price?
   a. $33,125
   b. $66,250
   c. $132,500
   d. $530,000

3. The Rand family owned the entire SW¼ of section 5. They sold the S½ of the SW¼ of the SW¼ of section 5 at $22,000 per acre. They also sold the SW¼ of the SE¼ of the SW¼ of section 5 at $25,000 per acre. How much money did the Rands receive from the sale of these parcels?
   a. $250,000
   b. $375,000
   c. $440,000
   d. $690,000

4. A woman owned acreage described as the NW¼ of section 7. She sold half of her property for $5,000 per acre and a quarter of the balance for $4,500 per acre. What was the total sales price?
   a. $400,000
   b. $450,000
   c. $490,000
   d. $500,000

5. Two brothers owned section 17. They sold the following three tracts of land: W½ of the SW¼, NE¼ of the SW¼, and N½ of the SE¼. Their remaining acreage totals
   a. 320.
   b. 400.
   c. 440.
   d. 460.

6. Which of the following tracts is the largest?
   a. NW¼ of the NW¼ of the SE¼ of section 1
   b. S½ of the SE¼ of the SE¼ of the NW¼ of section 3
   c. SE¼ of the SE¼ of the NW¼ and the SW¼ of the NE¼ of section 7
   d. All three tracts are of equal size

7. Which of the following tracts totals 20 acres?
   a. N½ of the SW¼ of the NE¼ of the SW¼ of section 6
   b. NW¼ of the SE¼ of the NW¼ of section 9
   c. S½ of the NE¼ of the SW¼ of section 8
   d. S½ of the S½ of the S½ of section 10

8. What price per acre was paid for the W½ of the NE¼ of the NE¼ of section 1 and the SE¼ of the NE¼ of the NE¼ of section 1 if the total parcel sold for $180,000?
   a. $600
   b. $3,000
   c. $4,500
   d. $6,000

9. How many square feet are in the following tract of land?

   ". . . to a point of beginning; thence, due South for 400 feet; thence North 45° West 562.5 feet; thence due East 400 feet to the point of beginning."
   a. 80,000
   b. 112,500
   c. 160,000
   d. 225,000

10. How many acres are in the tract of land described in problem 9?
   a. 1.84
   b. 2.58
   c. 3.67
   d. 5.17

11. Henry owned the SW¼ of a section of land. He sold the W½ of the NW¼ of the SW¼ at $275 an acre and he sold the SW¼ of the SW¼ at $250 an acre. How much money did he receive for the land?
   a. $5,500
   b. $10,000
   c. $12,500
   d. $15,500

12. Which section of a township is set aside for school purposes and referred to as a *school section?*
   a. 1
   b. 16
   c. 18
   d. 24

13. A family recently purchased 35 percent of section 26 and intend to utilize the land for an animal rescue sanctuary. How many acres do they have?
   a. 56
   b. 210
   c. 224
   d. 280

14. How many acres are contained in the following tract of land?

   ". . . to a point of beginning; thence South 45°0'0" West 300 feet; thence North 45°0'0" West 350 feet; thence North 45°0'0" East 300 feet; thence South 45°0'0" East 350 feet to the point of beginning."
   a. 2.07
   b. 2.41
   c. 2.81
   d. 3.6

15. How many acres are in the W½ of the NE¼ of the SW¼ of the NW¼ of Section 34?
   a. 2.5
   b. 5
   c. 40
   d. 50

SOLUTIONS: PROBLEMS IN CHAPTER 7

1. $640 \times 0.25 \times 0.25 = 40$ or $4 \times 4 = 16, 640 \div 16 = 40$

2. $640 \times 0.25 \times 0.25 \times 0.25 = 10$ or $4 \times 4 \times 4 = 64, 640 \div 64 = 10$

3. a. $640 \times 0.25 = 160$
   b. $640 \times 0.5 \times 0.5 \times 0.25 = 40$
   c. $640 \times 0.5 \times 0.25 = 80$
   d. $640 \times 0.25 \times 0.25 = 40$
   e. $640 \times 0.5 \times 0.25 \times 0.25 = 20$
   f. $640 \times 0.5 \times 0.5 \times 0.25 = 40$
   g. $640 \times 0.5 \times 0.5 \times 0.5 \times 0.25 = 20$ or $2 \times 2 \times 2 \times 4 = 32, 640 \div 32 = 20$
   h. $640 \times 0.25 \times 0.25 \times 0.25 = 10$
   i. $640 \times 0.5 \times 0.25 \times 0.25 \times 0.25 = 5$

4. $640 \times 0.5 \times 0.25 = 80$ or $2 \times 4 = 8, 640 \div 8 = 80$

5. $640 \times 0.25 \times 0.25 = 40$

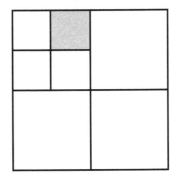

6. $640 \times 0.5 \times 0.5 \times 0.5 = 80$

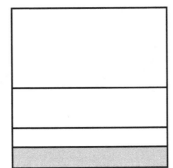

7. $640 \times 0.25 \times 0.25 = 40$
   $\$1,240 \times 40 = \$49,600$

8. $640 \times 0.5 \times 0.5 \times 0.5 \times 0.25 = 20$ or $2 \times 2 \times 2 \times 4 = 32$, $640 \div 32 = 20$
   $\$120,000 \div 20 = \$6,000$

9. $640 \times 0.25 = 160$
   $160 \times 0.5 = 80$
   $160 - 80 = 80$

10. $640 \times 0.25 \times 0.25 = 40$
    $\$144,000 \div 40 = \$3,600$
    $640 \times 0.5 \times 0.25 \times 0.25 = 20$
    $20 \times \$3,600 = \$72,000$

11. a. $640 \times 0.5 \times 0.25 \times 0.25 \times 0.25 = 5$
    $640 \times 0.25 \times 0.25 \times 0.25 = 10$
    $10 + 5 = 15$
    $15 \times 500 = 7,500$
    b. $640 \times 0.25 \times 0.25 \times 0.25 \times 0.25 = 2.5$
    $640 \times 0.5 \times 0.25 = 80$
    $80 + 2.5 = 82.5$
    $82.5 \times 500 = 41,250$

SOLUTIONS: ADDITIONAL PRACTICE

1. (b) $640 \times 0.5 \times 0.25 \times 0.25 = 20$ or $2 \times 4 \times 4 = 32$, $640 \div 32 = 20$
   $20 \times \$1,150 = \$23,000$

2. (b) $640 \times 0.5 \times 0.25 \times 0.25 \times 0.25 = 5$
   $5 \times \$13,250 = \$66,250$

3. (d) $640 \times 0.5 \times 0.25 \times 0.25 = 20$
   $20 \times \$22,000 = \$440,000$
   $640 \times 0.25 \times 0.25 \times 0.25 = 10$
   $10 \times \$25,000 = \$250,000$
   $250,000 + \$440,000 = \$690,000$

4. (c) $640 \times 0.25 = 160$
   $160 \times 0.5 = 80$
   $80 \times 0.25 = 20$
   $80 \times \$5,000 = \$400,000$
   $20 \times \$4,500 = \$90,000$
   $\$90,000 + \$400,000 = \$490,000$

5. (c) $640 \times 0.5 \times 0.25 = 80$
   $640 \times 0.25 \times 0.25 = 40$
   $640 \times 0.5 \times 0.25 = 80$
   $80 + 40 + 80 = 200$
   $640 - 200 = 440$

6. (c) a. $640 \times 0.25 \times 0.25 \times 0.25 = 10$
   b. $640 \times 0.5 \times 0.25 \times 0.25 \times 0.25 = 5$
   c. $640 \times 0.25 \times 0.25 \times 0.25 = 10$
   $640 \times 0.25 \times 0.25 = 40$
   $40 + 10 = 50$

7. (c) a. $640 \times 0.5 \times 0.25 \times 0.25 \times 0.25 = 5$
   b. $640 \times 0.25 \times 0.25 \times 0.25 = 10$
   c. $640 \times 0.5 \times 0.25 \times 0.25 = 20$
   d. $640 \times 0.5 \times 0.5 \times 0.5 = 80$

8. (d) $640 \times 0.5 \times 0.25 \times 0.25 = 20$
   $640 \times 0.25 \times 0.25 \times 0.25 = 10$
   $10 + 20 = 30$
   $\$180,000 \div 30 = \$6,000$

9. (a)
   400'
   Point of beginning
   562.5'
   400'
   $400' \times 400' \div 2 = 80,000$ square feet

10. (a) 80,000 square feet $\div$ 43,560 square feet
    = 1.84 acres (rounded)

11. (d) $640 \times 0.5 \times 0.25 \times 0.25 = 20$
    $20 \times \$275 = \$5,500$
    $640 \times 0.25 \times 0.25 = 40$
    $40 \times \$250 = \$10,000$
    $\$5,500 + \$10,000 = \$15,500$

12. (b) Section 16

13. (c) $640 \times 0.35 = 224$ acres

14. (b) $300' \times 350' = 105,00$ square feet
    105,000 square feet $\div$ 43,560 = 2.41 acres (rounded)

15. (b) $640 \times 0.5 \times 0.25 \times 0.25 \times 0.25 = 5$

CHAPTER

8

Area and Volume

Land is frequently sold by the front foot or by the square foot of land area. Building materials are sold by the square foot, square yard, or cubic yard. In most areas, improved real estate is sold or leased by the square foot. It is imperative that real estate practitioners be able to accurately measure and calculate linear, square, and cubic measure.

At the conclusion of your work in this chapter, you will be able to accurately calculate

- the front feet of a lot,
- square feet and square yards, and
- cubic feet and cubic yards.

Before attempting to calculate area or volume problems, it is important to do the following:

1. Convert all dimensions to feet.

EXAMPLE: 8 feet, 6 inches becomes 8.5 feet.

To convert inches to feet, divide the inches by 12.

$$\frac{6 \text{ inches}}{12 \text{ inches}} = 0.50 \text{ feet}$$

2. Become familiar with the information in Table 8.1.

TABLE 8.1

Common Conversions

Linear measure = A line
12 inches = 1 foot
3 feet = 1 yard
1 link = 7.92 inches
1 vara = 33.333 inches
1 rod = 16.5 feet = 5.5 yards
1 mile = 5,280 feet = 320 rods
1 chain = 66 feet = 4 rods = 100 links
Square measure = Area
Length (L) × Width (W) = Area (A) (in square unit measurements)
12" × 12" = 144 square inches = 1 square foot 3' × 3' = 9 square feet = 1 square yard
To convert square yards to square feet, multiply square yards by 9. To convert square feet to square yards, divide square feet by 9.
1 acre = 43,560 square feet
To convert acres to square feet, multiply acres by 43,560. To convert square feet to acres, divide square feet by 43,560.
1 section = 640 acres
To convert sections to acres, multiply sections by 640. To convert acres to sections, divide acres by 640.
Cubic Measure = Volume
Length (L) × Width (W) × Height (H) = Volume (V) (in cubic unit measurements)
12" × 12" × 12" = 1,728 cubic inches = 1 cubic foot 3' × 3' × 3' = 27 cubic feet = 1 cubic yard
To convert cubic yards to cubic feet, multiply cubic yards by 27. To convert cubic feet to cubic yards, divide cubic feet by 27.

LINEAR

Front Feet (Inches or Yards)

The price of a tract of land may be priced by the front foot. Typically, this occurs where the tract *fronts* onto or faces something desirable. Therefore, the frontage is the major element of value because it is the frontage of a tract that provides access to something of value, such as a main street, a river, or a lake. This avenue of access then becomes quite valuable, so much so that it assumes the pricing burden of the entire tract.

For example, consider a tract of land facing (or fronting on) Eagle Mountain Lake:

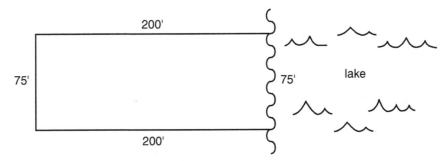

Because lakefront lots are so desirable, this lot is priced at $1,200 per front foot, while non-fronting lots in the subdivision are priced at only $3 per square foot.

Therefore, the lakefront lot shown would be valued at $90,000 (75 feet × $1,200 = $90,000), while a lot of equal size not fronting on the lake would be valued at half as much, or $45,000 (75 feet × 200 feet = 15,000 square feet; 15,000 square feet × $3 = $45,000).

1. Eagle Mountain Lake regulates the length of piers. A pier cannot exceed 80 percent of the lot's frontage on the water. How many feet long may a pier be constructed?

2. What would be the cost of the above pier at $12 per linear foot?

When the dimensions of a lot are given, front feet are always listed first. Thus, a lot 60 feet by 125 feet has 60 front feet.

To calculate the price per front foot, divide the sales price by the number of front feet:

Sales price ÷ Front feet = Price per front foot

E X A M P L E :   If a lot 60 feet by 125 feet sold for $168,000, how much was its selling price per front foot?

$168,000 ÷ 60 feet = $2,800 per front foot

3. A property on Market Street is valued at $262,500. What is its value per front foot if it has a frontage of 35 feet?

Linear—Perimeter

The cost of constructing fences will usually be quoted as dollars per linear foot. Fences are frequently installed on the property lines or perimeter of the property to enclose an area. The perimeter is simply the total linear feet of the sides that enclose an area.

E X A M P L E :   A man purchased a tract of land that he wants to enclose with a fence. The tract is 960 feet by 2,200 feet. The desired fence can be purchased at $2.10 per linear foot.

960' + 2,200' + 960' + 2,200' – 6,320 linear feet

6,320 linear feet × $2.10 = $13,272 cost of fence

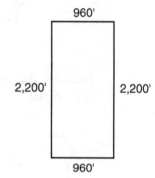

AREA

Square Feet (Inches or Yards)

It is imperative that every real estate professional be able to calculate square footage and area accurately because

-   commercial real estate is leased at dollars per square foot,
-   vacant lots are sold at dollars per square foot or dollars per acre when not sold at dollars per square foot, and
-   homes are sold at dollars per square foot.

Before you start working area problems, let's review some basics about shapes and measurements.

The space inside a two-dimensional shape is called its *area.*

A right angle is the angle formed by one-fourth of a circle. Because a full circle is 360 degrees, and one-fourth of 360 degrees is 90 degrees, a right angle is a 90-degree angle.

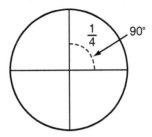

A rectangle is a closed figure with four sides that are at right angles to one another. In other words, each angle in a rectangle is 90 degrees.

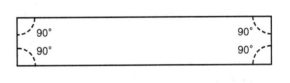

4. A square is a special type of rectangle. Which statement below best describes a square (illustrated below)?

   a. All sides of a square are of equal length.

   b. Only the opposite sides of a square are of equal length.

   c. Squares are rectangles with four sides of equal length.

   d. Rectangles are squares.

   e. Squares are rectangles with equal angles.

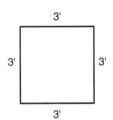

5. Which of the following figures is(are) a square(s)? Which is(are) a rectangle(s)?

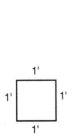
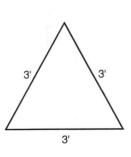
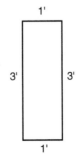
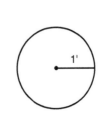

In math, the word square may be defined as a

- shape with four sides of equal length and each angle containing 90 degrees,
- unit for measuring the area of various shapes, or
- multiple of a number by or times itself.

E X A M P L E :   The number 9 is the square of 3 because if you multiply 3 × 3, the answer is 9.

Units of measurement can be treated in the same manner as numbers, and a clear understanding of this fact greatly simplifies math. For example, if 3 times 3 equals 9, which is the square of 3, then yards multiplied by yards equals square yards. Or to illustrate this example further:

$$3 \text{ yards} \times 3 \text{ yards} = ?$$

Step 1. Multiply the numbers together:

$$3 \times 3 = 9$$

Step 2. Multiply the units of measurement together:

$$\text{Yards} \times \text{Yards} = \text{Square yards}$$

Now let's look at some square units.

A square whose four sides measure one inch each is a square inch or one inch square. Likewise, one square mile is one mile on each of the four sides, or one mile square, which amounts to 640 acres.

E X A M P L E :   one square inch (sq in)

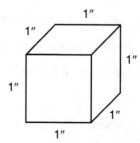

A square whose four sides measure one foot each is a square foot.

E X A M P L E :   one square foot (sq ft)

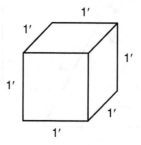

To calculate the area inside a shape, measure the number of square units inside the shape. One way to find the number of square units is to place the shape on a larger number of square units and count the number of square units inside the shape.

6. Count the number of square foot units inside the square below.

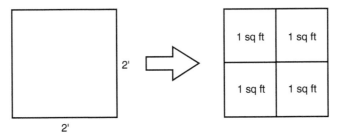

What is the area of this square?

7. Count the number of square foot units inside the rectangle below.

What is the area of this rectangle?

Area of Squares and Rectangles

Because counting squares is cumbersome, use the following formula to compute the area of any rectangle:

$$\textbf{Length} \times \textbf{Width} = \textbf{Area}$$
or
$$\text{L} \times \text{W} = \text{A}$$

Check your figures in questions 6 and 7, applying this formula. The formula should give you the same answers that counting squares did.

$$2' \times 2' = 4 \text{ square feet} \qquad 1' \times 3' = 3 \text{ square feet}$$

8. Compute the area of the following rectangle, using the formula L × W = A:

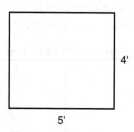

Your answer to Exercise 8 should have been 20 square feet.

Remember, when inches are multiplied by inches, the answer must be in square inches. Likewise, recalling our previous discussion:

Feet × Feet = Square feet

9. What is the area of the rectangle below?

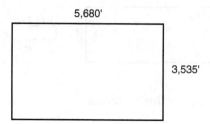

10. What is the area of the square below?

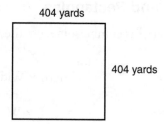

Now you can apply what you have learned about the area of a rectangle to a practical real estate problem.

11. A management company leases a parking lot that measures 80 feet by 150 feet. How much rent is paid each year if the lot rents for $6.60 per square foot per year?

Conversion—Using Like Measures for Area

When an area is computed, all of the dimensions used must be given in the same kind of unit. When you found areas in problems 6 and 7 by counting square units, all of the units you counted were of the same kind—feet. When you use a formula to find an area, you must also use units of the same kind for each element of the formula, with the answer as square units of that kind. So inches must be multiplied by inches to arrive at square inches, feet must be multiplied by feet to arrive at square feet, and yards must be multiplied by yards to arrive at square yards.

If the two dimensions you want to multiply are in different units of measure, you must convert one to the other.

Remember:

There are 43,560 square feet per acre.

It is best to convert all units to feet; therefore, you will

- multiply *yards* by 3 to get feet and
- divide *inches* by 12 to get feet.

12. Convert and solve the following:

   a. 36" × 3' = _____ square feet

   b. 15" × 1.5' = _____ square feet

   c. 72" × 7' = _____ square feet

   d. 6 yards × 5' = _____ square feet

   e. 17 yards × 24" = _____ square feet

It is best to calculate square feet, then convert to square inches or square yards:

■ To convert square feet to square inches, multiply the number of square feet by 144 square inches (12" × 12").

■ To convert square feet to square yards, divide the number of square feet by 9 square feet (3' × 3').

13. Convert the answers in problem 12 to square inches.

14. Convert the answers in problem 12 to square yards.

15. A house is on a lot that is 90 feet by 720 inches. What is the area of the lot?

NOTE: In the real estate business, lot sizes are generally calculated in square feet.

16. Compute the area of the lot below in square feet.

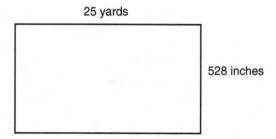

25 yards

528 inches

17. A broker sold a lot with 66 feet and 9 inches of street frontage and a depth of 150 feet to an alley. The sale price was $4 per square foot. Compute the amount the broker received from this sale if her commission rate was 6 percent.

18. You have contracted to build a sidewalk in front of your house. It is to be 5 feet wide by 27 feet and 6 inches long. If the contractor charges $200 per square yard for concrete and labor, how much will the sidewalk cost you?

Area of Triangles

 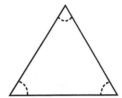 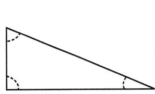 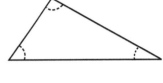

A *triangle* is a closed figure with three straight sides and three angles. *Tri* means three.

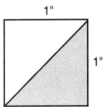

The square-inch figure at the right has been cut in half by a straight line drawn through the opposite corners to make two equal triangles.

19. How many square inches are in the shaded part of the above square?

20. How many square inches are contained in the triangle below when it is placed on a square-inch grid?

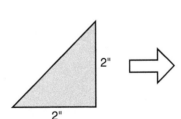 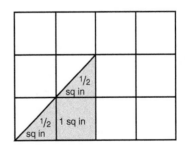

21. What is the area of the triangle below?

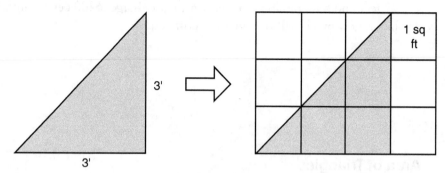

As before, the square-unit grid is cumbersome for computing large areas. It is more convenient to use the following formula for finding the area of a triangle:

½ (Base × Height) = Area of a triangle
½ (BH) = A

or

$$\frac{B \times H}{2} = \text{Area of a triangle}$$

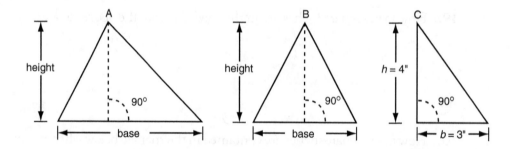

The base is the side on which the triangle sits.

The height is the straight line distance from the top of the uppermost angle to the base. The height line must form a 90-degree angle to the base.

22. Compute the area of triangle C.

23. The diagram below shows a lakefront lot. Compute its area.

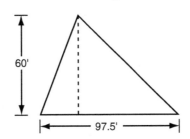

24. A man purchased the following lot at $4.75 per square foot. His broker received a 10 percent commission on the sale. How much was the broker's commission?

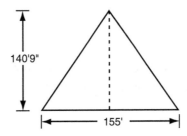

Area of Irregular Closed Figures

25. Use the following drawing of two neighboring lots to answer the questions below.

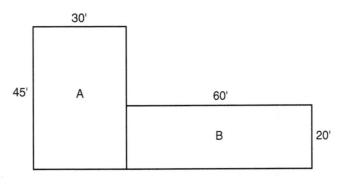

   a. What is the area of lot A?

   b. What is the area of lot B?

    c. What is the total area of both lots?

26. Make two rectangles by drawing one straight line inside the figure below.

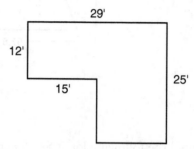

27. Using the measurements given in problem 26, compute the total area of the figure. (Find the area of each rectangle and add them.)

The area of an irregular figure can be found by dividing it into regular figures, computing the area of each regular figure, and adding all the areas together to obtain the total area.

28. Divide the following figure into rectangles and calculate its square footage.

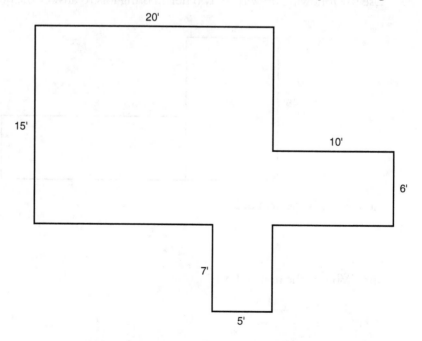

When calculating the square footage of most houses, it is easier to square off a figure and subtract the missing pieces than it is to try to divide it. To demonstrate, let's look at two ways to calculate the square footage of the following home.

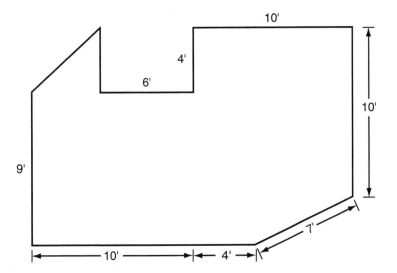

The more complicated way is to divide it into rectangles and triangles, calculate the square feet in each, and then add the areas to arrive at the total square feet.

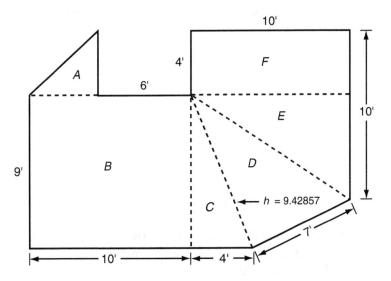

NOTE: It is very difficult, if not impossible, to obtain an accurate dimension for the height of the triangle identified as "D."

A. $4' \times 4' \div 2$ = 8 square feet
B. $10' \times 9'$ = 90 square feet
C. $4' \times 9' \div 2$ = 18 square feet
D. $7' \times 9.42857' \div 2$ = 33 square feet (rounded)
E. $10' \times 6' \div 2$ = 30 square feet
F. $10' \times 4'$ = 40 square feet
              Total 219 square feet

An easier, and usually more accurate, way to calculate the total area is to (1) square off the figure, (2) calculate the square footage of the squared-off figure, and then (3) calculate the square footage of and subtract the missing pieces.

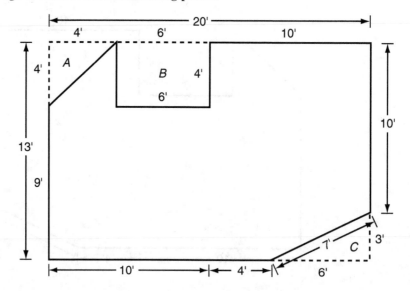

The missing pieces are identified as A, B and C in the above figure.

$$
\begin{array}{lll}
\text{The total figure is } 20' \times 13' & = 260 \text{ square feet} \\
\text{Less:} \quad \text{A. } 4' \times 4' \div 2 & = <8> \text{ square feet} \\
\qquad \text{B. } 6' \times 4' & = <24> \text{ square feet} \\
\qquad \text{C. } 6' \times 3' \div 2 & = \underline{<9>} \text{ square feet} \\
\qquad\qquad\qquad \text{Total } 219 \text{ square feet}
\end{array}
$$

In your real estate practice, most of your area calculations will be related to the square footage of a lot or house. When calculating the square feet of living area (heated and air-conditioned area) in a house, use the following five steps:

1. Sketch the foundation.
2. Measure and record the dimensions of all outside walls, remembering to convert inches to the decimal equivalent of a foot.
3. Square off your sketch and identify the missing areas of living space. These include the attached garage, patios, breezeways, porches, and so on.
4. Calculate the total square feet.
5. Subtract the missing areas.

29. Calculate the living area of the house shown here.

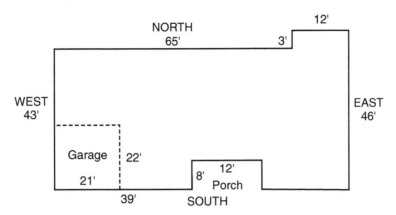

Area of Trapezoids

The shape of the figure in the following exercise is called a trapezoid. You can compute its area by applying the formula

$$\frac{a+b}{2} \times h = A$$

Substituting, we have:

Step 1. $\dfrac{16' + 20'}{2} \times 6' = A$

Step 2. $\dfrac{36'}{2} \times 6' = A$

Step 3. $18' \times 6' = A$

Step 4. 108 square feet = A

OR

You can divide a trapezoid into a rectangle and a triangle.

E X A M P L E :

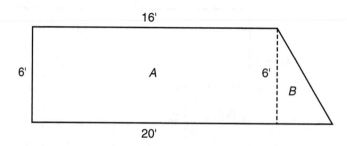

A. $16' \times 6' \quad = 96$ square feet
B. $4' \times 6' \div 2 = \underline{12}$ square feet
              Total 108 square feet

VOLUME

Cubic Feet (Inches or Yards)

When a shape encloses a space, the shape has volume.

The space that a three-dimensional object occupies is called its volume.

Technically speaking, each shape with three dimensions can also be measured in terms of its surface area. For example, a bedroom has volume because it has three dimensions—length, width, and height; however, one wall can be measured as a surface area, or length times height equals area.

30. **a.** Which of the following shapes have volume?

    b. Which have only area?

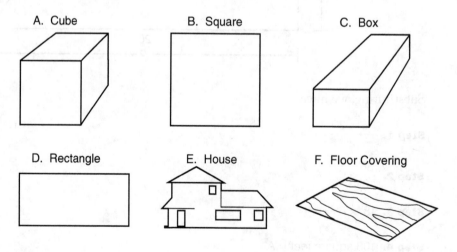

Flat shapes squares, rectangles, triangles, and so on—do not have volume. Flat shapes have two dimensions (length and width or height), and shapes with volume have three dimensions (length, width, and height).

Cubic Units

A cube is made up of six squares. Look at the six sides of the following cube:

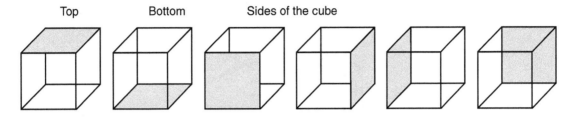

Top   Bottom   Sides of the cube

Volume is measured in cubic units. Look at the following cube:

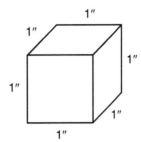

Each side measures one inch. The figure represents 1 cubic inch, abbreviated cu. in. Just as yards times yards equals square yards, a multiple of three units of space equals cubic units, or:

$$\text{Inches} \times \text{Inches} \times \text{Inches} = \text{Cubic inches}$$

31. How many cubic inches are there in the following figure?

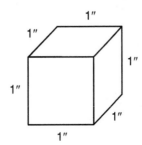

1 cu in

The following figure represents 1 cubic foot, abbreviated cu ft:

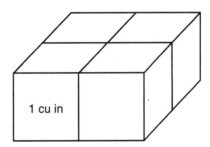

32. How many cubic feet are represented by the following figure?

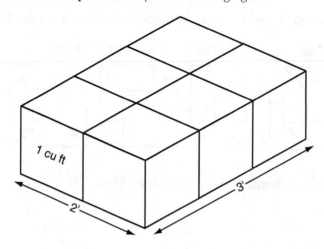

Volume of Box Shapes

Use the following formula for computing volume:

$$L \text{ (length)} \times W \text{ (width)} \times H \text{ (height)} = V \text{ (volume)}$$

33. Find the volume of each of the boxes below.

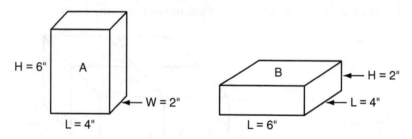

34. How many cubic feet of dirt must be excavated to dig a hole 5 feet long, 4 feet wide, and 4 feet deep? (Depth is the equivalent of height.)

35. A building cost $90,000. It is 50 feet long, 35 feet wide, and 40 feet high, including the basement. What was the cost of this building per cubic foot?

Volume of Triangular Prisms

To compute the volume of a three-dimensional triangular figure, called a prism (e.g., an A-frame house), use the following formula:

$$\tfrac{1}{2}\,(b \times h \times w) = V \text{ (volume)}$$

E X A M P L E :   To compute the volume of the following house:

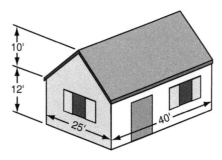

Step 1. Divide the house into shapes: prism and box

Step 2. Find the volume of the prism.
$$V = \tfrac{1}{2}\,(b \times h \times w)$$
$$= \tfrac{1}{2}\,(25' \times 10' \times 40')$$
$$= \tfrac{1}{2}\,(10{,}000 \text{ cubic feet}) = 5{,}000 \text{ cubic feet}$$

Step 3. Find the volume of the box.
$$V = L \times W \times H$$
$$= 25' \times 40' \times 12' = 12{,}000 \text{ cubic feet}$$

Step 4. Find the total volumes of the prism and the box.
$$5{,}000 \text{ cubic feet} + 12{,}000 \text{ cubic feet} = 17{,}000 \text{ cubic feet}$$

36. A family purchased a two-story rental house for $123,500. The house is 35 feet long and 20 feet wide and the first story is 10 feet high. The second story is A-shaped, with a roof 8 feet high at the tallest point. How many cubic feet of space does the house contain? What was its cost per cubic foot?

37. How many cubic feet of space are there in a flat-roofed cabin 27 feet long, 18 feet wide, and 9 feet high?

38. What is the cost of pouring a concrete driveway 20 feet wide, 80 feet long, and 4 inches thick if concrete costs $60 per cubic yard and the finishing costs are $2.28 per square foot, including setting the forms and furnishing the steel?

39. What will it cost to excavate a basement 9 feet deep for a ranch-style house 65 feet by 45 feet if the cost of excavation is $4.50 per cubic yard?

ADDITIONAL PRACTICE

When you have finished these problems, check your answers at the end of the chapter. If you miss any of the problems, review this chapter before going on to chapter 9.

Using the diagram below, answer the first five questions:

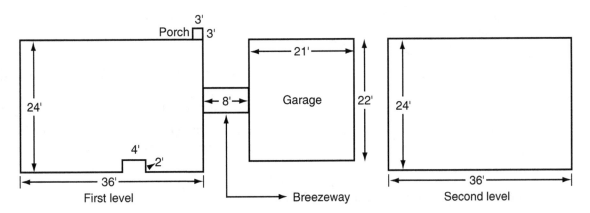

1. The total square feet of living area on the first floor of this house is
   a. 856.
   b. 864.
   c. 873.
   d. 905.

2. The total square feet of living area in the entire house is
   a. 1,720.
   b. 1,761.
   c. 1,769.
   d. 1,796.

3. At $18 per square foot, what would it cost to build the garage?
   a. $7,548
   b. $8,316
   c. $8,696
   d. $8,780

4. At $53 per square foot, what was the cost of building the house if the porch cost $1,800 and the breezeway cost $2,850 to construct?
   a. $91,160
   b. $92,960
   c. $94,010
   d. $95,810

5. If the house and garage sit on a lot 75 feet by 150 feet that cost $4 per square foot, what was the total cost to buy the lot and to build the house and garage?
   a. $137,960
   b. $140,810
   c. $146,276
   d. $149,126

6. This simple storage building will cost $48 per cubic yard to build. What is the cost of this building?

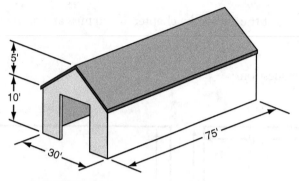

   a. $40,000
   b. $50,000
   c. $108,000
   d. $135,000

7. The area of a rectangle that is 5 feet by 17 feet is

   a. 22 feet.
   b. 44 linear feet.
   c. 44 square feet.
   d. 85 square feet.

8. A single woman owned a tract of land 150 feet wide and 700 feet long, with the 150 feet fronting on an east-west road. She sold the northern 300 feet (linear, not square feet) of this tract. The remaining land was leased to a neighbor at the annual rate of $500 an acre. The neighbor's approximate yearly rent is

   a. $515.50.
   b. $650.
   c. $666.66.
   d. $688.70.

9. A west Texas broker sold a triangular tract of land for $1,750 an acre. What is the amount of his commission at 8 percent if the land had a base length of 1,200 feet and the height of the triangle measured 700 feet?

   a. $1,012.20
   b. $1,156.80
   c. $1,349.88
   d. $16,870

10. A seller owned a rectangular ten-acre tract of land with a frontage of 726 feet along the south side of a paved road. After selling the southern half of this tract, the owner fenced the remaining land at a cost of $2.50 per running, or linear, foot. The fence cost

   a. $2,565.
   b. $2,652.
   c. $4,576.
   d. $5,130.

11. A U-shaped barn consists of two rectangles 30 feet by 75 feet and a connecting section 20 feet by 50 feet. The approximate cost (rounded to whole dollars) of a concrete floor 4 inches thick, at the rate of $36 per cubic yard, is

   a. $1,444.
   b. $2,222.
   c. $2,444.
   d. $44,000.

12. A building has been razed to make parking spaces and the basement area must be filled with earth and solid fill. The hole is 35 feet wide by 79 feet long and is 6 feet deep. Approximately how many cubic yards of fill are required?

   a. 614
   b. 2,765
   c. 5,530
   d. 18,590

13. What is the cost of $\frac{2}{5}$ of 174,240 square feet of land if the price per acre is $1,500?

   a. $1,200
   b. $1,500
   c. $2,400
   d. $6,000

14. A 60 foot by 175 foot lot has a 35 foot by 70 foot right triangle alley easement on one corner. The square feet of usable area is

   a. 8,050.
   b. 9,275.
   c. 10,395.
   d. 10,500.

15. What is the square footage of the living area of the house shown in the illustration below?
    a. 2,750
    b. 3,486
    c. 3,531
    d. 3,738

16. You bought a lot 70 feet by 150 feet for $15 per square foot and assumed a paving lien of $876. For how much must you sell it in order to pay a 7 percent broker's commission, pay off the paving lien, and realize a 15 percent profit on your investment.
    a. $169,462
    b. $170,297
    c. $170,400
    d. $195,700

17. There is a tract of land that is 1.25 acres. The lot is 150 feet deep. How much will the lot sell for at $2,650 per front foot?
    a. $93,280
    b. $144,292
    c. $397,500
    d. $961,950

18. A parking lot 200 feet by 380 feet earns annual gross income of $168,000. If each space, including access, uses 190 square feet, what is the monthly rent per space?
    a. $35
    b. $42
    c. $420
    d. $499

19. A 2,000 square foot house is located on a lot 50 feet by 75 feet. What percentage of the lot does the house occupy?
    a. 47.7 percent
    b. 50 percent
    c. 53.3 percent
    d. 75 percent

20. A rectangular lot 600 feet by 1,250 feet is divided into 12 lots of 55,000 square feet each. The tract of land has a road through the center. What percentage of the tract does the road take up?
    a. 12 percent
    b. 13.64 percent
    c. 88 percent
    d. 92.67 percent

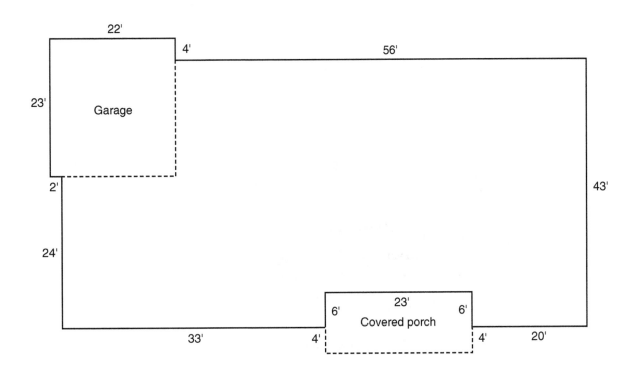

SOLUTIONS: PROBLEMS IN CHAPTER 8

1. $75' \times 0.8 = 60'$

2. $60' \times \$12 = \$720$

3. $\$262,500 \div 35' = \$7,500$

4. (c) Squares are rectangles with four sides of equal length.

5. Figure A is a square. Figures A and C are rectangles. Remember, a square is a rectangle with four sides of equal length.

6. 4 square feet

7. 3 square feet

8. $5' \times 4' = 20$ square feet

9. $5,680' \times 3,535' = 20,078,800$ square feet

10. 404 yards $\times$ 404 yards $= 163,216$ square yards

11. $80' \times 150' = 12,000$ square feet
   $12,000$ square feet $\times \$6.60 = \$79,200$

12. a. $36'' \div 12 = 3'$
      $3' \times 3' = 9$ square feet
   b. $15'' \div 12 = 1.25'$
      $1.25' \times 1.5' = 1.875$ square feet
   c. $72'' \div 12 = 6'$
      $6' \times 7' = 42$ square feet
   d. 6 yards $\times 3 = 18'$
      $18' \times 5' = 90$ square feet
   e. 17 yards $\times 3 = 51'$
      $24'' \div 12 = 2'$
      $51' \times 2' = 102$ square feet

13. a. 9 square feet × 144 = 1,296 square inches

   b. 1,875 square feet × 144 = 270 square inches

   c. 42 square feet × 144 = 6,048 square inches

   d. 90 square feet × 144 = 12,960 square inches

   e. 102 square feet × 144 = 14,688 square inches

14. a. 9 square feet ÷ 9 = 1 square yard

   b. 1.875 square feet ÷ 9 = 0.2083 square yard

   c. 42 square feet ÷ 9 = 4.6667 square yards

   d. 90 square feet ÷ 9 = 10 square yards

   e. 102 square feet ÷ 9 = 11.3333 square yards

15.   720" ÷ 12 = 60'

   90' × 60' = 5,400 square feet

16.   25 yards × 3 = 75'

   528" ÷ 12 = 44'

   75' × 44' = 3,300 square feet

17.   9" ÷ 12 = 0.75'

   0.75' + 66' = 66.75'

   66.75' × 150' = 10,012.5 square feet

   10,012.5 square feet × $4 = $40,050

   $40,050 × 0.06 = $2,403

18.   6" ÷ 12 = 0.5'

   0.5' + 27' = 27.5'

   27.5' × 5' = 137.5 square feet

   137.5 square feet ÷ 9 = 15.27778 square yards

   15.27778 square yards × $200 = $3055.56 (rounded)

19.   1" × 1" ÷ 2 = 0.5 square inch

20.   2" × 2" ÷ 2 = 2 square inches

21.   3' × 3' ÷ 2 = 4.5 square feet

22.   3" × 4" ÷ 2 = 6 square inches

23.   97.5' × 60' ÷ 2 = 2,925 square feet

24.   9" ÷ 12 = 0.75'

0.75' + 140' = 140.75'

155' × 140.75' = 21,816.25 square feet

21,816.25 square feet ÷ 2 = 10,908.125 square feet

10,908.125 square feet × $4.75 = $51,813.59375

$51,813.59375 × 0.1 = $5,181.36 (rounded)

25. a. 30' × 45' = 1,350 square feet

   b. 60' × 20' = 1,200 square feet

   c. 1,350 square feet + 1,200 square feet = 2,550 square feet

26.

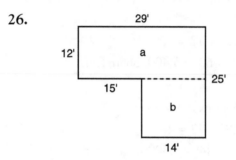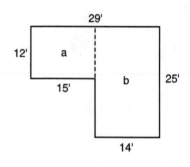

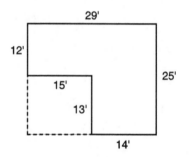

27. a. 29' × 12' = 348 square feet

   b. 14' × 13' = <u>182</u> square feet

       Total 530 square feet

       or

   a. 15' × 12' = 180 square feet

   b. 14' × 25' = <u>350</u> square feet

       Total 530 square feet

       or

       29' × 25' =   725 square feet

       15' × 13' = <u><195></u> square feet

       Total 530   square feet

28. a. 20' × 15' = 300 square feet

b.   5' × 7' = 35 square feet

c. 10' × 6' = <u>60</u> square feet

       Total 395 square feet

29.

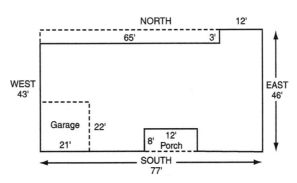

77' × 46'   = 3,542 square feet

Less: 65' × 3' = <195> square feet

Less: 21' × 22' = <462> square feet

Less: 8' × 12'   = <u><96></u> square feet

       Total   2,789 square feet

30. A. cube

B. square

C. box

D. rectangle

E. house

F. floor covering

31.   4 cubic inches

32.   6 cubic feet

33. A. 4" × 2" × 6" = 48 cubic inches

B. 6" × 4" × 2" = 48 cubic inches

34.   5' × 4' × 4' = 80 cubic feet

35.   50' × 35' × 40' = 70,000 cubic feet

$90,000 ÷ 70,000 cubic feet = $1.29 (rounded)

36.   35' × 20' × 10'   = 7,000 cubic feet
35' × 20' × 8' ÷ 2 = 2,800 cubic feet
Total 9,800 cubic feet
$123,500 ÷ 9,800 cubic feet = $12.60 per cubic foot

37.   27' × 18' × 9' = 4,374 cubic feet

38.   4" ÷ 12 = 0.333'
80' × 20' × $\frac{4}{12}$ = 533.33333 cubic feet
533.33333 cubic feet ÷ 27 = 19.75309 cubic yards
19.75309 cubic yards × $60 = $1,185.18519
80' × 20' = 1,600 square feet
1,600 × $2.28 = $3,648
$1,185.18519 + $3,648 = $4,833.19 (rounded)

39.   65' × 45' × 9' = 26,325 cubic feet
26,325 cubic feet ÷ 27 = 975 cubic yards
975 cubic yards × $4.50 = $4,387.50

SOLUTIONS: ADDITIONAL PRACTICE

First level. 36' × 24' = 864 square feet

864 square feet – (2' × 4') = 856 square feet

Second level. 36' × 24' = 864 square feet

Garage. 21' × 22' = 462 square feet

1. (a) 856 square feet

2. (a) 856 square feet + 864 square feet = 1,720 square feet

3. (b) 462 square feet × $18 = $8,316

4. (d) 1,720 square feet × $53 = $91,160
   $91,160 + $1,800 + $2,850 = $95,810

5. (d) 75' × 150' = 11,250 square feet
   11,250 square feet × $4 = $45,000
   $95,810 + $8,316 + $45,000 = $149,126

6. (b) 75' × 30' × 10' = 22,500 cubic feet
   75' × 30' × 5' ÷ 2 = 5,625 cubic feet
   22,500 cubic feet + 5,625 cubic feet = 28,125 cubic feet
   28,125 cubic feet ÷ 27 = 1,041.66667 cubic yards
   1,041.66667 cubic yards × $48 = $50,000

7. (d) 5' × 17' = 85 square feet

8. (d) 150' × 700' = 105,000 square feet
   150' × 300' = 45,000 square feet
   105,000 square feet – 45,000 square feet = 60,000 square feet
   60,000 square feet ÷ 43,560 square feet = 1.37741 acres
   1.37741 acres × $500 = $688.70

9. (c) 1,200' × 700' ÷ 2 = 420,000 square feet
   420,000 square feet ÷ 43,560 square feet = 9.642 acres
   9.642 acres × $1,750 = $16,873.50
   $16,873.50 × 0.08 = $1,349.88

10. (d) 10 acres × 43,560 square feet = 435,600 square feet

435,600 square feet ÷ 726' = 600'

600' ÷ 2 = 300'

726' + 300' + 726' + 300' = 2,052'

2,052' × $2.50 = $5,130

11. (c) 30' × 75' = 2,250 square feet

2,250 square feet × 2 = 4,500 square feet

20' × 50' = 1,000 square feet

4,500 square feet + 1,000 square feet = 5,500 square feet

5,500 square feet × $\frac{4}{12}$ = 1,833.33333 cubic feet

1,833.33333 cubic feet ÷ 27 = 67.90123 cubic yards

67.90123 cubic yards × $36 = $2,444.44 (rounded)

12. (a) 35' × 79' × 6' = 16,590 cubic feet

16,590 cubic feet ÷ 27 = 614.444 cubic yards, or 614 (rounded)

13. (c) 2 ÷ 5 = 0.4

0.4 × 174,240 square feet = 69,696 square feet

69,696 square feet ÷ 43,560 square feet = 1.6 acres

1.6 acres × $1,500 = $2,400

14. (b) 60' × 175' = 10,500 square feet

35' × 70' ÷ 2 = 1,225 square feet

10,500 square feet – 1,225 square feet = 9,275 square feet

15. (a)

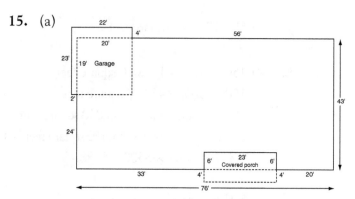

House. 76' × 43' = 3,268 square feet

Garage. 20' × 19' = 380 square feet

Porch. 23' × 6' = 138 square feet

3,268 square feet – 380 square feet – 138 square feet = 2,750 square feet

16. (d) 7% = 0.07   15% = 0.15
70' × 150' = 10,500 square feet
10,500 × $15 = $157,500
1 + 0.15 = 1.15
$157,500 × 1.15 = $181,125 + $876 = $182,001
$182,001 ÷ 0.93 = $195,700

17. (d) 1.25 × 43,560 = 54,450 square feet
54,450 ÷ 150' = 363 front feet
363' × $2,650 = $961,950

18. (a) 200' × 380' = 76,000 square feet
76,000 ÷ 190 = 400
$168,000 ÷ 400 = $420
$420 ÷ 12 = $35

19. (c) 50' × 75' = 3,750 square feet
2,000 ÷ 3,750 = 0.53333333 = 53.3%

20. (a) 600' × 1,250' = 750,000 square feet
55,000 × 12 = 660,000 square feet
750,000 − 660,000 = 90,000 square feet
90,000 ÷ 750,000 = 0.12 = 12%

ECONOMICS OF REAL ESTATE

2

PART

Interest

Interest is the cost (rent paid) of using someone else's money. When money is borrowed, interest is charged for the use of that money for a specific time period. That charge is typically expressed as a percentage (rate) of the loan amount (total) that is charged on an annual basis.

In this chapter, you will learn to

- calculate the interest paid when given the time, rate, and principal,

- calculate the principal loan amount when given the time, rate, and interest paid, and

- determine the interest rate when given the time, principal, and interest paid.

Mathematically, interest problems are another type of calculation using concepts learned in Chapter 1:

Total (loan amount) × Rate (annual interest rate) = Part (annual $ interest)
Part (annual $ interest) ÷ Total (loan amount) = Rate (annual interest rate)
Part (annual $ interest) ÷ Rate (annual interest rate) = Total (loan amount)

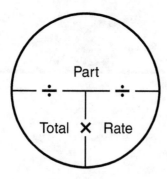 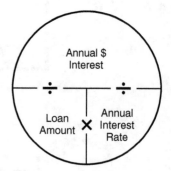

Interest, as stated earlier, is the cost of using someone else's money. A person who borrows money is required to repay the loan plus a charge for interest. This charge will depend on the amount borrowed (*principal*), the length of *time* the money is used (*time*), and the percentage of interest agreed on (*rate*). Repayment, then, involves the *return* of the principal plus a return on the principal, which is called *interest*.

A person who signs a 10 percent interest-bearing note for $500 that will mature in one year will be required to pay interest for one year (time) at 10 percent (rate) on the $500 (principal), as well as the face value of the note itself ($500).

Interest rates are expressed as annual rates, although interest may be paid monthly. A 10 percent interest rate means that the interest charged annually will be 10 percent of the principal.

There are two types of interest: simple interest and compound interest. The first part of this chapter will deal with simple interest, and the latter section will cover compound interest. Most real estate loans involve simple interest paid in *arrears*, or *after* the use of the money has occurred.

SIMPLE INTEREST

The basic formula for finding simple interest is:

Principal (Loan amount) × Interest rate × Time = Annual interest

While simple interest is generally charged for borrowing money for short periods of time, interest-only home loans can be for up to ten years in some cases. Interest only loans will be discussed with more depth in the next chapter.

Principal (total) × Annual interest rate (rate) = Annual $ interest (part)

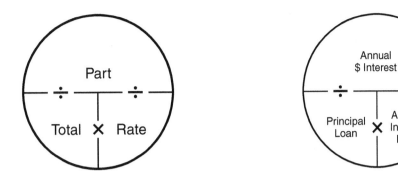

EXAMPLE: What is the annual interest earned by a bank on a $50,000 loan at 6 percent annual interest?

$50,000 (total) × 0.06 (rate) = $3,000 (part)

or

$50,000 (loan) × 0.06 (annual rate) = $3,000 (annual interest)

Often loans are paid back at intervals greater than one year. If a loan is paid back at the end of multiple years, multiply the dollars of annual interest by the number of years for which interest is owed.

EXAMPLE: What amount of simple interest would be due at the end of two years on a $25,000 loan at 8 percent annual interest?

$25,000 (total) × 0.08 (rate) = $2,000 (part)

or

$25,000 (loan) × 0.08 (annual rate) = $2,000 (annual interest)

$2,000 (annual interest) × 2 (years) = $4,000

Loans may also be paid back at the end of a time period less than one year. When this is the case, determine a monthly or daily amount of interest and multiply it by the number of months or days for which interest is owed. Using concepts learned in an earlier chapter, we can express different units of time as fractions or decimals. Six months = $^6\!/_{12}$ = ½ or 0.5 year, and 15 months = $^{15}\!/_{12}$ = $^5\!/_4$ = 1.25 years. This is very powerful in that you can include different time periods of rented money in a very simple mathematical expression.

EXAMPLE: What amount of simple interest would be due at the end of three months on a $6,000 loan at 10 percent annual interest?

$6,000 (total) × 0.1 (rate) = $600 (part)

or

$6,000 (loan) × 0.1 (annual rate) = $600 (annual interest)

$600 (annual interest) ÷ 12 (months) × 3 (months due) = $150

Using what you have just learned, solve the following interest problems.

1. Calculate the interest on a $10,000 small business loan at 7 percent for three years.

2. Find the amount of interest on a $6,000 office equipment loan at 8 percent for nine months.

3. A homeowner borrowed $4,000 to paint her house, and the lender charged 9.5 percent interest. The loan was repaid in three months. What amount was repaid (the loan in full plus interest)?

When two elements in the interest formula are known, the third can be calculated.

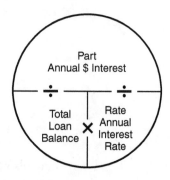

Loan amount × Rate = Annual $ interest
Annual $ interest ÷ Rate = Loan amount
Annual $ interest ÷ Loan amount = Rate

EXAMPLE: What amount of money was loaned if the borrower paid $450 in interest at the end of four months and was charged 9 percent annual interest?

$450 ÷ 4 (months) × 12 (months) = $1,350 (annual interest)

$1,350 (part) ÷ 0.09 (rate) = $15,000 (total)

EXAMPLE: What interest rate did the borrower pay if she borrowed $23,000 and paid $2,070 in interest at the end of nine months?

$2,070 ÷ 9 (months) × 12 (months) = $2,760 (annual interest)

$2,760 (part) ÷ $23,000 (total) = 0.12, or 12% (rate)

Use what you have just learned to solve the following problems.

4. If the interest rate is 10 percent per year, how much money will you have to lend to earn $75 interest for six months?

5. A borrower paid $24 in interest charges at the end of three months. If the annual interest rate was 8 percent, what was the amount of the loan?

6. How many months will it take for $800 to yield $95 in interest at a rate of 9.5 percent?

7. The bank received $750 in interest on a loan to a customer of $12,000 for six months. What interest rate was charged by the bank?

Interest payments may be made annually (once a year), semiannually (twice a year), quarterly (four times a year), or monthly (twelve times a year). To calculate the interest payment amount, compute the annual interest amount, then divide by the number of payments per year.

EXAMPLE: What will the quarterly interest payments be on a loan of $5,000 at 10 percent per annum?

Step 1. Compute the annual interest.

$$\$5,000 \times 0.105 = \$525$$

Step 2. Divide by the number of payments per year.

$$\$525 \div 4 = \$131.25$$

The quarterly interest payments will be $131.25 each.

8. What will be the quarterly interest payments for a $600,000 loan with an interest rate of $5\frac{7}{8}$ percent?

9. A loan for $15,000 with an interest rate of 6¾ percent requires monthly interest payments of how much?

10. If the appraised value of a house is $210,000, how much will semiannual interest payments be on a simple interest loan of $168,000 at 5¼ percent interest?

11. A signature loan has an interest rate of 6 percent and requires quarterly interest payments of $750. What is the principal amount of the loan?

12. A cash advance loan has an interest rate of 8.5 percent and requires semiannual interest payments of $637.50. What is the principal amount of the loan?

13. A short term $10,000 loan requires quarterly interest payments of $200. What is the interest rate of the loan?

14. A $76,000 loan requires semiannual interest payments of $2,152.50. What annual interest rate is being charged?

15. The interest on a $90,000 loan is to be paid every two months. At 6 percent annual interest, what will be the amount of the interest payment for 2 months?

COMPOUND INTEREST

Compound interest is interest that is paid on both the principal and on the interest earned on the principal from past years. The term *compound interest* means that the interest is periodically added to the principal, with the result that the new balance (principal plus interest) draws interest. The annual interest rate may be calculated at different intervals, such as annually, semiannually, quarterly, monthly, or daily. When the interest comes due during the compounding period (for instance, at the end of the month), the interest is calculated and accrues or is added to the principal.

E X A M P L E :   Consider a savings account with a starting balance of $10,000, earning compound interest at 10 percent per year, compounded annually. To determine how much money will be in the account at the end of two years, use the following steps:

Step 1. Calculate the interest for the first earning period.

$$\$10,000 \times 0.1 = \$1,000$$

Step 2. Add the first period's interest to the principal balance of the loan.

$$\$10,000 + \$1,000 = \$11,000$$

Step 3. Calculate the interest for the next earning period on the new principal balance.

$$\$11,000 \times 0.1 = \$1,100$$

If you want to compound for additional periods, simply repeat steps 2 and 3 as many times as necessary.

The example problem asks for the balance at the end of two years.

$10,000   beginning balance
$+1,000   first year's interest
$11,000   balance at end of first year
$+1,100   second year's interest
$12,100   balance at end of second year

The balance at the end of the second year includes the original principal amount of $10,000 plus the accrued compound interest calculated annually at the rate of 10 percent.

If this account were earning only simple interest, the interest would be calculated as follows:

$10,000 (principal) × 0.1 (rate) = $1,000 (annual interest)
$1,000 × 2 (years) = $2,000

Compound interest made a difference of:

$2,100 (compound interest) – $2,000 (simple interest) = $100

16. In 2000, you had a $20,000 certificate of deposit earning interest at the rate of 4.5 percent annually, but the interest was compounded monthly, what was your account balance at the end of three months?

Remember, the compounding period and the interest rate per year (called the *nominal* rate) do not have to be the same. When they are not, you must first compute the interest rate per *compounding period*. In our problem, this is

Rate: 4.5 percent or 0.045 annual rate   = 0.00375 monthly rate
Compounding period: 12 months

Now, the calculation proceeds as in the previous example.

Table 9.1 compares $10,000 earning simple interest and the same amount earning compound interest. The term is five years. The annual interest rate is 7 percent.

TABLE 9.1

Earned Interest

	Simple		Compound	
	Interest Earned	**Balance**	**Interest Earned**	**Balance**
Beginning		$10,000		$10,000
Year 1	$700	10,700	$700.00	10,700
Year 2	700	11,400	749.00	11,449
Year 3	700	12,100	801.43	12,25.43
Year 4	700	12,800	857.53	13,107.96
Year 5	700	13,500	917.56	14,025.52
Total	$3,500		$4,025.52	

Simple interest is computed only on the principal. *Compound interest* is computed on the principal plus accrued interest.

ADDITIONAL PRACTICE

When you have finished these problems, check your answers at the end of the chapter. If you miss any of the problems, review this chapter before going on to Chapter 10.

1. A woman borrowed $2,000 against her credit card at 10.5 percent interest. The loan will be repaid in nine months. What amount will be repaid when the nine months have elapsed?
   a. $157.70
   b. $210
   c. $2,157.50
   d. $2,210

2. The interest on a 10 percent cash advance loan was $72 for six months. What was the principal amount of the loan?
   a. $720
   b. $1,440
   c. $2,480
   d. $2,482

3. How many months will it take for $15,000 to yield $1,125 at 10 percent interest?
   a. 8
   b. 9
   c. 12
   d. 15

4. A man was charged $1,295 on a $14,000 loan from a retail store for one year. What was the rate of interest?
   a. 9 percent
   b. 9¼ percent
   c. 9¾ percent
   d. 9⅞ percent

5. What will quarterly interest payments be on a $16,500 loan at 6.5 percent interest for one year?
   a. $253.75
   b. $255.38
   c. $265.50
   d. $268.13

6. A woman has invested $12,000 at 6 percent annual interest compounded monthly. What is the balance in her account at the end of eight months?
   a. $12,180
   b. $12,364.53
   c. $12,480
   d. $12,488.49

7. A man had $6,945.75 at the end of three years in a money market account at his credit union, which compounded interest annually. If he was paid 5 percent per annum, what was the original amount deposited in the account?
   a. $6,000
   b. $6,305
   c. $6,450
   d. $6,630.50

8. A homeowner borrows $1,500 from a lender to install a new furnace at 11 percent interest. When this loan is paid off at the end of seven months, the total paid, including principal, will be
   a. $96.25.
   b. $1,500.
   c. $1,596.25.
   d. $1,642.50.

9. A couple spent $1,200 on furnishings at a department store, charging it on their credit card. They were out of town and did not pay their bill when due. The following month's bill showed a finance charge of $18 added to the $1,200. What was the rate of interest used to compute the finance charge?

   a. 6 percent
   b. 12 percent
   c. 18 percent
   d. 24 percent

10. Andrea took her $5,000 certificate of deposit to the bank as collateral for a loan of $2,300, which she wanted to buy furniture and equipment for her new office. The bank gave her the loan and had her sign a six-month note at 8 percent interest. The amount of interest Andrea will owe when the note matures is

   a. $90.
   b. $92.
   c. $94.
   d. $94.50.

11. A bank issued a home improvement loan of $20,000 at 7.5 percent simple interest for 4½ years. If the loan was paid in full at the end of 4½ years, how much principal and interest did the bank receive?

   a. $9,900
   b. $11,450
   c. $21,900
   d. $26,750

12. If a bank wished to earn $9,000 on a small business loan of $20,000 over 4½ years, what simple interest rate would it have to charge?

   a. 9 percent
   b. 10 percent
   c. 12.2 percent
   d. 45 percent

13. Which of the following short-term loans will yield the greatest amount of interest?

   a. $2,000 at 20 percent for 2½ years
   b. $10,000 at 5 percent for 2 years
   c. $60,000 at 10 percent for 2 months
   d. All of the above yield the same interest

14. If an interest payment of $90 is made every three months on a $5,000 business equipment loan, what is the interest rate?

   a. 3.1 percent
   b. 5.9 percent
   c. 6.2 percent
   d. 7.2 percent

15. An interest-only loan is given for 80 percent of the appraised value of a house. If the interest on the loan is $6,250 semi-annually at an annual rate of 5 percent, what is the appraised value of the house?

   a. $312,500
   b. $400,000
   c. $500,000
   d. $$625,000

16. A bank issued a loan of $21,000 at 11 percent simple interest to a client with marginal credit for 2½ years. If the loan was paid in full at the end of 2½ years, how much interest was paid to the bank?

   a. $4,620
   b. $5,775
   c. $6,006.43
   d. $6,612.53

17. If a bank wished to earn $3,000 on a loan of $50,000 over 12 months, what interest rate would the bank have to charge?

   a. 5 percent
   b. 5.5 percent
   c. 5.75 percent
   d. 6 percent

18. If a bank loans a woman $15,000 for a short term loan and charges her 8.5 percent simple interest, what will she pay the bank at the end of seven months to pay off the loan?

    a. $743.75
    b. $1,275
    c. $15,743.75
    d. $16,275

19. What is the balance in Steve's saving account at the end of four years if he deposits $18,000 and is paid 4 percent annual interest compounded semiannually (no money is withdrawn)?

    a. $18,720
    b. $19,468.80
    c. $20,247.55
    d. $21,089.87

20. A money market account in 1999 had a balance of $48,605.36 at the end of four years. If interest was compounded at an annual rate of 6 percent, what amount was originally deposited in the account?

    a. $38,500
    b. $40,425
    c. $42,446
    d. $45,854

SOLUTIONS: PROBLEMS IN CHAPTER 9

1. $10,000 × 0.07 = $700
   $700 × 3 = $2,100

2. $6,000 × 0.08 = $480
   $480 ÷ 12 × 9 = $360

3. $4,000 × 0.095 = $380
   $380 ÷ 12 × 3 = $95 (rounded)
   $4,000 + $95 = $4,095

4. $75 ÷ 6 × 12 = $150
   $150 (part) ÷ 0.1 (rate) = $1,500 (total)

5. $24 ÷ 3 × 12 = $96
   $96 (part) ÷ 0.08 (rate) = $1,200 (total)

6. $800 × 0.095 = $76
   $95 ÷ $76 = 1.25
   1.25 × 12 = 15

7. $750 ÷ 6 × 12 = $1,500
   $1,500 (part) ÷ $12,000 (total) = 0.125
   or 12.5% (rate)

8. 5⅞ percent = 0.05875 as a decimal equivalent
   $600,000 (total) × 0.05875 (rate) = $35,250 (part)
   $35,250 ÷ 12 × 3 = $8,812.50
   or
   $35,250 ÷ 4 = $8,812.50

9. $15,000 (total) × 0.0675 (rate) = $1,012.50 (part)
   $1,012.50 ÷ 12 = $84.38 (rounded)

10. $168,000 (total) × 0.0525 (rate) = $8,820 (part)
    $8,820 ÷ 12 × 6 = $4,410

11. $750 \div 3 \times 12 = \$3,000$
         $\$3,000$ (part) $\div 0.06$ (rate) $= \$50,000$ (total)

12. $\$637.50 \div 6 \times 12 = \$1,275$
         $\$1,275$ (part) $\div 0.085$ (rate) $= \$15,000$ (total)

13. $\$200 \div 3 \times 12 = \$800$ (rounded)
         $\$800$ (part) $\div \$10,000$ (total) $= 0.08$
         or 8% (rate)

14. $\$2,152.50 \div 6 \times 12 = \$4,305$
         $\$4,305$ (part) $\div \$76,000$ (total) $= 0.0566$
         or 5.66% (rate)

15. $\$90,000$ (total) $\times 0.06$ (rate) $= \$5,400$ (part)
         $\$5,400 \div 12 \times 2 = \$900$

16. $0.045 \div 12 = 0.00375$
         $\$20,000 \times 1.00375 \times 1.00375 \times 1.00375 = \$20,225.84$ (rounded)

SOLUTIONS: ADDITIONAL PRACTICE

1. (c) $2,000 × 0.105 = $210
   $210 ÷ 12 × 9 = $157.50
   $2,000 + $157.50 = $2,157.50

2. (b) $72 ÷ 6 × 12 = $144
   $144 ÷ 0.1 = $1,440

3. (b) $15,000 × 0.1 = $1,500
   $1,125 ÷ $1,500 = 0.75
   0.75 × 12 = 9

4. (b) $1,295 ÷ $14,000 = 0.0925 or 9¼%

5. (d) $16,500 × 0.065 = $1,072.50
   $1,072.50 ÷ 12 × 3 = $268.13 (rounded)

6. (d) 0.06 ÷ 12 = 0.005
   $12,000 × 1.005 × 1.005 × 1.005 × 1.005 × 1.005 × 1.005 × 1.005 × 1.005 = $12,488.49

7. (a) $6,945.75 ÷ 1.05 ÷ 1.05 ÷ 1.05 = $6,000

8. (c) $1,500 × 0.11 = $165
   $165 ÷ 12 × 7 = $96.25
   $96.25 + $1,500 = $1,596.25

9. (c) $18 × 12 = $216
   $216 ÷ $1,200 = 0.18 or 18%

10. (b) $2,300 × 0.08 = $184
    $184 ÷ 12 × 6 = $92 (rounded)

11. (d) $20,000 × 0.075 = $1,500
    $1,500 × 4.5 = $6,750
    $6,750 + $20,000 = $26,750

12. (b) $9,000 \div 4.5 = \$2,000$
$\$2,000 \div \$20,000 = 0.1$ or 10%

13. (d) a. $\$2,000 \times 0.2 = \$400$
$\$400 \times 2.5 = \$1,000$
b. $\$10,000 \times 0.05 = \$500$
$\$500 \times 2 = \$1,000$
c. $\$60,000 \times 0.1 = \$6,000$
$\$6,000 \div 12 = \$500$
$\$500 \times 2 = \$1,000$

14. (d) $\$90 \div 3 \times 12 = \$360$
$\$360 \div \$5,000 = 0.072$ or 7.2%

15. (a) $\$6,250 \div 6 \times 12 = \$12,500$ (rounded)
$\$12,500 \div 0.05 = \$250,000$
$\$250,000 \div 0.8 = \$312,500$

16. (b) $21,000 \times 0.11 = \$2,310$
$\$2,310 \times 2.5 = \$5,775$

17. (d) $\$3,000 \div \$50,000 = 0.06 = 6\%$

18. (c) $\$15,000 \times 0.085 = \$1,275$
$\$1,275 \div 12 \times 7 = \$743.75$
$\$743.75 + \$15,000 = \$15,743.75$

19. (d) $0.04 \div 2$ periods per year $= 0.02$ per period
4 years = 8 compounding periods
Multiply the principal by 100% + 2% (or 1.02)
$\$18,000 \times 1.02 \times 1.02 \times 1.02 \times 1.02$
$\times 1.02 \times 1.02 \times 1.02 \times 1.02 = \$21,089.87$ (rounded)

20. (a) $\$48,605.36 \div 1.06 \div 1.06 \div 1.06 \div 1.06 = \$38,500$ (rounded)

CHAPTER 10

The Mathematics of Real Estate Finance

Real estate finance is such a critical area of the real estate business that entire courses and textbooks are devoted to it. The purpose of this chapter is to introduce the student to some of the basic calculations involved in the area of real estate finance.

In this chapter, you will be introduced to the calculation of loan qualification ratios, loan-to-value ratios, down payments, mortgage amounts, loan discount points, mortgage insurance premiums, amortization, funding fees, and commitment fees. At the conclusion of your work in this chapter, you will be able to

- calculate a loan amount,
- calculate a down payment,
- calculate a monthly payment for an amortized loan payment,
- calculate points,
- compute an amortized loan payment, and
- use the lender's qualifying ratios to determine how much verifiable gross monthly income a purchaser must show to qualify for a particular loan amount.

LOAN-TO-VALUE RATIO

Remember:

LTV = Loan to value = The maximum loan amount.

It is based on the sales price or appraised value, whichever is lower.

In the financing of real estate, the lender will typically loan a certain percentage of the sales price or the appraised value, whichever is less. The relationship between the value (sales price) and the loan amount is known as the loan-to-value ratio (LTV). The interest, then, is charged only on the amount of the loan, not on the sales price.

E X A M P L E : $200,000 sales price (value)
                       $180,000 loan

This describes a 90 percent loan-to-value ratio. Here is how it works:

$$\frac{\$180,000 \text{ loan}}{\$200,000 \text{ value}} = 0.9, \text{ or } 90\% \text{ LTV loan}$$

1. If a buyer obtains an 80 percent loan on a $290,000 sale, what is the loan amount?

2. If the loan in problem 1 has a 5.5 percent interest rate, what is the amount of interest due for the first month? (*See* Chapter 9 if you need help.)

The amount of interest charged and the total amount of money to be repaid relate only to the loan amount (the loan principal) and not to the sales price or value. (A VA loan, however, can have a 100 percent loan-to-value ratio.)

AMORTIZED LOANS

In Chapter 9, you learned to calculate simple interest. Loans earn a return, or profit, on the principal loan amount. Before the 1930s, the typical real estate loan was a term loan, which required the borrower to pay interest only (monthly, quarterly, or annually) until the maturity date, when the entire principal balance became due and payable in full.

Following the Great Depression, lenders decided that it was better to have the borrower make periodic payments, which would, over the term of the loan, liquidate the indebtedness as well as pay all of the interest. This is what is known as an amortized loan. An amortized loan calls for a fixed monthly payment over the term of the loan.

E X A M P L E :   A $200,000 loan is granted for 30 years at 6 percent annual interest, with monthly payments of $1,200 principal plus accrued interest. The first three payments would look like this:

	Total Payment	Principal	Interest	Ending Balance
Payment 1	$1,200	$200	$1,000	$199,800
Payment 2	$1,200	$201	$999	$199,599
Payment 3	$1,200	$202	$998	$199,397

Amortized loans have a *fixed* monthly payment, which includes principal and interest, but with a changing amount being credited to each.

E X A M P L E :   Assume a $90,000 construction loan at 10 percent interest with a fixed monthly payment amount of $967.15, the first three payments would be:

	Total Payment	Principal	Interest	Ending Balance
Payment 1	$967.15	$217.15	$750.00	$89,782.85
Payment 2	$967.15	$218.96	$748.19	$89,563.89
Payment 3	$967.15	$220.78	$746.37	$89,343.11

Lenders prefer amortized loans because it enables the borrower to qualify for a larger loan due to the smaller initial payments toward principal and because there is a reduced amount of risk connected with level-payment loans.

To calculate the monthly payment for a level-payment amortized loan:

- Use a financial calculator. (Be sure to check the owner's manual for the specific steps for the proper operation of your calculator.)

  number of = $\boxed{\text{N}}$

  annual interest rate ÷ 12 = $\boxed{\text{%i}}$

  loan amount = $\boxed{\text{PV}}$

  compute for $\boxed{\text{PMT}}$

- Refer to a loan amortization book.
- Use a loan constant chart.
- Use a loan payment factor from a chart such as Table 10.1.

Loan Amortization Formula

Loan amount ÷ $1,000 × Loan payment factor = Monthly principal and interest payment
(P&I)

LOAN PAYMENT FACTORS

Table 10.1 shows a family of numbers known as loan payment factors. These factors are based on a $1,000 loan. Therefore, it is necessary to divide the loan amount by 1,000. To use these factors, just locate the appropriate interest rate in the left-hand column and relate this to the appropriate loan term or length of repayment period. For simplicity, we show only 30-, 25-, 20-, and 15-year terms. After choosing the correct factor, multiply it by the amount of the loan divided by 1,000, as discussed above.

To illustrate, suppose that we wish to know the payment required to amortize a $200,000 loan at 6 percent interest over a 30-year term. First divide the $200,000 loan amount by 1,000 ($200,000 ÷ 1,000 = 200). Then locate 6 percent in the left-hand column and find the factor that corresponds to the 30-year repayment term. This factor happens to be is $6. Now multiply this factor by 200, the number of thousands in the loan amount. This calculation yields a $1,200 monthly payment. This a benchmark number to remember. **A 30-year amortized loan of $200,000 at 6 percent is a monthly P&I payment of $1,200.**

T A B L E 10.1

Loan Payment Factors
Monthly Principal and Interest Payment Factors (per $1,000)

RATE	TERM				RATE	TERM			
	30 Yrs.	25 Yrs.	20 Yrs.	15 Yrs.		30 Yrs.	25 Yrs.	20 Yrs.	15 Yrs.
4.000%	4.78	5.28	6.06	7.40	6.750%	6.49	6.91	7.60	8.85
4.125	4.85	5.35	6.13	7.46	6.875	6.57	6.99	7.68	8.92
4.250	4.92	5.42	6.20	7.53	7.000	6.65	7.07	7.75	8.99
4.375	5.00	5.49	6.26	7.59	7.125	6.74	7.15	7.83	9.06
4.500	5.07	5.56	6.33	7.65	7.250	6.82	7.23	7.90	9.13
4.625	5.15	5.63	6.40	7.72	7.375	6.91	7.31	7.98	9.20
4.750	5.22	5.71	6.47	7.78	7.500	6.99	7.39	8.06	9.27
4.875	5.30	5.78	6.54	7.85	7.625	7.08	7.47	8.13	9.34
5.000	5.37	5.85	6.60	7.91	7.750	7.16	7.55	8.21	9.41
5.125	5.45	5.92	6.67	7.98	7.875	7.25	7.64	8.29	9.48
5.250	5.53	6.00	6.74	8.04	8.000	7.34	7.72	8.36	9.56
5.375	5.60	6.07	6.81	8.11	8.125	7.42	7.80	8.44	9.63
5.500	5.68	6.15	6.88	8.18	8.250	7.51	7.83	8.52	9.70
5.625	5.76	6.22	6.95	8.24	8.375	7.60	7.97	8.60	9.77
5.750	5.84	6.30	7.03	8.31	8.500	7.69	8.05	8.68	9.85
5.875	5.92	6.37	7.10	8.38	8.625	7.78	8.14	8.76	9.92
6.000	6.00	6.44	7.16	8.44	8.750	7.87	8.22	8.84	9.99
6.125	6.08	6.52	7.24	8.51	8.875	7.96	8.31	8.92	10.07
6.250	6.16	6.60	7.31	8.57	9.000	8.05	8.39	9.00	10.14
6.375	6.24	6.67	7.38	8.64	9.125	8.14	8.48	9.08	10.22
6.500	6.32	6.75	7.46	8.71	9.250	8.23	8.56	9.16	10.29
6.625	6.40	6.83	7.53	8.78	9.375	8.32	8.65	9.24	10.37

TABLE 10.1

Loan Payment Factors (continued)
Monthly Principal and Interest Payment Factors (per $1,000)

RATE	TERM 30 Yrs.	25 Yrs.	20 Yrs.	15 Yrs.	RATE	TERM 30 Yrs.	25 Yrs.	20 Yrs.	15 Yrs.
9.500%	8.41	8.74	9.32	10.44	13.375	11.36	11.56	11.98	12.90
9.625	8.50	8.82	9.40	10.52	13.500	11.45	11.66	12.07	12.98
9.750	8.59	8.91	9.49	10.59	13.625	11.55	11.75	12.16	13.07
9.875	8.68	9.00	9.57	10.67	13.750	11.65	11.85	12.25	13.15
10.000	8.78	9.09	9.65	10.75	13.875	11.75	11.94	12.34	13.23
10.125	8.87	9.18	9.73	10.82	14.000	11.85	12.04	12.44	13.32
10.250	8.96	9.26	9.81	10.90	14.125	11.95	12.13	12.53	13.40
10.375	9.05	9.35	9.90	10.98	14.250	12.05	12.23	12.62	13.49
10.500	9.15	9.44	9.98	11.05	14.375	12.15	12.33	12.71	13.57
10.625	9.24	9.53	10.07	11.13	14.500	12.25	12.42	12.80	13.66
10.750	9.33	9.62	10.15	11.18	14.625	12.35	12.52	12.89	13.74
10.875	9.43	9.71	10.24	11.29	14.750	12.44	12.61	12.98	13.83
11.000	9.52	9.80	10.32	11.37	14.875	12.54	12.71	13.08	13.91
11.125	9.62	9.89	10.41	11.44	15.000	12.64	12.81	13.17	14.00
11.250	9.71	9.98	10.49	11.52	15.125	12.74	12.91	13.26	14.08
11.375	9.81	10.07	10.58	11.60	15.250	12.84	13.00	13.35	14.17
11.500	9.90	10.16	10.66	11.68	15.375	12.94	13.10	13.45	14.25
11.625	10.00	10.26	10.75	11.76	15.500	13.05	13.20	13.54	14.34
11.750	10.09	10.35	10.84	11.84	15.625	13.15	13.30	13.63	14.43
11.875	10.19	10.44	10.92	11.92	15.750	13.25	13.39	13.73	14.51
12.000	10.29	10.53	11.01	12.00	15.875	13.35	13.49	13.82	14.60
12.125	10.38	10.62	11.10	12.08	16.000	13.45	13.59	13.91	14.69
12.250	10.48	10.72	11.19	12.16	16.125	13.55	13.69	14.01	14.77
12.375	10.58	10.81	11.27	12.24	16.250	13.65	13.79	14.10	14.86
12.500	10.67	10.90	11.36	12.33	16.375	13.75	13.88	14.19	14.95
12.625	10.77	11.00	11.45	12.41	16.500	13.85	13.98	14.29	15.04
12.750	10.87	11.09	11.54	12.49	16.625	13.95	14.08	14.38	15.13
12.875	10.96	11.18	11.63	12.57	16.750	14.05	14.18	14.48	15.21
13.000	11.06	11.28	11.72	12.65	16.875	14.16	14.28	14.57	15.30
13.125	11.16	11.37	11.80	12.73	17.000	14.26	14.38	14.67	15.39
13.250	11.26	11.47	11.89	12.82					

We can simplify this process by combining the steps this way:

$$\frac{\$200,000}{\$1,000} \times \$6 = \$1,200$$

Calculate the loan payment if the term is shortened to 20 years at 6 percent.

Use the calculation below to check your answer:

$$\frac{\$200,000}{\$1,000} \times \$7.16 = \$1,432$$

MORTGAGE INSURANCE PREMIUMS

Because of the increased risk to lenders that results from making a loan with a high loan-to-value ratio, lenders demand additional protection. This has come to be known as mortgage insurance. Do not confuse this with credit life insurance, which is designed to pay off a loan if the borrower dies. Mortgage insurance helps protect the lender if the buyer defaults and the property does not sell for a sufficient amount at a foreclosure or short sale to pay off the defaulted loan.

FHA MORTGAGE INSURANCE PREMIUMS (MIPS)

The Federal Housing Administration (FHA) originated the concept of mortgage insurance premiums (MIP). As of April 2011, the MIP rates for FHA insured loans have changed again. For a loan greater than or equal 95 percent loan, there is an up-front, one time, premium of 1 percent of the loan amount and an annual premium of 1.15 percent of the loan amount. The annual premium is paid on a monthly prorated basis as part of the regular monthly payment. When the LTV gets to around 78 percent, the mortgage insurance should stop being collected. In 2006, FHA was 4 percent of the purchase money loans and just 2 percent of the purchase money in terms of dollars. In 2010, it was 19 percent.

The FHA insurance premium is identified as MIP. Check with your lender or local FHA field office for current premiums for a particular loan program.

The following example shows how to calculate the MIPs required for an FHA-insured loan.

E X A M P L E : Assume the loan amount totals $180,000:

Up-front premium: $180,000 × 0.0100 = $1,800
Annual premium: $180,000 × 0.0115 = $2,070
$2,070 ÷ 12 months = $172.25 monthly premium

Therefore, $172.50 is added to the monthly payment.

VA FUNDING FEES

VA-guaranteed loans are underwritten by the Department of Veterans Affairs and require that the veteran borrower, who must have a documented certificate of eligibility, pay an upfront funding fee. This fee is always subject to change. No down payment requires 2.15 points. A down payment of 5 percent or more requires 1.5 points. A down payment of 10 percent or more requires 1.25 points.

E X A M P L E :　Assume a home has a purchase price of $225,000:

No down payment:

$225,000 × 0.0215 = $4,837.50

5 percent down payment:

$225,000 × 0.05 = $11,250 down payment
$225,000 – $11,250 = $213,750 loan
$213,750 × 0.015 = $3,206.25 funding fee

PRIVATE MORTGAGE INSURANCE (PMI) PREMIUMS

Loans that are neither insured nor guaranteed by the government are known as conventional loans. When a lender grants a conventional loan for an amount greater than 80 percent of the sales price or the appraised value, whichever is less, the borrower will be required to obtain private mortgage insurance (PMI).

The premiums for PMI are expressed and calculated in points. The premium cost will depend on several factors, such as the amount of coverage required, the loan-to-value ratio, the repayment term of the loan, the geographic location of the property, and other factors related to the lender's risk associated with a particular loan.

The premium amount will also be influenced by how and when premiums are paid. A variety of options are available to purchasers of PMI. The insurance premium may be paid

- upfront, in a one-time amount;
- by financing it in the loan;
- in an up-front payment, followed by annual renewal premiums; or
- only in annual premiums.

PMI can be required only until the loan balance is reduced to an amount less than 78 percent of the acquisition date market value, or purchase price of the property. There is usually an automatic trigger in the amortization schedule when the remaining loan gets to 78 percent or less. A current appraisal of market value could also be presented to the lender for consideration.

When you know the required current charges for a particular loan, use the following formula to compute the dollar amount of the up-front or annual premium:

Loan amount × Required points = PMI premium

E X A M P L E : A lender requires a monthly PMI premium of ½ of the 0.52 point collected with the monthly PITI payment on a $195,000 loan.

$195,000 × 0.0052 = $1,014.00

$1,014 ÷ 12 = $84.50 monthly PMI premium

LOAN COMMITMENT FEES

If a builder desires to finance the construction of a new house, a short-term construction loan (also called an interim loan) is required. However, before the short-term lender funds the loan, it will require a loan commitment from a long-term lender to pay off its short-term loan and take it out of that property—hence, the term take-out, or stand-by, commitment. The long-term lender charges a commitment fee for this service of committing funds for a permanent loan. A typical commitment fee is 1 percent of the amount of the new long-term loan. This fee is generally nonrefundable. However, in some cases, it is credited against the total loan discount charged to the seller. If such is the case, it is greatly to the builder's benefit to require that the buyer obtain the loan from the same lender that provided the builder's commitment.

E X A M P L E : If a proposed long-term or permanent loan is $650,000 and the commitment fee is 1 percent, how much must the builder pay to the lender?

$650,000 × 0.01 = $6,500

Loan commitment fees are not restricted to new construction loans. They frequently are charged on nonresidential loans and may be charged on certain residential loans, particularly the larger ones.

LOAN ORIGINATION FEES

Lenders charge a service fee to originate a new loan. This fee is usually expressed in points, although some lenders charge a flat fee. The most typical loan requires a 1-point origination fee. This fee can vary dramatically and can be impacted by loan discount points.

E X A M P L E : A buyer is getting a $325,000 loan to purchase a new home. The lender will charge a ½-point loan commitment fee and a 1-point loan origination fee.

The commitment fee will be paid at loan approval and the origination fee will be paid at closing. How much will each be?

Commitment Fee: $325,000 × 0.005 = $1,625
Origination Fee: $325,000 × 0.01 = $3,250

LOAN DISCOUNT POINTS

A point always equals 1 percent of the loan amount. As discussed earlier in this chapter, FHA mortgage insurance premiums, VA funding fees, private mortgage insurance premiums, loan commitment fees, and loan origination fees are stated in points.

Lenders may also charge discount points to adjust the yield or profit on a loan. Sometimes these points are called buydowns because they enable the lender to offer a lower face rate.

To calculate one point, simply multiply the loan amount by 1 percent, or 0.01.

EXAMPLE: A lender requires 1¾ discount points on a $325,000 loan.

1¾ points = 0.0175 points
$325,000 × 0.0175 = $5,687.50 for discount points

BUYER'S LOAN QUALIFICATION RATIOS

Prior to approving a prospective buyer's loan application, the lender wants to be sure that the applicant has the financial ability to repay the loan and that the applicant has a history of paying off other debts satisfactorily. Likewise, before a real estate licensee invests a great deal of time and expense in working with a buyer, the licensee should ensure as best as possible that the buyer is pre-qualified for a loan.

Lenders verify a buyer applicant's income and relate this to (1) the amount of the payments on the requested loan and (2) the total amount of all other payments now owed by the buyer. To accomplish this, lenders use arbitrary ratios. In the case of FHA and VA loans, the U.S. government sets these ratios. Secondary market institutions such as Fannie Mae (formerly the Federal National Mortgage Association or FNMA) and Freddie Mac (formally the Federal Home Loan Mortgage Corporation or FHLMC) set the ratios. Or if a lender plans to retain the loan in its own portfolio, the ratios are set individually. It is important to remember that each agency or lender is free to change the numbers in each ratio, as well as which items are included in that ratio. These ratios also may vary depending on the loan-to-value ratio and whether the interest is fixed or is subject to adjustment. Therefore, our discussion is intended to be general in nature.

Qualification ratios are usually described as PITI and LTD (long-term debt) ratios. The PITI ratio is a percentage of the buyer's income to be applied to the principal, interest, tax, and insurance payment; the LTD ratio is a percentage of the buyer's income to be applied to all of the buyer's present monthly payments plus the PITI payment, as described above. Buyers must satisfy both ratios to obtain loan approval.

Qualification Ratios

Let us now explore the calculation of these loan qualification ratios. Suppose that the PITI and LTD ratios for a 90 percent loan are 28 percent and 36 percent (expressed as 28/36), respectively. This means that the buyer's PITI payment should not exceed 28 percent of the buyer's gross monthly income and that the mortgage loan payment plus all other debts should not exceed 36 percent of gross monthly income. (If the buyer is able to obtain a 95 percent loan, the lender may require ratios of 25/33 owing to the fact that the loan has more risk because of the buyer's smaller cash investment.)

$$\text{Total} \times \text{Rate} = \text{Part}$$
$$\text{Income} \times \text{Ratio} = \text{Allowable payment amount}$$

NOTE: Qualification ratios on conventional residential mortgages may go as high as 33/45 as compared to 28/36, which has been the norm for many years. It depends upon many factors including the leader, the program, the loan itself, and/or other qualification considerations of a buyer.

EXAMPLE: A young couple have a combined gross monthly income of $3,600. They have selected a $100,000 house and plan to obtain a $90,000 loan at 6 percent for 30 years. The monthly principal and interest payment on this house is $540, the hazard insurance premium is $41, the taxes are $95, and the financed private mortgage insurance premium is $26.25. Their only long-term debt is a $300 car payment. Can they qualify for the loan?

$540 principal and interest + $41 insurance + $95 taxes + $26.25 PMI = $702.25 total house
payment

$702.25 total house payment ÷ $3,600 income = 19.5% (rounded—must not exceed 28%)

$702.25 total house payment + $300 car payment = $1,002.25 total debt payment

$1,002.25 total debt payment ÷ $3,600 income = 27.8% (rounded—must not exceed 36%)

This couple should qualify for the loan because their ratios are less than those required.

Now you try a few simple loan qualification problems.

3. A newly married couple wish to obtain a home loan. Their combined monthly income is $5,200. What amount of monthly house payment can they qualify for if the lender uses the 28/36 ratios and if they have no other debts?

4. A couple buying their first home have been told that the monthly payment for PITI on the house they have selected is $1,234.56. If area conventional lenders are qualifying prospective buyers at 28/36, what is the required monthly income for the this couple?

5. A single buyer has a monthly income is $5,000. What monthly PITI can he qualify for if area conventional lenders are qualifying at 28/36?

6. What is the maximum monthly total debt including the house payment (*see* problem 5) that the single buyer can have and still qualify for the loan? How much is available for debt other than the monthly house payment?

CALCULATION OF LOAN AMOUNTS AND DOWN PAYMENTS

The amount of money that a lender requires a buyer to pay toward the purchase price is called the down payment. The difference between the sales price and this down payment is the amount of money that the lender is willing to loan on the subject property. This loan amount must be substantiated by an appraisal of the property. The amount of the down payment and the loan amount (the loan-to-value ratio) are determined by the type of loan to be obtained.

VA Loans

A VA-guaranteed loan can require no down payment up to the maximum allowable loan amount, which is based on the amount of the veteran's entitlement. Of course, the buyer may make a down payment to keep the payments lower and to reduce the funding fees discussed earlier.

FHA Loans

FHA-insured loans today comprise a significant percentage of all residential loans and are especially attractive to first-time buyers. They include a variety of down payment and loan amounts. Most FHA buyers prefer to make a minimum down payment and therefore obtain the maximum loan amount. For a buyer to obtain the maximum loan for FHA mortgage insurance purposes, the FHA permits the buyer to add the amount of the buyer's closing costs (not including the prepaid items) to the sales price. This amount is called the FHA acquisition cost. It is the basis on which the loan amount is calculated.

Check with your instructor or a real estate finance text of current date for current MIP (mortgage insurance premium), allowable closing cost to be paid by borrower, and down payment requirements for the currently available FHA-insured loan programs in your area. They change frequently. Remember that FHA insures loans to make housing more available to the public; FHA does not loan money.

Conventional Loans

Since the financial crisis in 2008, the minimum down payment requirements for a loan have increased and are subject to stringent underwriting requirements for high loan-to-value ratio loans. Private mortgage insurance is required by the lender on any loan greater than 80 percent of the market value (or the sales price, whichever is less). The amount of the premium for this PMI varies among insurers and also among types of loans. For example, a fixed-rate loan will have a smaller PMI premium than an adjustable-rate loan.

EXAMPLE: If the sales price is $200,000 and the buyer requests a 90 percent loan, how much cash down payment must the buyer make if the property appraises for $197,000?

Remember, the loan amount is based on the lesser of the sales price or the appraised value. In this case, the seller may not be willing to reduce the sales price to an amount equal to the appraised value. Thus, the buyer may either terminate the contract (which is a typical contract provision) or pay a larger down payment. Let's look at the figures:

$197,000 appraised value × 0.9 = $177,300 maximum loan amount

$200,000 sales price − $177,300 maximum loan amount = $22,700 required down payment

If the seller reduces the sales price to the appraised value of $97,000, the down payment will be $19,700.

MORTGAGE LOANS—OVERVIEW

Mortgage loans are usually made with a repayment period of 15 or 30 years. Payments of both principal (face value of the mortgage) and interest are required during the term of the loan. As discussed earlier, a mortgage debt divided into equal, regular payments (usually monthly) over a period of time is called an amortized mortgage.

Under the terms of an amortized loan, the borrower makes a fixed monthly payment that includes one month's interest on the unpaid principal, plus a payment of part of the principal. The beginning monthly installments pay primarily interest, and only a small portion of each payment is applied to the reduction of the principal. As the principal is gradually repaid and the balance reduced, also reducing the interest to be paid, an increasing percentage of the monthly payment will be applied to repayment of the principal, until the loan is repaid entirely.

A chart of typical amortized loan payments is shown in Figure 10.1. Notice how the amount of principal paid in monthly installment increases while the amount of interest paid decreases. The reason for this is that interest is charged only on the outstanding balance of the loan. Each payment on such a loan involves only principal reduction and interest on the balance, although the percentages change with each payment.

TABLE 10.2

Amortized Mortgage over 25 Years
$220,000 loan at 4.75 percent interest

Payments	Yearly Total	Principal Paid	Interest Paid	Balance
Year 1 (1–12)	$15,051.10	$4,703.00	$10,348.00	$215,297.40
Year 2 (13–24)	$15,051.10	$4,931.00	$10,120.00	$210,366.50
Year 3 (25–36)	$15,051.10	$5,170.00	$9,881.00	$205,196.21
Year 4 (37–48)	$15,051.10	$5,421.00	$9,630.00	$199,774.91
Year 5 (49–60)	$15,051.10	$5,684.00	$9,367.00	$194,090.43
Year 6 (61–72)	$15,051.10	$5,960.00	$9,091.00	$188,129.97
Year 7 (73–84)	$15,051.10	$6,250.00	$8,801.00	$181,880.15
Year 8 (85–96)	$15,051.10	$6,553.00	$8,498.00	$175,326.91
Year 9 (97–108)	$15,051.10	$6,871.00	$8,180.00	$168,455.52
Year 10 (109–120)	$15,051.10	$7,205.00	$7,846.00	$161,250.54
Year 11 (121–132)	$15,051.10	$7,555.00	$7,496.00	$153,695.78
Year 12 (133–144)	$15,051.10	$7,922.00	$7,130.00	$145,774.25
Year 13 (145–156)	$15,051.10	$8,306.00	$6,745.00	$137,468.14
Year 14 (157–168)	$15,051.10	$8,709.00	$6,342.00	$128,758.80
Year 15 (169–180)	$15,051.10	$9,132.00	$5,919.00	$119,626.63
Year 16 (181–192)	$15,051.10	$9,576.00	$5,476.00	$110,051.11
Year 17 (193–204)	$15,051.10	$10,040.00	$5,011.00	$100,010.72
Year 18 (205–216)	$15,051.10	$10,528.00	$4,523.00	$89,482.90
Year 19 (217–228)	$15,051.10	$11,039.00	$4,012.00	$78,443.97
Year 20 (229–240)	$15,051.10	$11,575.00	$3,476.00	$66,869.12
Year 21 (241–252)	$15,051.10	$12,137.00	$2,914.00	$54,732.34
Year 22 (253–264)	$15,051.10	$12,726.00	$2,325.00	$42,006.34
Year 23 (265–276)	$15,051.10	$13,344.00	$1,707.00	$28,662.53
Year 24 (277–288)	$15,051.10	$13,992.00	$1,059.00	$14,670.89
Year 25 (289–300)	$15,051.10	$14,671.00	$380.00	$0.00
Totals	**$376,277.46**	**$220,000.00**	**$156,277.46**	

In addition to the monthly principal and interest payment, many mortgage lenders require that the borrower pay one-twelfth of the annual ad valorem tax and one-twelfth of the annual homeowners' insurance premium to establish a reserve to pay real estate taxes and insurance premiums when they become due. The amount of this reserve will be indicated when it is to be included in a problem in this text. It is not a part of the loan payment, however.

AMORTIZATION CALCULATIONS

You should be able to handle all the problems in this chapter by applying what you have learned about percentages, principal, and interest. Work all dollar amounts out to three decimal places and round off to two places only in the last step of a problem. Work carefully. If your answer does not agree with the one given, review until you understand the correct solution. Then adjust your work before going on to the next problem.

7. A homeowner wants to purchase a residence valued at $277,000 and has been granted a 30-year mortgage loan equal to 75 percent of the value of the property. If the interest rate is 5 percent, compute the amount of interest charged for the first month of the loan. (Remember the loan-to-value ratio; in this example, it is 75 percent.)

8. Using Table 10.1 on pages 180–181, what will the homeowner's monthly principal and interest payment be (*see* problem 7)?

EXAMPLE: Using the information in problem 7, if the homeowner's monthly payment is $310.12, what will be the balance of the principal of her loan next month?

Step 1. Compute the monthly interest on the full principal. This was calculated in the last problem. The answer is $865.63

Step 2. Find the amount of payment that will be applied to reducing the principal.

$1,156.62   total payment
−$ 865.63   monthly interest
$ 290.99   amount applied to principal

Step 3. Compute the new principal balance.

$207,750.00   old principal balance
−   290.99   reduction
$207,459.01   new principal balance

NOTE: There will be a difference of a few cents in the answer if you leave the numbers in the calculator and perform the chain functions, as opposed to writing down each answer, clearing the calculator, then reentering the numbers for the next step in the problem. Greater accuracy with a calculator is obtained if the numbers are left in the calculator and the next calculation is then performed.

9. Now calculate the balance of the principal of this loan when the interest for the third payment is computed.

Accrued Interest and Loan Reduction

Typically, interest on a real estate loan is paid after it has been earned, or accrued, by the lender. For this reason, interest is paid in arrears, which means that the June payment on a loan includes both the interest earned during May and a remainder, which reduces the principal.

Because a loan may be finalized, or closed, on any day of the month, the buyer at closing usually pays interest from that day of closing through the end of the month. This is called prepaid interest. Then the first regular monthly payment will be on the first day of the following month. That payment will include the interest for the intervening first full month of the loan. The buyer is not getting a free ride, as some think.

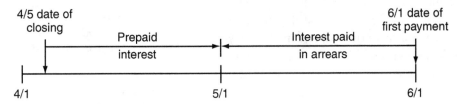

10. A buyer took out a loan of $275,000 at 4.5 percent interest. The loan was amortized over a 20-year period at $1,740.75 per month. How much of the first monthly payment was applied to interest and how much was applied to principal?

11. Using the information in problem 10, divide the second monthly payment between interest and principal.

ADDITIONAL PRACTICE

1. Two discount points cost a seller $3,300. What is the amount of his loan?
   - a. $3,300
   - b. $164,950
   - c. $165,000
   - d. $165,500

2. For how much monthly PITI payment can a prospective buyer qualify if he earns $3,300 monthly and the lender applies 28/36 qualifying ratios?
   - a. $924
   - b. $925
   - c. $1,150
   - d. $1,188

3. A couple moving to Dallas can get a 90 percent conventional loan for 20 years at 4 percent. It will require a monthly principal and interest payment of $6.06 per $1,000 of the loan amount. For how much financing can they qualify if their combined monthly income is $6,800? (The lender will permit them to devote up to 25 percent of their gross monthly income to a principal and interest payment.)
   - a. $1,687.50
   - b. $181,000
   - c. $267,900
   - d. $280,528

4. Using the information in problem 3, calculate the price of the house this couple can purchase. Divide loan amount by loan-to-value ratio to get purchase price.
   - a. $286,281
   - b. $289,000
   - c. $299,420
   - d. $311,698

5. If a lender agrees to make an 80 percent loan on a house that sells for $290,000 and that appraises for $280,000, what is the amount of the loan?
   - a. $222,000
   - b. $224,000
   - c. $232,000
   - d. $232,500

6. To obtain an FHA-insured loan, the buyers will have to pay a MIP of 1.75 points, which will be financed into the loan. What will be the amount of their loan if FHA insures 96.5 percent of the appraised value and this property appraises for $210,000. (The maximum loan the FHA will insure in their area is $271,000.)
   - a. $180,750
   - b. $204,349
   - c. $204,500
   - d. $206,196.38

7. A couple earn a combined annual income of $96,400. They can get a 20-year, 90 percent conventional loan at 4.75 percent interest that will require monthly payments of $6.46 per $1,000 borrowed. A house they really like has annual taxes of $3,200 and can be insured for $1,500 per year. If the lender uses 28/36 qualifying ratios and they have no other debts, how much financing can they qualify for?
   - a. $210,142.53
   - b. $254,449.12
   - c. $263,492.12
   - d. $287,563.46

8. Using the information in problem 7, calculate the maximum sales price this couple can afford.
   - a. $210,142.91
   - b. $233,491.70
   - c. $254,449.10
   - d. $319,514.95

9. If this couple (*see* problems 7 and 8) is required to pay a 1.5-point origination fee, a 0.75-point PMI premium, and 1 discount point plus $2,860 in other closing costs, how much cash will they need to bring to the closing if they have already deposited $10,000 earnest money with the escrow officer?
    a. $20,178.80
    b. $34,157.31
    c. $35,178.80
    d. $36,200.80

10. If a prospective buyer has an annual gross income of $48,000, for how much monthly PITI payment can he qualify if the lender uses 29/41 qualifying ratios?
    a. $1,160
    b. $1,180
    c. $1,401
    d. $1,640

11. What is the 1.75-point MIP on a $170,000 FHA-insured loan?
    a. $2,905
    b. $2,970
    c. $2,975
    d. $2,990

12. What is the maximum amount of money a new homebuyer would have available for a car note if he earns $65,400 per year, wants to obtain the maximum amount of home loan possible, and can get a 95 percent conventional loan for 30 years at 5.25 percent? (The lender will require 25/33 qualifying ratios and a monthly payment of $5.52 per $1,000 borrowed.)
    a. $436
    b. $1,362.50
    c. $5,250
    d. $5,450

13. A buyer can obtain an 80 percent conventional loan to purchase a home selling for $428,000. If the property appraises for $425,000, what will be the required down payment if she buys it for the appraised value?
    a. $42,500
    b. $43,500
    c. $85,000
    d. $$85,600

14. How much verifiable gross monthly income will a couple need in order to purchase a new home for $286,000 if they can obtain an 80 percent conventional loan for 15 years at 4 percent annual interest? (The annual insurance premium will be 2 percent of the value of the home, and the ad valorem taxes are $7,161. The loan will require a monthly principal and interest payment of $4.77 for each $1,000 of the loan amount, and the lender will use 28/36 qualifying ratios. The property appraises for $286,000 and the newlyweds have no other debts.)
    a. $2,976
    b. $7,731.43
    c. $7,861
    d. $10,599.60

15. If the newlyweds (*see* problem 14) pay 2 discount points to obtain the loan, what amount will be charged on the closing statement?
    a. $4,576
    b. $4,976
    c. $5,238
    d. $5,498.65

16. If a homebuyer obtains a loan for $346,500 and is required to pay 1.5 discount points, a 1-point loan origination fee, and a private mortgage insurance premium of 0.873 points, how much cash will he need to deliver to the closing table, including his down payment of $38,500?
    a. $47,162.50
    b. $50,187.45
    c. $52,986.05
    d. $52,999.09

17. A couple relocating to North Carolina want to purchase a home for $235,000 with a 95 percent conventional loan. The lender uses a qualifying ratio of 28 percent of gross monthly income for the principal and interest payment. How much verifiable gross monthly income must they show to qualify for a 15-year loan at 4 percent that requires monthly payments of $7.40 per $1,000 of the loan amount?

    a. $4,201.84
    b. $5,885.85
    c. $5,900.18
    d. $5,905.42

18. A relocating executive moving to Fargo can obtain a 30-year, 90 percent nonconforming conventional loan at 4.75 percent. The loan requires monthly principal and interest payments of $5.22 per $1,000. If the annual insurance premium is $1,800 and the annual ad valorem tax bill is calculated at $3.80 per $100 of value—using an assessment ratio of 53 percent of market value—what will be his monthly PITI payment if he purchases a home for $456,000?

    a. $2,998.85
    b. $3,057.61
    c. $3,087.26
    d. $4,125.35

19. A buyer has decided to offer $335,000 for a home that she really likes. The bank will loan her 80 percent of the purchase price for 30 years at 5 percent interest. What will be the amount of her principal and interest payment if the requirement is $5.68 per thousand of the loan amount?

    a. $1,405.45
    b. $1,522.24
    c. $1,562.12
    d. $1,613.10

20. A first-time home buyer can obtain a 90 percent loan on a home selling for $385,000. The required cash down payment will be

    a. $38,500.
    b. $77,000.
    c. $308,500.
    d. $346,500.

SOLUTIONS: PROBLEMS IN CHAPTER 10

1. $290,000 × 0.8 = $232,000

2. $232,000 × 0.055 ÷ 12 = $1063.33

3. $5,200 × 0.28 = $1,456

4. $1,234.56 ÷ 0.28 = $4,409.14 (rounded)

5. $5,000 × 0.28 = $1,400

6. $5,000 × 0.36 = $1,800
   $1,800 − $1,400 = $400

7. $277,000 × 0.75 = $207,750
   $207,750 × 0.05 ÷ 12 = $865.63 (rounded)

8. $207,750 ÷ $1,000 × $5.37 = $1,156.62 (rounded)

9. Pmt 2: $207,459.01 × 0.05 ÷ 12 = $864.41
   $1,156.62 − $864.41 = $292.21
   $207,459.01 − $292.21 = $207,166.80
   Pmt 3: $207,166.80 × 0.05 ÷ 12 = $863.20
   $1,156.62 − $863.20 = $293.42
   $207,166.80 − $293.42 = $206,873.38

10. $275,000 × 0.0450 ÷ 12 = $1,031.25 to interest
    $1,740.75 − $1031.25 = $709.50 to principal

11. $275,000 − $709.50 = $274,290.50
    $274,290.50 × 0.0450 ÷ 12 = $1,028.58 to interest
    $1,740.75 − $1,028.58 = $712.17 to principal

SOLUTIONS: ADDITIONAL PRACTICE

1. (c) $3,300 ÷ 0.02 = $165,000

2. (a) $3,300 × 0.28 = $924

3. (d) 60,000 ÷ 12 + $1,800 = $6,800
   $6,800 × 0.25 = $1,700
   $1,700 ÷ $6.06 × $1,000 = $280,528 (rounded)

4. (d) $280,528 ÷ 0.9 = $311,698 (rounded)

5. (b) $280,000 × 0.8 = $224,000

6. (d) $210,000 × 0.965 = $202,650
   $202,650 × 0.0175 = $3,546.38
   $202,650 + $3,546.38 = $206,196.38

7. (d) $96,400 ÷ 12 × 0.28 = $2,249.33 (rounded)
   $3,200 + $1,500 = $4,700
   $4,700 ÷ 12 = $391.67 (rounded)
   $2,249.33 − $391.67 = $1,857.66
   $1,857.66 ÷ $6.46 × $1,000 = $287,563.46

8. (d) $287,563.46 ÷ 0.9 = $319,514.95

9. (b) $319,514.95 × 0.1 = $31,951.50
   1.5 + 0.75 + 1 = 3.25
   $287,563.46 × 0.0325 = $9,345.81 (rounded)
   $9,345.81 + $2,860 + $31,951.50 − $10,000 = $34,157.31

10. (a) $48,000 ÷ 12 = $4,000
    $4,000 × 0.29 = $1,160

11. (c) 1.75 points = 1.75% = 0.0175
    $170,000 × 0.0175 = $2,975

12. (a) 33% − 25% = 8%

$65,400 ÷ 12 = $5,450

$5,450 × 0.08 = $436

13. (c) $425,000 × 0.2 = $85,000

14. (b) $286,000 × 0.8 = $228,800

$228,800 ÷ $1,000 × $4.77 = $1,091.38

$286,000 × 0.02 = $5,720

$7,161 + $5,720 ÷ 12 = $1,073.42

$1,091.38 + $1,073.42 = $2,164.80

$2,164.80 ÷ 0.28 = $7,731.43

15. (a) $286,000 × 0.8 × 0.02= $4,576

16. (b) 1.5 + 1 + 0.873 = 3.373

3.373 = 3.373% or 0.03373

$346,500 × 0.03373 = $11,687.45 (rounded)

$11,687.45 + $38,500 = $50,187.45

17. (c) $235,000 × 0.95 = $223,250

$223,250 ÷ $1,000 = 223.25

223.25 × $7.40 = $1,652.05

$1,652.05 ÷ 0.28 = $5,900.18

18. (b) 456,000 × 0.9 = $410,400

$410,400 ÷ $1,000 × $5.22 =
$2,142.29 (rounded)

$456,000 × 0.53 ÷ $100 × $3.80 = $9,183.84

$9,183.84 + $1,800 ÷ 12 = $915.32

$2,142.29 + $915.32 = $3,057.61

19. (b) $335,000 × 0.8 = $268,000

$268,000 ÷ $1,000 = 268

268 × $5.68 = $1,522.24

20. (a) $385,000 × 0.9 = $346,500

$385,000 − $346,500 = $38,500

Appraisal Methods

This chapter presents methods and formulas used in estimating property value. First you will be given a general description of the most commonly used methods of appraising property, including the

- sales comparison approach,
- cost approach, and
- income capitalization approach.

Then you will analyze each method in detail. Appraisal is not a science. An appraisal is an estimate of value, which depends on the experience and common sense of an appraiser, who must evaluate the data involved.

Appraisals are done by state-licensed or state-certified appraisers. In most states, sales associates and brokers are not legally permitted to do appraisals. However, they are frequently called on to do broker price opinions (BPOs) and comparative market analyses (CMAs). This is especially true in the case of foreclosures and short sales. The purpose of this chapter is to help you understand the appraisal process. An in-depth discussion of appraisals is beyond the scope of this text.

At the conclusion of your work in this chapter, you will be able to

- ▣ adjust comparables, applying the sales comparison approach,
- ▣ accurately calculate the replacement or reproduction cost and accrued depreciation for the application of the cost approach, and
- ▣ capitalize annual net operating income into an indication of value for an income-producing property.

VALUE

Value is not a static number but rather a concept involving the benefits the item returns to its owner or prospective owner. A real estate appraisal is a type of value, stated as an opinion, that presumes the transfer or sale of a property as of a certain date, under specific conditions set forth in the definition of the term identified by the appraiser as applicable in an appraisal.

It is easier to understand the use of the term *value* not only in real estate practice but in other areas, as well. For example, how much would you pay for five gallons of gasoline if your car ran out of fuel as it rolled into the service station driveway? How much would you pay for that same five gallons of gasoline if your car ran out of fuel 50 miles from a service station at midnight on a cold February night? Did the *value* of the fuel change for the service station owner? Did it change for you?

Or how about the value of a 2,500-square-foot, four-bedroom house bought when energy was cheap and the children were all living at home compared to that same house today, when all of the children are married, both spouses are in poor health and retired, and energy is expensive. Is the value still similar for the owners? Do the owners currently receive the same benefits of ownership that they once did?

Exact property values are not possible to obtain. In the field of real estate, varying methods of estimating property value are used. Real estate is traditionally appraised by three methods: the sales comparison approach (also called the market data approach), the cost approach, and the income capitalization approach.

The *sales comparison approach* is used to estimate the value of a parcel of real estate by

- ▣ comparing the given real estate to comparable (or similar) properties in the subject neighborhood; and
- ▣ making plus or minus dollar adjustments to each comparable's sales price for significant differences between the comparable and the subject property.

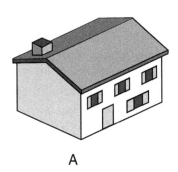
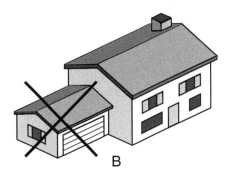

A   B

For example, if House A (pictured above) is being appraised via the sales comparison approach to value, the appraiser finds a comparable house—for example, House B, which sold for $156,000. In comparing the two, the only major difference between the houses may be that House B has a garage, valued at $4,000, whereas House A has no garage. Therefore, $4,000 must be subtracted from the sales price of House B to arrive at the sales comparison approach appraisal of House A, which is $152,000.

In estimating value by the *cost approach*, the appraiser will

- estimate the cost of replacing the buildings on the land at current prices,
- subtract the estimated amount of accumulated depreciation from the cost of the buildings,
- estimate the value of the land, and
- add the land value to the depreciated building value to arrive at the current property value.

The *income capitalization approach* is used to estimate the value of a property on the basis of the income it produces. It is calculated by

- subtracting the operating expenses from the gross income of the property to determine the net operating income; and
- dividing the net operating income by an appropriate capitalization rate—a rate that is estimated to represent the proper relationship between the value of that property and the net operating income it produces.

Market Value

Market value is an estimate of the most probable price a property would bring if exposed for sale in the open market. Reasonable time is allowed in which to find a purchaser who buys with the knowledge of all of the uses and purposes for which the property is adapted and for which it is capable of being used.

SALES COMPARISON APPROACH

The sales comparison approach to value is the method most frequently used in estimating the value of residential properties. Many salespeople do not use the other two approaches to value because the salespeople typically provide broker price opinions or CMAs, not appraisals.

Belonging to a multiple-listing service (MLS) with reliable, up-to-date information greatly simplifies the use of the sales comparison approach to value. For instance, if a salesperson can find only one similar, or comparable, house, as shown in the example, the estimate of the value of House A depends completely on the information obtained from the sale of House B and the similarities between the two. However, if a salesperson scans a list of similar properties and selects three or four of those most similar to the subject house, the salesperson's estimate of value will be much more accurate. The larger database provides better statistics.

In selecting similar or comparable houses, a salesperson must be careful to consider the following:

- Sales or financing concessions
- Date of sale/time
- Location
- Quality of construction
- Age
- Condition
- Amenities and features
- Room count and square footage
- Lot size
- Style or type of house
- Any unusual features, such as a converted garage now used as a bedroom or the large size of a particular model when compared with the rest of the neighborhood

Without printed data furnished by an appraisal file or from an MLS, a sales comparison approach would be much more difficult and subjective rather than objective. Most real estate offices also have forms or computer programs used to accumulate data on current listings and similar houses that have sold. Similar houses currently on the market tend to establish the maximum value of the property being appraised. Furthermore, these comparisons allow owners to recognize their competition before they list or market their property.

The dates of sale of similar houses and information about how they were financed also greatly influence the adjusted values of houses. Because the market changes, it is more accurate to use the most recent sales.

For example, during a period of rapid economic expansion, house values may increase, or appreciate, by large amounts. Inflation certainly enters into this, and prices sometimes increase dramatically. By considering the date of sale, a salesperson can determine a comparative sales price by using the current rate of appreciation within a particular market.

Older sales figures particularly must be adjusted to allow for the lapse of time since the sales. When an adjustment is made for the date of sale, a method similar to computing simple interest is used. For example, if you choose 6 percent per year as your appreciation adjustment factor (i.e., the amount you estimate real estate has gained in value due to inflation and other causes), you can reduce that to a monthly factor of 0.5 percent ($0.06 \div 12 = 0.005$, or 0.5%). The monthly factor can then be multiplied by the number of months elapsed since the sale you are evaluating.

1. If housing prices appreciate at a rate of 8 percent per year, what is the adjusted value of a house that sold for $153,000 three years ago? (Round to the nearest dollar.)

The type of financing used in each sale affects the net amount received by the seller, and this has an indirect bearing on the probable sales price of the house. For example, some buyers may be able to pay cash for a house. This type of sale tends to be the most reliable because financing plays no part at all. Another seller with an assumable loan at a below-market interest rate might obtain a higher price for her house. Still another seller might have to pay very large loan costs in order to sell, which results in a much lower net price received by the seller. In this case, some of the high loan costs could be included in the sales price. Therefore, these costs must be subtracted from the sales price in order to remove this effect of financing from the sales price. Still another seller might have such a compelling reason to sell that he will carry a large second lien note at a below-market interest rate. If each of the foregoing sales involved similar models in the same subdivision within a short period of time, the sales prices could vary considerably, depending on the type of financing. Appraisers obtain this data from various sources, including MLS membership and verification from the seller or buyer or from a broker involved in the sale.

TABLE 11.1

Gathering Data on Similar Homes

House	Age	Rooms	Extras	Sales Price	Sale Date	Time Adjusted Price	How Financed	Final Adjustment	Size	$ per Sq Ft
1	5 years	3-2-2	Fireplace Pool <$15,000>	$185,000 <15,000> $170,000	Jan. 1 (11 months ago)	$170,000 + 9,500 $179,500	Cash	$179,500	1,500 sq ft	$119.33
2	4 years	3-2-2	No fireplace +$2,500	$174,472 + 2,500 $176,972	Dec. 1 (current date)	$176,972 -0- $176,972	Equity <$1,000>	$176,972 <1,000> $175,972	1,480 sq ft	$118.90
3	5 years	3-2-2	Fireplace	$175,172	June 1 (6 months ago)		FHA <$1,800>		1,460 sq ft	
4*	5 years	3-2-2	Fireplace	$176,300	Aug. 1 (4 months ago)		Equity + 2nd +2,000		1,500 sq ft	
Subject	4 years	3-2-2	Fireplace		Dec. 1 (current date)				1,490 sq ft	

* This house involved a distress sale and the seller agreed to carry back a large second lien note.

Table 11.1 shows a useful format for gathering data concerning the sale of houses that are similar to and located near the subject house. It permits the user to adjust the sales prices for differences in extras, date of sale, and method of financing. For this exercise, use an appreciation rate of 6 percent per year, or 0.5 percent per month. (Note: The use of a factor for appreciation or depreciation depends on a great many variables, such as prevailing economic conditions, geographic location of the property, and so on. Therefore, careful use should be made of such a factor.) After you read the explanation of the chart, fill in the missing amounts, considering appreciation and financing.

In Table 11.1, the first adjustment is for *extras*. For House 1, subtract $15,000 for the pool because the subject house does not have one. This gives an estimate of the sales price for a house that, like the subject house, has no pool.

$185,000   actual sales price for House 1
− 15,000   estimated value of pool
$170,000   price of House 1 adjusted for pool

Next adjust House 1's price for the sale date. Use an appreciation factor of 6 percent per year (or 0.5 percent per month) to account for elapsed time between sale dates.

$170,000 × 0.005 = $850   monthly appreciation
$850 × 11 months = $9,500   total appreciation (rounded to the nearest $500)
$170,000 + $9,500 = $179,500 adjusted price

Because this was a cash sale, no adjustment is made for financing, so the final adjustment leaves the price at $179,500.

This house has 1,500 square feet of living area (excluding garages and open porches), so:

$179,500 ÷ 1,500 square feet = $119.33 per square foot

The procedure is the same for House 2. First add $2,500 for a fireplace because all of the similar houses, including the subject house, have one. This results in an adjusted sales price of $176,972. The sale date is current, so no adjustment for date of sale is necessary. However, the house may have sold for about $1,000 more because of an attractive low-interest loan. Therefore, adjust downward by this $1,000 to $175,972. The house has 1,480 square feet of living area, which yields a rate of $118.90 per square foot:

$175,972 ÷ 1,480 square feet = $118.90 per square foot

2. Now fill in the missing data for Houses 3 and 4 in Table 11.1.

Check your answers against the completed table in the answer key. These numbers can help you estimate a value for the subject house. Many real estate associates calculate a numerical average of the adjusted sales price per square foot for the comparables and use that average as the value per square foot of the subject property. The average value is multiplied by the square footage to estimate the value of the subject house. This method is acceptable because the final calculation represents an estimate of value, not an appraisal. It is very important to evaluate the properties themselves for inclusion in the comparison or average. Each property must be considered as being representative of the subdivision or area.

To compute an average, add the individual values together, then divide by the number of values you have added.

E X A M P L E :   To compute the average of a set of numbers such as 12, 17, 23, and 14.2, first add those numbers:

$$12 + 17 + 23 + 14.2 = 66.2$$

Four values are being averaged, so divide by 4:

$$66.2 \div 4 = 16.55$$

Thus, the average of the four values is 16.55.

The next step in estimating the value of the subject house would be to take the average value per square foot and multiply it by the number of square feet in the subject house, to arrive at the total estimated value or price. Please note that a professional appraiser would probably use a more sophisticated method of arriving at the value per square foot of the subject house. Multiplying this different value per square foot by the square footage of the subject house would give the appraiser a different estimate of the value of the subject house.

Forms

The simple form that you used for accumulating data illustrates how the date of sale and the financing affect the accuracy of the data. In times when appreciation or inflation is great, the sales price must be adjusted to reflect the date of sale of each comparable property.

Another form used nationwide is the Uniform Residential Appraisal Report produced by Fannie Mae, illustrated in Figure 11.1. Notice that this is an appraisal form and not one just for estimating value. Therefore, it provides for adjustments to account for date of each sale, differences in amenities, features or improvements, and the effects of financing on each property. Because this form is so detailed and elicits data not customarily used in a simple estimate of value (as in the solicitation of a listing), most brokers have devised forms similar to the one used in the example.

Please note that this chapter describes estimation of market value by a real estate associate rather than appraisal of a property by a licensed or certified appraiser. There is a distinct difference.

FIGURE 11.1

Uniform Residential Appraisal Report

Uniform Residential Appraisal Report File

The purpose of this summary appraisal report is to provide the lender/client with an accurate, and adequately supported, opinion of the market value of the subject property.

SUBJECT

Property Address	City	State	Zip Code
Borrower	Owner of Public Record	County	
Legal Description			

Assessor's Parcel #   Tax Year   R.E. Taxes $

Neighborhood Name   Map Reference   Census Tract

Occupant ☐ Owner ☐ Tenant ☐ Vacant   Special Assessments $ ☐ PUD   HOA $ ☐ per year ☐ per month

Property Rights Appraised ☐ Fee Simple ☐ Leasehold ☐ Other (describe)

Assignment Type ☐ Purchase Transaction ☐ Refinance Transaction ☐ Other (describe)

Lender/Client   Address

Is the subject property currently offered for sale or has it been offered for sale in the twelve months prior to the effective date of this appraisal? ☐ Yes ☐ No

Report data source(s) used, offering price(s), and date(s).

CONTRACT

I ☐ did ☐ did not analyze the contract for sale for the subject purchase transaction. Explain the results of the analysis of the contract for sale or why the analysis was not performed.

Contract Price $ Date of Contract   Is the property seller the owner of public record? ☐ Yes ☐ No   Data Source(s)

Is there any financial assistance (loan charges, sale concessions, gift or downpayment assistance, etc.) to be paid by any party on behalf of the borrower? ☐ Yes ☐ No
If Yes, report the total dollar amount and describe the items to be paid.

NEIGHBORHOOD

Note: Race and the racial composition of the neighborhood are not appraisal factors.

Neighborhood Characteristics	One-Unit Housing Trends	One-Unit Housing	Present Land Use %
Location ☐ Urban ☐ Suburban ☐ Rural	Property Values ☐ Increasing ☐ Stable ☐ Declining	PRICE AGE	One-Unit %
Built-Up ☐ Over 75% ☐ 25–75% ☐ Under 25%	Demand/Supply ☐ Shortage ☐ In Balance ☐ Over Supply	$ (000) (yrs)	2-4 Unit %
Growth ☐ Rapid ☐ Stable ☐ Slow	Marketing Time ☐ Under 3 mths ☐ 3–6 mths ☐ Over 6 mths	Low	Multi-Family %
Neighborhood Boundaries		High	Commercial %
		Pred.	Other %

Neighborhood Description

Market Conditions (including support for the above conclusions)

SITE

Dimensions	Area	Shape	View
Specific Zoning Classification	Zoning Description		

Zoning Compliance ☐ Legal ☐ Legal Nonconforming (Grandfathered Use) ☐ No Zoning ☐ Illegal (describe)

Is the highest and best use of the subject property as improved (or as proposed per plans and specifications) the present use? ☐ Yes ☐ No   If No, describe

Utilities	Public	Other (describe)		Public	Other (describe)	Off-site Improvements—Type	Public	Private
Electricity	☐	☐	Water	☐	☐	Street	☐	☐
Gas	☐	☐	Sanitary Sewer	☐	☐	Alley	☐	☐

FEMA Special Flood Hazard Area ☐ Yes ☐ No   FEMA Flood Zone   FEMA Map #   FEMA Map Date

Are the utilities and off-site improvements typical for the market area? ☐ Yes ☐ No   If No, describe

Are there any adverse site conditions or external factors (easements, encroachments, environmental conditions, land uses, etc.)? ☐ Yes ☐ No   If Yes, describe

IMPROVEMENTS

General Description	Foundation	Exterior Description materials/condition	Interior materials/condition
Units ☐ One ☐ One with Accessory Unit	☐ Concrete Slab ☐ Crawl Space	Foundation Walls	Floors
# of Stories	☐ Full Basement ☐ Partial Basement	Exterior Walls	Walls
Type ☐ Det. ☐ Att. ☐ S-Det./End Unit	Basement Area sq. ft.	Roof Surface	Trim/Finish
☐ Existing ☐ Proposed ☐ Under Const.	Basement Finish %	Gutters & Downspouts	Bath Floor
Design (Style)	☐ Outside Entry/Exit ☐ Sump Pump	Window Type	Bath Wainscot
Year Built	Evidence of ☐ Infestation	Storm Sash/Insulated	Car Storage ☐ None
Effective Age (Yrs)	☐ Dampness ☐ Settlement	Screens	☐ Driveway # of Cars
Attic ☐ None	Heating ☐ FWA ☐ HWBB ☐ Radiant	Amenities ☐ Woodstove(s) #	Driveway Surface
☐ Drop Stair ☐ Stairs	☐ Other Fuel	☐ Fireplace(s) # ☐ Fence	☐ Garage # of Cars
☐ Floor ☐ Scuttle	Cooling ☐ Central Air Conditioning	☐ Patio/Deck ☐ Porch	☐ Carport # of Cars
☐ Finished ☐ Heated	☐ Individual ☐ Other	☐ Pool ☐ Other	☐ Att. ☐ Det. ☐ Built-in

Appliances ☐ Refrigerator ☐ Range/Oven ☐ Dishwasher ☐ Disposal ☐ Microwave ☐ Washer/Dryer ☐ Other (describe)

Finished area **above** grade contains: Rooms   Bedrooms   Bath(s)   Square Feet of Gross Living Area Above Grade

Additional features (special energy efficient items, etc.)

Describe the condition of the property (including needed repairs, deterioration, renovations, remodeling, etc.).

Are there any physical deficiencies or adverse conditions that affect the livability, soundness, or structural integrity of the property? ☐ Yes ☐ No   If Yes, describe

Does the property generally conform to the neighborhood (functional utility, style, condition, use, construction, etc.)? ☐ Yes ☐ No   If No, describe

Uniform Residential Appraisal Report   File

There are	comparable properties currently offered for sale in the subject neighborhood ranging in price from $			to $		
There are	comparable sales in the subject neighborhood within the past twelve months ranging in sale price from $			to $		

FEATURE	SUBJECT	COMPARABLE SALE # 1		COMPARABLE SALE # 2		COMPARABLE SALE # 3	
Address							
Proximity to Subject							
Sale Price	$		$		$		$
Sale Price/Gross Liv. Area	$ sq. ft.	$ sq. ft.		$ sq. ft.		$ sq. ft.	
Data Source(s)							
Verification Source(s)							
VALUE ADJUSTMENTS	DESCRIPTION	DESCRIPTION	+(-) $ Adjustment	DESCRIPTION	+(-) $ Adjustment	DESCRIPTION	+(-) $ Adjustment
Sale or Financing Concessions							
Date of Sale/Time							
Location							
Leasehold/Fee Simple							
Site							
View							
Design (Style)							
Quality of Construction							
Actual Age							
Condition							
Above Grade	Total Bdrms. Baths	Total Bdrms. Baths		Total Bdrms. Baths		Total Bdrms. Baths	
Room Count							
Gross Living Area	sq. ft.	sq. ft.		sq. ft.		sq. ft.	
Basement & Finished Rooms Below Grade							
Functional Utility							
Heating/Cooling							
Energy Efficient Items							
Garage/Carport							
Porch/Patio/Deck							
Net Adjustment (Total)		☐ + ☐ -	$	☐ + ☐ -	$	☐ + ☐ -	$
Adjusted Sale Price of Comparables		Net Adj. % Gross Adj. %	$	Net Adj. % Gross Adj. %	$	Net Adj. % Gross Adj. %	$

I ☐ did ☐ did not research the sale or transfer history of the subject property and comparable sales. If not, explain

My research ☐ did ☐ did not reveal any prior sales or transfers of the subject property for the three years prior to the effective date of this appraisal.

Data source(s)

My research ☐ did ☐ did not reveal any prior sales or transfers of the comparable sales for the year prior to the date of sale of the comparable sale.

Data source(s)

Report the results of the research and analysis of the prior sale or transfer history of the subject property and comparable sales (report additional prior sales on page 3).

ITEM	SUBJECT	COMPARABLE SALE # 1	COMPARABLE SALE # 2	COMPARABLE SALE # 3
Date of Prior Sale/Transfer				
Price of Prior Sale/Transfer				
Data Source(s)				
Effective Date of Data Source(s)				

Analysis of prior sale or transfer history of the subject property and comparable sales

Summary of Sales Comparison Approach

Indicated Value by Sales Comparison Approach $

Indicated Value by: Sales Comparison Approach $ Cost Approach (if developed) $ Income Approach (if developed) $

This appraisal is made ☐ "as is", ☐ subject to completion per plans and specifications on the basis of a hypothetical condition that the improvements have been completed, ☐ subject to the following repairs or alterations on the basis of a hypothetical condition that the repairs or alterations have been completed, or ☐ subject to the following required inspection based on the extraordinary assumption that the condition or deficiency does not require alteration or repair:

Based on a complete visual inspection of the interior and exterior areas of the subject property, defined scope of work, statement of assumptions and limiting conditions, and appraiser's certification, my (our) opinion of the market value, as defined, of the real property that is the subject of this report is $, as of   , which is the date of inspection and the effective date of this appraisal.

Uniform Residential Appraisal Report

File #

ADDITIONAL COMMENTS

(blank lined area)

COST APPROACH TO VALUE (not required by Fannie Mae)

Provide adequate information for the lender/client to replicate the below cost figures and calculations.

Support for the opinion of site value (summary of comparable land sales or other methods for estimating site value)

ESTIMATED ☐ REPRODUCTION OR ☐ REPLACEMENT COST NEW	OPINION OF SITE VALUE .... = $
Source of cost data	Dwelling Sq. Ft. @ $ .... = $
Quality rating from cost service Effective date of cost data	Sq. Ft. @ $ .... = $
Comments on Cost Approach (gross living area calculations, depreciation, etc.)	Garage/Carport Sq. Ft. @ $ .... = $
	Total Estimate of Cost-New .... = $
	Less Physical	Functional	External
	Depreciation = $( )
	Depreciated Cost of Improvements .... = $
	"As-is" Value of Site Improvements .... = $
Estimated Remaining Economic Life (HUD and VA only) Years	Indicated Value By Cost Approach .... = $

INCOME APPROACH TO VALUE (not required by Fannie Mae)

Estimated Monthly Market Rent $ X Gross Rent Multiplier   = $ Indicated Value by Income Approach

Summary of Income Approach (including support for market rent and GRM)

PROJECT INFORMATION FOR PUDs (if applicable)

Is the developer/builder in control of the Homeowners' Association (HOA)? ☐ Yes ☐ No   Unit type(s) ☐ Detached ☐ Attached

Provide the following information for PUDs ONLY if the developer/builder is in control of the HOA and the subject property is an attached dwelling unit.

Legal name of project

Total number of phases   Total number of units   Total number of units sold

Total number of units rented   Total number of units for sale   Data source(s)

Was the project created by the conversion of an existing building(s) into a PUD? ☐ Yes ☐ No   If Yes, date of conversion

Does the project contain any multi-dwelling units? ☐ Yes ☐ No   Data source(s)

Are the units, common elements, and recreation facilities complete? ☐ Yes ☐ No   If No, describe the status of completion.

Are the common elements leased to or by the Homeowners' Association? ☐ Yes ☐ No   If Yes, describe the rental terms and options.

Describe common elements and recreational facilities

Uniform Residential Appraisal Report   File

This report form is designed to report an appraisal of a one-unit property or a one-unit property with an accessory unit; including a unit in a planned unit development (PUD). This report form is not designed to report an appraisal of a manufactured home or a unit in a condominium or cooperative project.

This appraisal report is subject to the following scope of work, intended use, intended user, definition of market value, statement of assumptions and limiting conditions, and certifications. Modifications, additions, or deletions to the intended use, intended user, definition of market value, or assumptions and limiting conditions are not permitted. The appraiser may expand the scope of work to include any additional research or analysis necessary based on the complexity of this appraisal assignment. Modifications or deletions to the certifications are also not permitted. However, additional certifications that do not constitute material alterations to this appraisal report, such as those required by law or those related to the appraiser's continuing education or membership in an appraisal organization, are permitted.

SCOPE OF WORK: The scope of work for this appraisal is defined by the complexity of this appraisal assignment and the reporting requirements of this appraisal report form, including the following definition of market value, statement of assumptions and limiting conditions, and certifications. The appraiser must, at a minimum: (1) perform a complete visual inspection of the interior and exterior areas of the subject property, (2) inspect the neighborhood, (3) inspect each of the comparable sales from at least the street, (4) research, verify, and analyze data from reliable public and/or private sources, and (5) report his or her analysis, opinions, and conclusions in this appraisal report.

INTENDED USE: The intended use of this appraisal report is for the lender/client to evaluate the property that is the subject of this appraisal for a mortgage finance transaction.

INTENDED USER: The intended user of this appraisal report is the lender/client.

DEFINITION OF MARKET VALUE: The most probable price which a property should bring in a competitive and open market under all conditions requisite to a fair sale, the buyer and seller, each acting prudently, knowledgeably and assuming the price is not affected by undue stimulus. Implicit in this definition is the consummation of a sale as of a specified date and the passing of title from seller to buyer under conditions whereby: (1) buyer and seller are typically motivated; (2) both parties are well informed or well advised, and each acting in what he or she considers his or her own best interest; (3) a reasonable time is allowed for exposure in the open market; (4) payment is made in terms of cash in U. S. dollars or in terms of financial arrangements comparable thereto; and (5) the price represents the normal consideration for the property sold unaffected by special or creative financing or sales concessions* granted by anyone associated with the sale.

*Adjustments to the comparables must be made for special or creative financing or sales concessions. No adjustments are necessary for those costs which are normally paid by sellers as a result of tradition or law in a market area; these costs are readily identifiable since the seller pays these costs in virtually all sales transactions. Special or creative financing adjustments can be made to the comparable property by comparisons to financing terms offered by a third party institutional lender that is not already involved in the property or transaction. Any adjustment should not be calculated on a mechanical dollar for dollar cost of the financing or concession but the dollar amount of any adjustment should approximate the market's reaction to the financing or concessions based on the appraiser's judgment.

STATEMENT OF ASSUMPTIONS AND LIMITING CONDITIONS: The appraiser's certification in this report is subject to the following assumptions and limiting conditions:

1. The appraiser will not be responsible for matters of a legal nature that affect either the property being appraised or the title to it, except for information that he or she became aware of during the research involved in performing this appraisal. The appraiser assumes that the title is good and marketable and will not render any opinions about the title.

2. The appraiser has provided a sketch in this appraisal report to show the approximate dimensions of the improvements. The sketch is included only to assist the reader in visualizing the property and understanding the appraiser's determination of its size.

3. The appraiser has examined the available flood maps that are provided by the Federal Emergency Management Agency (or other data sources) and has noted in this appraisal report whether any portion of the subject site is located in an identified Special Flood Hazard Area. Because the appraiser is not a surveyor, he or she makes no guarantees, express or implied, regarding this determination.

4. The appraiser will not give testimony or appear in court because he or she made an appraisal of the property in question, unless specific arrangements to do so have been made beforehand, or as otherwise required by law.

5. The appraiser has noted in this appraisal report any adverse conditions (such as needed repairs, deterioration, the presence of hazardous wastes, toxic substances, etc.) observed during the inspection of the subject property or that he or she became aware of during the research involved in performing this appraisal. Unless otherwise stated in this appraisal report, the appraiser has no knowledge of any hidden or unapparent physical deficiencies or adverse conditions of the property (such as, but not limited to, needed repairs, deterioration, the presence of hazardous wastes, toxic substances, adverse environmental conditions, etc.) that would make the property less valuable, and has assumed that there are no such conditions and makes no guarantees or warranties, express or implied. The appraiser will not be responsible for any such conditions that do exist or for any engineering or testing that might be required to discover whether such conditions exist. Because the appraiser is not an expert in the field of environmental hazards, this appraisal report must not be considered as an environmental assessment of the property.

6. The appraiser has based his or her appraisal report and valuation conclusion for an appraisal that is subject to satisfactory completion, repairs, or alterations on the assumption that the completion, repairs, or alterations of the subject property will be performed in a professional manner.

Uniform Residential Appraisal Report   File

APPRAISER'S CERTIFICATION: The Appraiser certifies and agrees that:

1. I have, at a minimum, developed and reported this appraisal in accordance with the scope of work requirements stated in this appraisal report.

2. I performed a complete visual inspection of the interior and exterior areas of the subject property. I reported the condition of the improvements in factual, specific terms. I identified and reported the physical deficiencies that could affect the livability, soundness, or structural integrity of the property.

3. I performed this appraisal in accordance with the requirements of the Uniform Standards of Professional Appraisal Practice that were adopted and promulgated by the Appraisal Standards Board of The Appraisal Foundation and that were in place at the time this appraisal report was prepared.

4. I developed my opinion of the market value of the real property that is the subject of this report based on the sales comparison approach to value. I have adequate comparable market data to develop a reliable sales comparison approach for this appraisal assignment. I further certify that I considered the cost and income approaches to value but did not develop them, unless otherwise indicated in this report.

5. I researched, verified, analyzed, and reported on any current agreement for sale for the subject property, any offering for sale of the subject property in the twelve months prior to the effective date of this appraisal, and the prior sales of the subject property for a minimum of three years prior to the effective date of this appraisal, unless otherwise indicated in this report.

6. I researched, verified, analyzed, and reported on the prior sales of the comparable sales for a minimum of one year prior to the date of sale of the comparable sale, unless otherwise indicated in this report.

7. I selected and used comparable sales that are locationally, physically, and functionally the most similar to the subject property.

8. I have not used comparable sales that were the result of combining a land sale with the contract purchase price of a home that has been built or will be built on the land.

9. I have reported adjustments to the comparable sales that reflect the market's reaction to the differences between the subject property and the comparable sales.

10. I verified, from a disinterested source, all information in this report that was provided by parties who have a financial interest in the sale or financing of the subject property.

11. I have knowledge and experience in appraising this type of property in this market area.

12. I am aware of, and have access to, the necessary and appropriate public and private data sources, such as multiple listing services, tax assessment records, public land records and other such data sources for the area in which the property is located.

13. I obtained the information, estimates, and opinions furnished by other parties and expressed in this appraisal report from reliable sources that I believe to be true and correct.

14. I have taken into consideration the factors that have an impact on value with respect to the subject neighborhood, subject property, and the proximity of the subject property to adverse influences in the development of my opinion of market value. I have noted in this appraisal report any adverse conditions (such as, but not limited to, needed repairs, deterioration, the presence of hazardous wastes, toxic substances, adverse environmental conditions, etc.) observed during the inspection of the subject property or that I became aware of during the research involved in performing this appraisal. I have considered these adverse conditions in my analysis of the property value, and have reported on the effect of the conditions on the value and marketability of the subject property.

15. I have not knowingly withheld any significant information from this appraisal report and, to the best of my knowledge, all statements and information in this appraisal report are true and correct.

16. I stated in this appraisal report my own personal, unbiased, and professional analysis, opinions, and conclusions, which are subject only to the assumptions and limiting conditions in this appraisal report.

17. I have no present or prospective interest in the property that is the subject of this report, and I have no present or prospective personal interest or bias with respect to the participants in the transaction. I did not base, either partially or completely, my analysis and/or opinion of market value in this appraisal report on the race, color, religion, sex, age, marital status, handicap, familial status, or national origin of either the prospective owners or occupants of the subject property or of the present owners or occupants of the properties in the vicinity of the subject property or on any other basis prohibited by law.

18. My employment and/or compensation for performing this appraisal or any future or anticipated appraisals was not conditioned on any agreement or understanding, written or otherwise, that I would report (or present analysis supporting) a predetermined specific value, a predetermined minimum value, a range or direction in value, a value that favors the cause of any party, or the attainment of a specific result or occurrence of a specific subsequent event (such as approval of a pending mortgage loan application).

19. I personally prepared all conclusions and opinions about the real estate that were set forth in this appraisal report. If I relied on significant real property appraisal assistance from any individual or individuals in the performance of this appraisal or the preparation of this appraisal report, I have named such individual(s) and disclosed the specific tasks performed in this appraisal report. I certify that any individual so named is qualified to perform the tasks. I have not authorized anyone to make a change to any item in this appraisal report; therefore, any change made to this appraisal is unauthorized and I will take no responsibility for it.

20. I identified the lender/client in this appraisal report who is the individual, organization, or agent for the organization that ordered and will receive this appraisal report.

Uniform Residential Appraisal Report   File

21. The lender/client may disclose or distribute this appraisal report to: the borrower; another lender at the request of the borrower; the mortgagee or its successors and assigns; mortgage insurers; government sponsored enterprises; other secondary market participants; data collection or reporting services; professional appraisal organizations; any department, agency, or instrumentality of the United States; and any state, the District of Columbia, or other jurisdictions; without having to obtain the appraiser's or supervisory appraiser's (if applicable) consent. Such consent must be obtained before this appraisal report may be disclosed or distributed to any other party (including, but not limited to, the public through advertising, public relations, news, sales, or other media).

22. I am aware that any disclosure or distribution of this appraisal report by me or the lender/client may be subject to certain laws and regulations. Further, I am also subject to the provisions of the Uniform Standards of Professional Appraisal Practice that pertain to disclosure or distribution by me.

23. The borrower, another lender at the request of the borrower, the mortgagee or its successors and assigns, mortgage insurers, government sponsored enterprises, and other secondary market participants may rely on this appraisal report as part of any mortgage finance transaction that involves any one or more of these parties.

24. If this appraisal report was transmitted as an "electronic record" containing my "electronic signature," as those terms are defined in applicable federal and/or state laws (excluding audio and video recordings), or a facsimile transmission of this appraisal report containing a copy or representation of my signature, the appraisal report shall be as effective, enforceable and valid as if a paper version of this appraisal report were delivered containing my original hand written signature.

25. Any intentional or negligent misrepresentation(s) contained in this appraisal report may result in civil liability and/or criminal penalties including, but not limited to, fine or imprisonment or both under the provisions of Title 18, United States Code, Section 1001, et seq., or similar state laws.

SUPERVISORY APPRAISER'S CERTIFICATION: The Supervisory Appraiser certifies and agrees that:

1. I directly supervised the appraiser for this appraisal assignment, have read the appraisal report, and agree with the appraiser's analysis, opinions, statements, conclusions, and the appraiser's certification.

2. I accept full responsibility for the contents of this appraisal report including, but not limited to, the appraiser's analysis, opinions, statements, conclusions, and the appraiser's certification.

3. The appraiser identified in this appraisal report is either a sub-contractor or an employee of the supervisory appraiser (or the appraisal firm), is qualified to perform this appraisal, and is acceptable to perform this appraisal under the applicable state law.

4. This appraisal report complies with the Uniform Standards of Professional Appraisal Practice that were adopted and promulgated by the Appraisal Standards Board of The Appraisal Foundation and that were in place at the time this appraisal report was prepared.

5. If this appraisal report was transmitted as an "electronic record" containing my "electronic signature," as those terms are defined in applicable federal and/or state laws (excluding audio and video recordings), or a facsimile transmission of this appraisal report containing a copy or representation of my signature, the appraisal report shall be as effective, enforceable and valid as if a paper version of this appraisal report were delivered containing my original hand written signature.

APPRAISER	SUPERVISORY APPRAISER (ONLY IF REQUIRED)
Signature_____	Signature_____
Name _____	Name_____
Company Name _____	Company Name _____
Company Address_____	Company Address_____
	_____
Telephone Number _____	Telephone Number _____
Email Address_____	Email Address_____
Date of Signature and Report _____	Date of Signature _____
Effective Date of Appraisal _____	State Certification #_____
State Certification #_____	or State License # _____
or State License #_____	State _____
or Other (describe) _____ State # _____	Expiration Date of Certification or License _____
State _____	
Expiration Date of Certification or License _____	SUBJECT PROPERTY
ADDRESS OF PROPERTY APPRAISED	☐ Did not inspect subject property
	☐ Did inspect exterior of subject property from street
_____	Date of Inspection _____
_____	☐ Did inspect interior and exterior of subject property
APPRAISED VALUE OF SUBJECT PROPERTY $ _____	Date of Inspection _____
LENDER/CLIENT	
Name _____	COMPARABLE SALES
Company Name _____	☐ Did not inspect exterior of comparable sales from street
Company Address_____	☐ Did inspect exterior of comparable sales from street
_____	Date of Inspection _____
Email Address_____	

COST APPROACH

The cost approach can be expressed as a formula:

Building replacement cost – Depreciation + Land value = Estimated property value

Building replacement cost is the dollar amount that would be required to build a comparable building today. Note that this would result in a new building. If the subject building is not new, depreciation must be considered.

Depreciation represents the difference (loss) in value between a new building of the same type as the subject (the replacement) and one in the present condition of the structure being appraised. This has nothing to do with IRS (Internal Revenue Service) depreciation cost recovery. When depreciation is used in calculating an appraisal, it involves the actual wearing out of an improvement based on its actual age and compared with its projected remaining economic life.

There are three types of depreciation that apply here—physical deterioration, functional obsolescence, and external obsolescence.

Remember:

Land + Improvement = Real estate or property

Land is not considered when calculating depreciation. The golden rule is that land does not depreciate.

Land value represents the present market value of the land alone. It does not include the value of improvements. Land value is arrived at through an analysis of current sales of comparable land in the area. It is computed separately because land is not depreciable.

Physical deterioration may be defined as the physical wearing out of a structure.

EXAMPLES:

- A building that needs a new roof
- Peeling paint and broken windows
- A furnace with a cracked heat exchanger

Functional obsolescence occurs as a result of an undesirable layout or an outdated design.

EXAMPLES:

- A two-story, five-bedroom house with only one bathroom that is located on the first floor
- A house with a coal furnace
- A house with multicolor shag carpeting and avocado green appliances
- A house with no dishwasher or garbage disposal in a neighborhood where all other homes have them

External (economic and/or environmental) obsolescence involves a loss of value from causes outside the property itself.

E X A M P L E S :

- Loss of value due to a new highway constructed adjacent to a property (dirt and noise)
- A machine shop, an elementary school, or a drive-through restaurant built across from an apartment hotel designed for retirees
- Excessive taxes, zoning changes, proximity of nuisances, and changes in land use

Now use the cost approach formula to arrive at an estimate of value for the real estate described in problems 3 through 7.

Building replacement cost – Depreciation + Land value = Estimated property value

3. An appraiser estimates the value of a piece of land at $60,000 and the replacement cost of the building on that land at $150,000. The depreciation has been calculated to be $20,000. What is the estimated value of the real estate?

 The estimated replacement cost of a building is often given as an amount per square foot or cubic foot.

4. A house has a total finished floor area of 1,450 square feet. An appraiser estimated its replacement cost at $85 per square foot.

 a. What is the estimated replacement cost of the building?

 b. If the value of the land is $30,000 and the depreciation is $8,200, what is the estimated value of the real estate?

5. Mr. Robinson's house is 24 feet by 37 feet, with a finished family room addition that measures 15 feet by 20 feet. An appraiser has estimated the replacement cost at $90 per square foot, the land value at $25,000, and the depreciation at $8,400. What is the estimated value of the real estate?

6. What is the estimated replacement cost of the building shown to the right if the cost estimate is $106 per square foot? What is the value of the real estate if the land is estimated at $30,000 and depreciation at $5,500?

Round off your answer to the nearest hundred dollars.

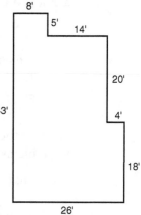

7. Compute the estimated value of the real estate pictured below.
An appraiser has told you that the replacement cost is $6.25 per cubic foot, the depreciation is $10,800, and the land value is $25,500. Round off your answer to the nearest hundred dollars.

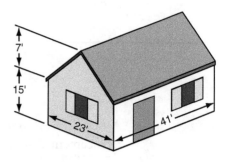

Calculating Depreciation

Depreciation is the loss of value suffered by a building or improvement. It is the difference between an existing building and a brand new building of like specifications.

Straight-Line Method   The *straight-line method* (also known as the economic age-life method) of depreciation spreads the total depreciation over the useful life of a building in equal annual amounts, using the formula below. Remember, this *useful life* has nothing at all to do with the life used for IRS depreciation or cost recovery.

$$\frac{\text{Replacement cost}}{\text{Years of useful life}} = \text{Annual depreciation charge}$$

Note:

The *useful life*, *economic life*, and *actual life* of a building are rarely the same.

A building most frequently becomes useless through external or functional obsolescence rather than physical deterioration. For this reason, appraisers often refer to the useful life of real estate as the *estimated economic life*.

An appraiser estimates the remaining economic life of a property after considering the physical, functional, and external factors.

E X A M P L E :   An appraiser has estimated the replacement cost of a building at $500,000. The building is ten years old and has an estimated useful life of 50 years. What is the annual depreciation charge? What is the total depreciation for ten years? What is the current value of the building?

Step 1. Compute the annual depreciation charge.

$$\frac{\text{Replacement cost}}{\text{Years of useful life}} = \text{Annual depreciation charge}$$

$$\frac{\$500,000}{50} = \$10,000$$

Step 2. Find the amount of depreciation over ten years.

Annual depreciation charge × Number of years = Total depreciation

$10,000 × 10 = $100,000

Step 3. Find the current value of the buildings.

Replacement cost − Depreciation = Current value of building

$500,000 − $100,000 = $400,000

8. If the building in the preceding example was 30 years old, what would its current value be?

9. If the building in the example was located on a piece of land worth $325,000, what would be the estimated value of the property after 30 years of use (computed in problem 8)?

10. If the building in the example originally cost $75,000, what would be the current estimated value of the property?

Depreciation can also be expressed as a percentage or rate. To find the depreciation rate by the straight-line method, divide the total value (100 percent) by the building's estimated useful years of life.

$$\frac{100\%}{\text{Years of useful life}} = \text{Annual depreciation rate}$$

EXAMPLE: If a building has a useful life of 25 years, 1/25 of the building's value is depreciated in one year. That is, the building depreciates at a rate of 4 percent per year.

$$\frac{100\%}{\text{Years of useful life}} = \text{Annual depreciation rate}$$

$$\frac{100\%}{25} = 4\%$$

11. a. If a building has an estimated useful life of 40 years, what is its annual rate of depreciation?

    b. By what percentage will that building depreciate in 15 years?

    c. If the building is 15 years old and has a current replacement cost of $180,000, what is the total amount that it has depreciated?

    d. If the land on which the building is located is valued at $40,000, what is the estimated value of the total real estate?

12. The replacement cost of a small building has been estimated at $350,000 and the building has an estimated useful life of 50 years. The building is nine years old.

    a. What is the annual depreciation rate?

    b. What is the total amount of depreciation that the appraiser will deduct?

INCOME CAPITALIZATION APPROACH

The *income capitalization approach* is a technique used in appraising income-producing real estate. It is a method of estimating the value of a property by dividing the annual net operating income (NOI—gross income minus expenses) produced by the property by the desired capitalization rate.

Net operating income is found by constructing an operating statement, using annual amounts for each line item (*see* Table 11.2).

Notice that in the income capitalization approach, expenses do not include payments of principal and interest on any note. To do so would distort the data because some properties are debt free. Therefore, the net remaining after expenses are subtracted ought to be sufficient to service any debt (make the payments). If it is not, negative cash flow occurs. Finally, note that the terms net annual income, cash flow, net spendable income and taxable income are not synonymous. Detailed discussion of each, however, is beyond the scope of this text.

T A B L E 11.2

Annual Operating Statement

Potential Gross Income (Rental income at 100 percent occupancy)	
Less:	**Allowance for vacancy and credit loss** (Reduction for unrented space and uncollectible rents)
Plus:	**Other income** (Laundry room coins, vending machine revenue, fees, parking charges, etc.)
	equals
Effective Gross Income	

Less:	**Annual operating expenses**
	 (The costs ordinary and necessary to keep the property open and operating)
	 1. **Fixed expenses**—real estate taxes, insurance, etc.
	       (Are not tied to occupancy)
	 2. **Variable expenses**—maintenance, utilities provided by owner, etc.
	       Items that increase or decrease with increased or decreased occupancy levels)
	 3. **Reserves for replacement**—appliances, carpet, etc.

	equals
Net Operating Income (NOI) (The income available to the property after all operating expenses have been paid)	

$$\frac{\text{Annual NOI}}{\text{Annual rate of return}} = \text{Value}$$

Does the formula look familiar? It's really the same formula you used in previous chapter:

$$\frac{\text{Annual NOI (part)}}{\text{Over-all capitalization rate (rate)}} = \text{Value (total)}$$

E X A M P L E :   What is the estimated value of an apartment building that is expected to produce an annual NOI of $14,000? An appraiser estimates that 10 percent is a suitable capitalization rate for comparable properties. This percentage is the rate of return demanded by an investor, but it is subject to limitations beyond the scope of this text. (For example, it ignores fluctuations in the projected income.)

By inserting the appropriate figures into the formula, you get:

NOI ÷ Rate = Value or
$14,000 ÷ 10% = ?
$14,000 ÷ 0.1 = $140,000

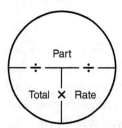

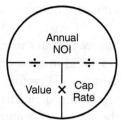

13. Fill in the following equations. Remember, total is the same as value, part is the same as NOI, and rate stands for overall capitalization rate.

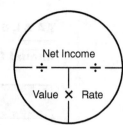

_____ × _____ = NOI

_____ ÷ _____ = Value

_____ ÷ _____ = Capitalization rate

14. If you had $120,000 to invest and you wanted a 10 percent return on your investment, what net income would a property have to produce to meet your required return?

a. First, fill in the known parts of the equation.
Value =   Rate =   Income =

b. Restate the problem.

c. What formula will you use?

d. Solve the problem.

Remember:

NOI = Net operating income

15. Assume that a property produces an NOI of $26,250 per year. What capitalization rate is this if you purchased the property for $210,000?

    a. Restate the problem.

    b. What formula will you use?

    c. Solve the problem.

16. An apartment building earns an NOI of $100,000 per year. What price would a buyer pay for the property if the capitalization rate is 10 percent?

    a. Restate the problem.

    b. What formula will you use?

    c. Solve the problem.

17. A purchaser paid $175,000 for an older fourplex that produced annual NOI of $16,850. Find the rate of return on the cost.

    a. Restate the problem.

    b. What formula will you use?

    c. Solve the problem.

18. A purchaser bought a parcel of commercial real estate for $820,000 and wants a 12 percent capitalization rate. What annual NOI does she expect?

   a. Restate the problem.

   b. What formula will you use?

   c. Solve the problem.

Remember:

Effective gross income minus expenses equals NOI.

19. The effective gross income from an apartment building is $270,500, and annual expenses total $140,000. If the owner expects to get a 9 percent return on his investment, what is the indicated value of his property?

A small change in the rate of return, or capitalization rate, makes a big difference in the value. So, again, be aware of the importance of estimates in all of the methods used in the appraisal, or estimation of value, of real estate.

Reconciliation of Data

After an appraiser has completed the tasks of gathering the data and calculating values based on the three methods (or approaches to value), a determination must be made as to which method is most valid for that specific appraisal. This involves the reconciliation of data and a comparison of the various values. It is quite important to note that the reconciliation of data is not the averaging of data. These reconciliation operations are beyond the scope of this text.

TABLE 11.3

Three Approaches to Value

Each of the three approaches to value must be used on an appropriate type of property. The following is a general list of types of property lending themselves to the various approaches or methods:

Sales comparison approach

- Single-family, owner-occupied homes, including condominiums
- Vacant lots
- Resort or recreation property

Cost approach

- All types of property with buildings and other improvements constructed thereon
- Especially well suited to newer buildings and special-use properties

Income capitalization approach

- Properties producing rent or income

TABLE 11.4

Gross Rent Multipliers (GRMs)

The income capitalization approach is used for income-producing properties. Residential properties are sometimes evaluated using a gross rent multiplier (GRM), which may be either a monthly multiplier or an annual multiplier.

To arrive at a multiplier, search the market to find houses that sold recently and that had tenants who occupied the properties at the time of sale.

Divide each sales price by the gross rent to find the GRM. Multiply the gross rent of the subject property by the GRM to find the indicated value of the subject property.

EXAMPLE: A house that rented for $500 per month recently sold for $60,000.

To find the monthly GRM:

$60,000 sales price ÷ $500 monthly gross rent = 120 monthly GRM

To find the annual GRM:

$500 monthly gross rent × 12 months = $6,000 annual gross rent

$60,000 sales price ÷ $6,000 annual gross rent = 10 annual GRM

The subject home rents for $625 per month. Find its indicated value.

Applying the monthly GRM:

$625 monthly gross rent × 120 monthly GRM = $75,000 indicated value

Applying the annual GRM:

$625 monthly gross rent × 12 months = $7,500 annual gross rent

$7,500 annual gross rent × 10 annual GRM = $75,000 indicated value

There are, of course, many appraisals made by professionals who use two or all three of these methods. In these appraisals, the appraiser must reconcile all of the data from all of the methods used and write a report supporting the appraisal presented.

ADDITIONAL PRACTICE

When you have finished these problems, check your answers at the end of the chapter. If you miss any of the problems, review this chapter before going on to Chapter 12.

1. A building, 100 feet by 250 feet by 20 feet, has a replacement cost of $6.50 per cubic foot. The land is valued at $150,000 and the building's depreciation has been estimated at $75,000. What is the value of this property via the cost approach to value?
   a. $3,175,000
   b. $3,325,000
   c. $4,225,000
   d. $4,500,000

2. The replacement cost of a building has been estimated at $150,000. The building was estimated to have a useful life of 50 years; it is now two years old. The land is valued at $50,000. What is the estimated value of this real estate via the cost approach to value?
   a. $192,000
   b. $194,000
   c. $198,000
   d. $200,000

3. An older building being used for storage is valued at $100,000 and produces a net operating income of $12,000 per year. What is the overall capitalization rate for this property?
   a. 10 percent
   b. 11.5 percent
   c. 12 percent
   d. 13.6 percent

4. If the owner is selling the property in problem 3 and a prospective buyer wishes a 15 percent capitalization rate, what amount will the buyer pay for this property?
   a. $80,000
   b. $80,500
   c. $85,500
   d. $95,000

5. In computing value by the cost approach, the appraiser estimated the remaining economic life, or years of useful life, of a building to be 40 years. The replacement cost of the building is estimated at $170,000 and the age of the building is eight years. The current value of the building is
   a. $127,000.
   b. $136,000.
   c. $164,687.
   d. $170,000.

6. In the appraisal of a seven-story commercial building, the appraiser estimated the replacement cost per square foot to be $120. If the building is 92 feet wide and 117 feet deep, the replacement cost is estimated at
   a. $6,250,000.
   b. $7,500,000.
   c. $8,500,000.
   d. $9,041,760.

7. What capitalization rate is indicated by a property producing $10,000 annual net operating income and for which an investor paid $120,000?
   a. 8.33 percent
   b. 9.6 percent
   c. 10 percent
   d. 12 percent

8. An appraiser has estimated the annual net operating income from a commercial building to be $142,700. When capitalized at a rate of 10.5 percent, the estimated property value is
   a. $1,359,048.
   b. $1,392,195.
   c. $1,427,000.
   d. $1,498,350.

9. An apartment fourplex has been appraised for $275,000, using a capitalization rate of 9.5 percent. The estimated annual net operating income is
   a. $26,125.
   b. 26,150.
   c. $26,160.
   d. $26,550.

10. If the effective gross annual income from a property is $112,000 and the total expenses for the year are $53,700, what capitalization rate was used to obtain a valuation of $542,325?
    a. 9.75 percent
    b. 10.25 percent
    c. 10.50 percent
    d. 10.75 percent

11. What is the current value of a house originally costing $235,000 if the house has appreciated 12 percent?
    a. $262,900
    b. $262,950
    c. $263,150
    d. $263,200

12. If the rate of straight line appreciation is 10 percent, what is the current value of a house that was appraised at $240,000 four years ago?
    a. $335,800
    b. $335,950
    c. $336,000
    d. $336,200

13. A man bought a condominium for $260,000. Six months later, he was transferred and had to sell the property for $230,000. Which of the following calculations would you use to find his percentage of loss?
    a. $30,000 ÷ $260,000
    b. $30,000 ÷ $230,000
    c. $230,000 ÷ $260,000
    d. $260,000 ÷ $230,000

14. What is the indicated value via the sales comparison approach of a three-bedroom, two-bath, two-car-garage home with a pool? Market research indicates that a pool is worth $6,000, a bathroom is worth $2,800, and a two-car garage is worth $5,000 more than a one-car garage. A similar four-bedroom, three-bath home recently sold for $127,500. It had a one-car garage and no pool.
    a. $121,100
    b. $124,700
    c. $135,700
    d. $141,300

15. The subject property is similar to the comparable property in every way other than it has no fireplace. The comparable sold last week for $86,700. Your market study determines that a fireplace is worth $1,200. What is the indicated value of the subject property via the sales comparison approach?
    a. $85,500
    b. $86,700
    c. $87,000
    d. $87,900

16. What is the estimated replacement cost of the following building if the cost is estimated to be $95 per square foot?
    a. $204,250
    b. $204,600
    c. $205,100
    d. $205,220

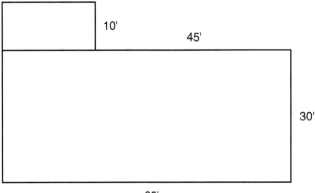

17. Using a replacement cost of the building in question 16, what is the value of the property if the building has $6,250 of accrued depreciation and is sitting on a $25,000 lot?
    a. $221,999
    b. $221,950
    c. $222,950
    d. $223,000

18. An apartment building earns an annual net operating income of $25,000. If the property sells for $175,000, what is the overall capitalization rate for this property.
    a. 14 percent
    b. 14.3 percent
    c. 14.5 percent
    d. 14.7 percent

19. If you were purchasing an apartment duplex for $265,000 and wished a 24 percent overall return on your investment, what annual net operating income would the property have to produce to meet your required return?
    a. $63,000
    b. $63,500
    c. $63,600
    d. $110,416.67

20. The subject property is a three-bedroom, two-and-a-half-bath house with no garage. Market research indicates that a two-car garage adds $7,500 value and a half-bath adds $1,800 value. A three-bedroom, two-bath house with a two-car garage on the next block sold for $115,600 two weeks ago. What is the indicated market value of the subject property by the sales comparison approach?
    a. $106,300
    b. $109,900
    c. $121,300
    d. $124,900

SOLUTIONS: PROBLEMS IN CHAPTER 11

1. 8% × 3 years = 24%

   24% = 0.24

   $153,000 × 0.24 = $36,720

   $153,000 + $36,720 = $189,720

2.

House	Age	Rooms	Extras	Sales Price	Sale Date	Time Adjusted Price	How Financed	Final Adjustment	Size	$ per Sq Ft
1	5 years	3-2-2	Fireplace Pool <$15,000>	$185,000 <15,000> $170,000	Jan. 1 11 months ago	$170,000 + 9,500 $179,500	Cash	$179,500	1,500 sq ft	$119.33
2	4 years	3-2-2	No fireplace +$2,500	$174,472 + 2,500 $176,972	Dec. 1 (current date)	$176,972 -0- $176,972	Equity <$1,000>	$176,972 <1,000> $175,972	1,480 sq ft	$118.90
3	5 years	3-2-2	Fireplace	$175,172	June 1 6 months ago	$175,172 + 5,255 $180,427	FHA <$1,800>	$180,427 <1,800> $178,627	1,460 sq ft	$122.35
4*	5 years	3-2-2	Fireplace	$176,300	Aug. 1 4 months ago	$176,300 + 3,536 $179,826	Equity + 2nd +2,000	$179,826 +2,000 $181,826	1,500 sq ft	$121.22
Subject	4 years	3-2-2	Fireplace		Dec. 1 (current date)			Estimated Value $178,800	1,490 sq ft	Average $120.00

* This house involved a distress sale and the seller agreed to carry back a large second lien note.

House 3

You need make no adjustment for extras because House 3 is similar to the subject house, but update the sales price at 0.5 percent per month, resulting in $180,427. Because this was a new FHA loan, estimate that the seller had to pay $1,800 in loan costs. Thus, after you subtract this amount to arrive at a cash equivalent price, the final adjusted price is $178,627. This house has 1,460 square feet of heated and cooled space (excluding the garage and covered porches), so its price per square foot is $122.35.

House 4

Again, no adjustment need be made for extras because House 4 is similar to the subject house, but you must account for the lapse of time since it sold. At 0.5 percent per month, this adjusts the sales price to $179,826. This was a distress sale, and the seller agreed to carry back a portion of the equity in the form of a second lien note. This might affect the sales price, so add $2,000, for a final adjusted price of $181,826. The house has 1,500 square feet of living area. This yields $121.22 as the price per square foot.

Please notice that several estimates were made in this problem. They must be based on experience and judgment. Remember, appraisal is not a science. These are some of the reasons that seem to make it more of an art.

Subject estimate

Find the average price per square foot for the four comparable properties.

$119.33 + $118.90 + $122.35 + $121.22 = $481.80

$481.80 ÷ 4 = $120.45 or (rounded) $120 per square foot

Multiply the area of the subject house in square feet by the estimated value per square foot.

1,490 square feet × $120 = $178,800 estimated value

3. $150,000 – $20,000 + $60,000 = $190,000

4. a. 1,450 square feet × $85 per square foot = $123,250
    b. $123,250 – $8,200 + $30,000= $145,050

5.   Compute the area.

$$L \times W = A$$

24' × 37' = 888 square feet

15' × 20' = 300 square feet

888 square feet + 300 square feet = 1,188 square feet

Compute the building replacement cost.

1,188 square feet × $90 = $106,920

Compute the estimated value

$106,920 – $8,400 + $25,000 = $123,520

6.   Compute the area.

43' × 26' = 1,118 square feet

4' × 20' = 80 square feet

5' × 18' = 90 square feet

1,118 – 80 – 90 = 948 square feet

Compute the building replacement cost.

948 square feet × $106 = $100,488

Compute the estimated value.

$100,488 – $5,500 + $30,000 = $124,988 or $125,000 (rounded)

7.   Compute the volume.

        $Volume_1 = L \times W \times H$

        $41' \times 23' \times 15' = 14{,}145$ cubic feet (first story)

        $Volume_2 = \frac{1}{2} (b \times h \times w)$

        $\frac{1}{2} (23' \times 7' \times 41') = 3{,}300.5$ cubic feet (second story)

        Total volume = 14,145 cubic feet + 3,300.5 cubic feet = 17,445.5 cubic feet

    Compute the building replacement cost.

        17,445.5 cubic feet × $6.25 = $109,034.37

    Compute the estimated value.

        $109,034.37 – $10,800 + $25,500 = $123,734.37 or $123,700 (rounded)

8. $10,000 × 30 = $300,000

    $500,000 – $300,000 = $200,000

9. $500,000 – $300,000 + $325,000 = $525,000

10.   The current value would remain the same—$525,000. The original value of the building is not considered in this formula—only the appraiser's estimate of its current replacement cost.

11. a.   Calculate the depreciation rate.

      100% ÷ 40 = 0.025

    b.   Calculate the depreciation rate for 15 years.

      0.025 × 15 = 0.375 or 37.5%

    c.   Calculate the depreciation value for 15 years.

      0.375 × $180,000 = $67,500

    d.   Calculate the estimated value.

      $180,000 – $67,500 + $40,000 = $152,500

12. a.   100% ÷ 50 = 0.02

    b.   0.02 × 9 = 0.18

      0.18 × $350,000 = $63,000

13.   Value × Capitalization rate = NOI

        NOI ÷ Capitalization rate = Value

        NOI ÷ Value = Capitalization rate

14. a. Value = $120,000   Rate = 10% income = Unknown (annual NOI needed)

    b. What is 10 percent of $120,000?

    c. Value × Rate = NOI

    d. $120,000 × 0.1 = $12,000

15. a. What percent of $210,000 is $26,250?

    b. NOI ÷ Total = Rate

    c. $26,250 ÷ $210,000 = 0.125 or 12.5%

16. a. $100,000 is 10 percent of what amount?

    b. NOI ÷ Rate = Value

    c. $100,000 ÷ 0.1 = $1,000,000

17. a. $16,850 is what percent of $175,000?

    b. NOI ÷ Total = Rate

    c. $16,850 ÷ $175,000 = 0.096 or 9.6%

18. a. What is 12 percent of $820,000?

    b. Value × Rate = NOI

    c. $820,000 × 0.12 = $98,400

19. a. First compute the net income.

    $270,500 – $140,000 = $130,500

    Then ask, $130,500 is 9 percent of what amount? (Use the formula NOI ÷ Rate = Value.)

    $130,500 ÷ 0.09 = $1,450,000

SOLUTIONS: ADDITIONAL PRACTICE

1. (b) 100' × 250' × 20' = 500,000 cubic feet
    500,000 cubic feet × $6.50 = $3,250,000
    $3,250,000 − $75,000 + $150,000 = $3,325,000

2. (b) $150,000 ÷ 50 = $3,000
    $3,000 × 2 = $6,000
    $150,000 − $6,000 = $144,000
    $144,000 + $50,000 = $194,000

3. (c) $12,000 ÷ $100,000 = 0.12 or 12%

4. (a) $12,000 ÷ 0.15 = $80,000

5. (b) $170,000 ÷ 40 × 8 = $34,000
    $170,000 − $34,000 = $136,000

6. (d) 92' × 117' × 7 × $120 = $9,041,760

7. (a) $10,000 ÷ $120,000 = 0.0833 (rounded) or 8.33%

8. (a) $142,700 ÷ 0.105 = $1,359,048

9. (a) $275,000 × 0.095 = $26,125

10. (d) $112,000 − $53,700 = $58,300
    $58,300 ÷ $542,325 = 0.1075 or 10.75%

11. (d) 12% = 0.12
    $235,000 × 0.12 = $28,200
    $235,000 + $28,200 = $263,200

12. (c) 10% = 0.1
    0.1 × 4 = 0.4
    $240,000 × 0.4 = $96,000
    $240,000 + $96,000 = $336,000

13. (a) $260,000 – $230,000 = $30,000
    $30,000 ÷ $260,000 = 0.1154 or 11.54%

14. (c) $127,500 + $5,000 + $6,000 – $2,800 = $135,700

15. (a) $86,700 – $1,200 = $85,500

16. (a) 30' × 65' = 1,950 square feet
    65' – 45' = 20'
    20' × 10' = 200 square feet
    1,950 square feet + 200 square feet = 2,150 square feet
    2,150 square feet × $95 = $204,250

17. (d) $204,450 – $6,250 + $25,000 = $223,000

18. (b) $25,000 ÷ $175,000 = 0.14286 = 14.3%

19. (c) $265,000 × 0.24 = $63,600

20. (b) $115,600 + $1,800 – $7,500 = $109,900

12

Tools of Investment Analysis

This chapter is designed simply to introduce you to some of the mathematical tools that investors might use to help them make informed decisions about the profit potential of a property under consideration. Real estate investment is in fact all about the numbers. The experienced investor understands that money has a time value. A good investment produces income over a long period and hopefully can be sold for an appreciated value in the future. Today's marketplace includes bank foreclosures, short sales, and other types of distressed properties. Such real estate properties continue to have an impact on the real estate values in various parts of the country.

At the conclusion of your work in this chapter, you will be able to

■ extract a capitalization rate from available market data,

■ identify the components of the investor's cash investment and accurately calculate cash-on-cash return, and

■ be familiar with the concept of the time value of money and be able to calculate discounted cash flows.

REAL ESTATE AS AN INVESTMENT

Throughout history, people have been well advised to save part of their earnings and invest them wisely to provide for a rainy day, their children's education, or their own retirement. Many investment vehicles are available to today's investor; however, real estate continues to be a historically wise choice. In the eyes of many, it is the ideal choice, because it offers the investor three types of financial return:

1. Income—A well-purchased and well-managed property offers the investor the opportunity to receive a monthly cash flow. One of the calculations that an investor may want to use in investment analysis is cash-on-cash return. The investor also may want to estimate future anticipated cash flows or income streams and discount them to a present value.

2. Appreciation—Historically, real estate increases in value over time. An investor anticipates that the land will increase in value and that the improvements will decrease in value over time. The discussion of this concept and the mathematical calculations used to apply it are discussed in Chapter 3.

3. Value gain—Property may appreciate in spite of the owner. This type of appreciation might be identified as unearned increment. Value also can be added to the property through the efforts of the investor/owner, who can apply management skills to increase the bottom line (net operating income, or NOI) by increasing revenues and decreasing operating expenses. Appraisers will apply the income approach to estimate the value of an income-producing property. Investors will apply the same income approach, or capitalization techniques, to help them determine what they should pay for a particular property. The discussion of how to estimate the value of an income-producing property by employing the income capitalization approach is discussed in Chapter 11.

Remember:

Investors look at the numbers and don't deal in emotion like a residential buyer might.

Those who regard real estate as the ideal investment vehicle, generally identify the following as the reasons it is an IDEAL investment.

I   Income—Real estate offers the opportunity for investors to enjoy an income stream that will enable those investors to recapture their investments and to experience a profit.

D   Depreciation and deductibility—It is good for the economy to have investors develop land and build rental properties. The government rewards the real estate investor by providing tax incentives in the form of depreciation deductions (cost recovery) and tax credits. See Chapter 3 for information about the allowable write-offs for real estate investment.

E   Equity—The buildup that occurs through appreciation and the fact that real estate investment property is usually leveraged adds to its attractiveness. Also, every time a tenant pays rent and an investor makes a mortgage payment, a little more equity (principal payment) is added.

A   Appreciation—Increase through unearned increment and through value gain is of great value to an investor.

L   Leverage—Leverage is the ability to use other people's money to make money for the investor. Chapter 10 teaches you about the mathematics of real estate finance.

CAPITALIZATION RATES

When an appraiser or an investor applies the income approach, an accurate operating statement must be constructed to estimate the correct annual net operating income (NOI) and an acceptable capitalization rate must be determined. The rate is used to convert the NOI into an indicated value.

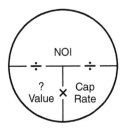

MARKET EXTRACTION OF DATA

The capitalization rate may be determined from market data when available. Locate recently sold comparable properties and obtain the sales price (SP) and the property's annual net operating income. Divide the NOI by the selling price to discover the cap rate.

E X A M P L E :   There are three recently sold properties similar to the subject property. You investigate and discover the following information.

Property 1: Generates annual NOI of $616,044 and sold three months ago for $5,600,400.

Property 2: Generates annual NOI of $483,000 and sold six months ago for $4,472,222.

Property 3: Generates annual NOI of $1,200,000 and sold last month for $10,169,500.

What is the indicated capitalization rate that needs to be applied to the NOI of the subject property?

Property 1:

Answer: 0.11 or 11%

Property 2:

Answer: 0.108 or 10.8%

Property 3:

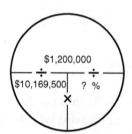

Answer: 0.118 or 11.8%

Average the three results.

$$0.11 + 0.108 + 0.118 \div 3 = 0.112 \text{ or } 11.2\%$$

The subject property generates annual NOI of $982,063. What is its capitalized value?

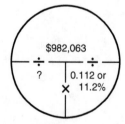

Answer: $8,768,420 (rounded)

Now you try one. Calculate the indicated value of the subject property.

1. Market data

Property 1:	Generates annual NOI of $78,400 and sold for $825,263.
Property 2:	Generates annual NOI of $43,860 and sold for $474,162.
Property 3:	Generates annual NOI of $186,400 and sold for $1,911,795.
Subject:	Generates annual NOI of $87,400.

CASH-ON-CASH RETURN

Cash-on-cash return is an extremely important ratio to focus on when evaluating the long-term performance of a real estate investment. This ratio considers the property's annual net cash flow as a percentage when divided by the net investment. Many investors prefer to evaluate a property by looking at the relationship between the cash invested and the cash flow of the property. A common error made by novice investors is the failure to look at the *real* cash it takes to invest in the property. The investor's total cash position includes cash down payment plus closing costs plus loan fees plus all evaluation costs. An investor who spends $9,500 having a feasibility study done, spends $4,600 in closing costs, and makes a cash down payment of $125,000 must add those three numbers together to identify the cash investment. Failure to do so gives a distorted result.

The rate of return in this analysis is solely at the discretion of the investor. Usually, the investor establishes the required rate by making a comparison of rates of return on other types of available investments.

EXAMPLE: An investor determines that 12 percent is an acceptable rate of return on the cash invested. The property under consideration generates cash flow (NOI less annual debt service equals cash flow before taxes) of $18,435. The property can be acquired for a down payment of $135,000 plus $9,000 closing costs plus $4,000 research fees plus $5,625 in loan origination fees including discount points. Is this a property that this investor should purchase?

$135,000	down payment
9,000	closing costs
4,000	research/property evaluation
5,625	loan costs
$153,625	total acquisition costs

Answer: 0.12 = 12%

The investor can buy this property and realize the desired return.

If the available cash flow and the total amount of the needed acquisition dollars are known, the investor can calculate the rate and compare it with other available investment opportunities.

EXAMPLE: It will take a total cash outlay of $18,600 to acquire a small rental property that produces an annual before-tax cash flow of $1,814. What cash-on-cash return will this investor receive?

Answer: 0.0975 or 9.75%

Now you try two problems.

2. An investor has the opportunity to purchase a property that generates annual cash flow of $22,300 that can be acquired for a cash down payment of $180,000 plus $5,833 in closing costs. What cash-on-cash return will this property generate for this investor?

3. If an investor demands a cash-on-cash return of 11 percent or more and is considering the acquisition of a property that generates $20,000 annual cash flow, what is the maximum total acquisition cash that can be invested?

DISCOUNTED CASH FLOWS

One fundamental concept in business finance is that money has a time value. Money that one has today is worth more than the same money received in the future. Money that you receive today can be invested today and as a result will be worth more in the future. Many investors and their brokers will try to estimate future cash flows for a predetermined period and then attempt to arrive at an offering price by discounting those cash flows to a present value. The whole concept of the discounting of cash flows is based on the concept that money in hand today is more valuable than money to be received at some future time. Money held today can be put to work earning a return for the owner.

The following equation is used to compute discounted value.

$$\frac{P}{P(1+I)^n} = \text{Discount factor}$$

For a one-year period at 8 percent (0.08) it would be

$$\frac{P}{P+8\%(0.08)}$$

Let's say that P is equal to $1.

$$\frac{\$1}{\$1+\$0.08} \text{ or } \frac{\$1}{\$1.08} = 0.92593$$

For a two-year period at 8 percent it would be

$$\frac{P}{(P+8\%)(P+8\%)}$$

Using $1 again, the factor would be

$$\frac{\$1}{\$1.08\times1.08} = \frac{\$1}{\$1.1664} = 0.8573$$

In the real world of practicing real estate, an investor or the investor's broker would simply refer to a "Present Worth" chart (*see* Table 12.1).

To discount cash flows, multiply the anticipated cash to be received by the appropriate present worth factor. If you do not have a present worth chart available, use the equation

$$\frac{P}{P(1+I)^n} = \text{Discount factor}$$

If you want to find the future value of money in hand today plus compounded earnings, you may use the same factors and divide instead of multiplying.

EXAMPLE: An investor wants to know the value of a $1,000 certificate of deposit at the end of 5 years. The certificate is earning 3 percent interest, with the interest being compounded annually.

$$\frac{\$1,000}{0.8626} = \$1,159.2858$$

Try a few using the chart on the following page.

4. An investor anticipates that a property will generate NOI of $12,000 in year one and $16,000 in year two. What is the present worth of each of the years assuming a 9 percent return?

Part 1: $_____ × _____ (factor) = $_____ discounted value

Part 2: $_____ × _____ (factor) = $_____ discounted value

Part 3: Add together parts 1 and 2 for the value of the 2 years' income stream.

TABLE 12.1

Present Worth Chart

Present Value Factors							
Years	1%	2%	3%	4%	5%	6%	7%
1	0.9901	0.9804	0.9709	0.9615	0.9524	0.9434	0.9346
2	0.9803	0.9612	0.9426	0.9246	0.9070	0.8900	0.8734
3	0.9707	0.9423	0.9151	0.8890	0.8638	0.8396	0.8163
4	0.9610	0.9238	0.8885	0.8548	0.8227	0.7921	0.7629
5	0.9515	0.9057	0.8626	0.8219	0.7835	0.7473	0.7130
6	0.9420	0.8880	0.8375	0.7903	0.7462	0.7050	0.6663
7	0.9327	0.8706	0.8131	0.7599	0.7107	0.6651	0.6228
8	0.9235	0.8535	0.7894	0.7307	0.6768	0.6274	0.5820
9	0.9143	0.8368	0.7664	0.7026	0.6446	0.5919	0.5439
10	0.9053	0.8203	0.7441	0.6756	0.6139	0.5584	0.5083
11	0.8963	0.8043	0.7224	0.6496	0.5847	0.5268	0.4751
12	0.8874	0.7885	0.7014	0.6246	0.5568	0.4970	0.4440
13	0.8787	0.7730	0.6810	0.6006	0.5303	0.4688	0.4150
14	0.8700	0.7579	0.6611	0.5775	0.5051	0.4423	0.3878
15	0.8613	0.7430	0.6419	0.5553	0.4810	0.4173	0.3624
16	0.8528	0.7284	0.6232	0.5339	0.4581	0.3936	0.3387
17	0.8444	0.7142	0.6050	0.5134	0.4363	0.3714	0.3166
18	0.8360	0.7002	0.5874	0.4936	0.4155	0.3503	0.2959
19	0.8277	0.6864	0.5703	0.4746	0.3957	0.3305	0.2765
20	0.8195	0.6730	0.5537	0.4564	0.3769	0.3118	0.2584
21	0.8114	0.6598	0.5375	0.4388	0.3589	0.2942	0.2415
22	0.8034	0.6468	0.5219	0.4220	0.3419	0.2775	0.2257
23	0.7954	0.6342	0.5067	0.4057	0.3256	0.2618	0.2109
24	0.7876	0.6217	0.4919	0.3901	0.3101	0.2470	0.1971
25	0.7798	0.6095	0.4776	0.3751	0.2953	0.2330	0.1842
26	0.7720	0.5976	0.4637	0.3607	0.2812	0.2198	0.1722
27	0.7644	0.5859	0.4502	0.3468	0.2678	0.2074	0.1609
28	0.7568	0.5744	0.4371	0.3335	0.2551	0.1956	0.1504
29	0.7493	0.5631	0.4243	0.3207	0.2429	0.1846	0.1406
30	0.7419	0.5521	0.4120	0.3083	0.2314	0.1741	0.1314

TABLE 12.1

Present Worth Chart (continued)

Present Value Factors							
Periods	8%	9%	10%	11%	12%	13%	14%
1	0.9259	0.9174	0.9091	0.9009	0.8929	0.8850	0.8772
2	0.8573	0.8417	0.8264	0.8116	0.7972	0.7831	0.7695
3	0.7938	0.7722	0.7513	0.7312	0.7118	0.6931	0.6750
4	0.7350	0.7084	0.6830	0.6587	0.6355	0.6133	0.5921
5	0.6806	0.6499	0.6209	0.5935	0.5674	0.5428	0.5194
6	0.6302	0.5963	0.5645	0.5346	0.5066	0.4803	0.4556
7	0.5835	0.5470	0.5132	0.4817	0.4523	0.4251	0.3996
8	0.5403	0.5019	0.4665	0.4339	0.4039	0.3762	0.3506
9	0.5002	0.4604	0.4241	0.3909	0.3606	0.3329	0.3075
10	0.4632	0.4224	0.3855	0.3522	0.3220	0.2946	0.2697
11	0.4289	0.3875	0.3505	0.3173	0.2875	0.2607	0.2366
12	0.3971	0.3555	0.3186	0.2858	0.2567	0.2307	0.2076
13	0.3677	0.3262	0.2897	0.2575	0.2292	0.2042	0.1821
14	0.3405	0.2992	0.2633	0.2320	0.2046	0.1807	0.1597
15	0.3152	0.2745	0.2394	0.2090	0.1827	0.1599	0.1401
16	0.2919	0.2519	0.2176	0.1883	0.1631	0.1415	0.1229
17	0.2703	0.2311	0.1978	0.1696	0.1456	0.1252	0.1078
18	0.2502	0.2120	0.1799	0.1528	0.1300	0.1108	0.0946
19	0.2317	0.1945	0.1635	0.1377	0.1161	0.0981	0.0829
20	0.2145	0.1784	0.1486	0.1240	0.1037	0.0868	0.0728
21	0.1987	0.1637	0.1351	0.1117	0.0926	0.0768	0.0638
22	0.1839	0.1502	0.1228	0.1007	0.0826	0.0680	0.0560
23	0.1703	0.1378	0.1117	0.0907	0.0738	0.0601	0.0491
24	0.1577	0.1264	0.1015	0.0817	0.0659	0.0532	0.0431
25	0.1460	0.1160	0.0923	0.0736	0.0588	0.0471	0.0378
26	0.1352	0.1064	0.0839	0.0663	0.0525	0.0417	0.0331
27	0.1252	0.0976	0.0763	0.0597	0.0469	0.0369	0.0291
28	0.1159	0.0895	0.0693	0.0538	0.0419	0.0326	0.0255
29	0.1073	0.0822	0.0630	0.0485	0.0374	0.0289	0.0224
30	0.0994	0.0754	0.0573	0.0437	0.0334	0.0256	0.0196

5. Calculate the present worth of $1,634,200 at 11 percent to be delivered 20 years from today.

Money does indeed have value over time!

Another way to calculate present or future value is to utilize a financial calculator. The four function keys that you will use are

Number of Periods   Interest Rates   Present Value   Future Value

You must carefully follow the instruction book and provide three of the known values to calculate for the unknown.

For Future Value you will need to supply

For Present Value you will need to supply

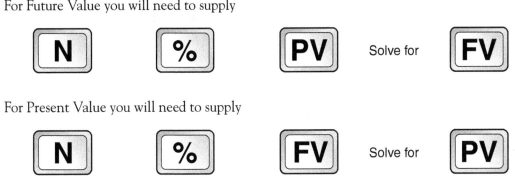

ADDITIONAL PRACTICE

Note: To work the problems involving the time value of money, you will need to refer to Table 12.1

1. If a property generates an annual NOI of $86,500 and requires $45,865 for annual debt service, what is its cash flow to an investor seeking an annual cash-on-cash return of 8 percent?
   a. $6,920
   b. $40,635
   c. $132.365
   d. $573,312.50

2. What cash flow would be required to deliver a 12.5 percent return to an investor who will need to invest $135,000 cash down payment and $13,500 in closing costs and other fees to acquire a particular property?
   a. $1,687.50
   b. $15,187.50
   c. $18,562.50
   d. $18,982.50

3. Using the Present Value chart in Table 12.1, what is the value of an income stream of $124,500 to be delivered in the fifth year of ownership to an investor seeking an 8 percent return?
   a. $84,734.70
   b. $94,451.36
   c. $115,278.28
   d. $188,809.54

4. What cash-on-cash return is being delivered to an investor who pays $16,400 cash down payment plus $500 attorney fees and $2,300 in other closing costs? The annual NOI is $6,824, which is reduced by $5,000 annual debt service.
   a. 9.25 percent
   b. 9.5 percent
   c. 9.75 percent
   d. 9.735 percent

5. At the end of three years, what is the value of $16,800 invested in a certificate of deposit earning 10 percent interest compounded annually using Table 12.1?
   a. $12,622.01
   b. $18,480.02
   c. $21,840.00
   d. $22,361.24

6. Property 1 sold for $8,600,000 with an NOI of $1,204,000. Property 2 sold for $86,000 with an NOI of $12,040. Property 3 sold for $20,000,000 with an NOI of $2,760,000. Which of the three properties generated the lowest capitalization rate?
   a. Property 1
   b. Property 2
   c. Property 3
   d. All three properties generated the same rate

7. Which of the following properties will give the investor the greatest cash-on-cash return?
   a. Property 1—total acquisition cash: $300,000; cash flow: $24,000
   b. Property 2—total acquisition cash: $321,212; cash flow: $26,500
   c. Property 3—total acquisition cash: $198,919; cash flow: $18,400
   d. Property 4—total acquisition cash: $150,000; cash flow: $15,000

8. What is the present value of a property that can be sold at the end of a three-year holding period for $1,500,000, assuming a rate of 8 percent? For the first year of ownership, it is estimated that the property can produce $90,000 NOI; in year two, $101,100 NOI; in year three, $119,075 NOI. What can the investor pay for it today according to the discounted value of the cash that he expects to receive if he wants to realize a 9 percent annual return?

    a. $1,158,270 (rounded)
    b. $1,417,880 (rounded)
    c. $1,468,445 (rounded)
    d. $1,759,610 (rounded)

9. What is the future value of $350,000 earning 11 percent compounded annually at the end of three years using Table 12.1?

    a. $255,916.50
    b. $465,500.00
    c. $478,671.75
    d. $840,438.92

10. If the NOI is $22,400, the monthly debt service is $1,500, and the investor is looking for a 12 percent return, how much cash can the investor put up front to cover the down payment, closing costs, loan expenses, and all other acquisition fees?

    a. $28,056
    b. $36,667
    c. $40,400
    d. $174,167

SOLUTIONS: PROBLEMS IN CHAPTER 12

1. $78,400 ÷ $825,263 = 0.095 or 9.5%
   $43,860 ÷ $474,162 = 0.0925 or 9.25%
   $186,400 ÷ $1,911,795 = 0.0975 or 9.75%
   0.095 + 0.0925 + 0.0975 ÷ 3 = 0.095 or 9.5%

2. $180,000 + $5,833 = $185,833
   $22,300 ÷ $185,833 = 0.12 or 12%

3. $20,000 ÷ 0.11 = $181,818.18

4. Part 1: $12,000 × 0.9174 = $11,008.80
   Part 2: $16,000 × 0.8417 = $13,467.20
   Part 3: $11,008.80 + $13,467.20 = $24,476 present value

5. $1,634,200 × 0.124 = $202,640.80

SOLUTIONS: ADDITIONAL PRACTICE

1. (b) $86,500 NOI − $45,865 debt service = $40,635

2. (c) $135,000 + $13,500 = $148,500 acquisition cash
   $148,500 × 0.125 = $18,562.50

3. (a) $124,500 × 0.6806 = $84,734.70

4. (b) $16,400 + $500 + $2,300 = $19,200 acquisition cash
   $6,824 NOI − $5,000 debt service = $1,824 cash flow
   $1,824 ÷ $19,200 = 0.095 or 9.5%

5. (d) $16,800 ÷ 0.7513 = $22,361.24 future value

6. (c) Property 1: $1,204,000 ÷ $8,600,000 = 0.14 or 14%
   Property 2: $12,040 ÷ $86,000 = 0.14 or 14%
   Property 3: $2,760,000 ÷ $20,000,000 = 0.138 or 13.8%

7. (d) Property 1: $24,000 ÷ $300,000 = 0.08 or 8%
   Property 2: $26,500 ÷ $321,212 = 0.0825 or 8.25%
   Property 3: $18,400 ÷ $198,919 = 0.0925 or 9.25%
   Property 4: $15,000 ÷ $150,000 = 0.1 or 10%

8. (b) Year 1: $90,000 × 0.91743 = $82,568.70 discounted value
   Year 2: $101,100 × 0.84168 = $85,093.85 discounted value
   Year 3: $119,075 × 0.77218 = $91,947.33 discounted value
   Year 4: $1,500,000 × 0.77218 = $1,158,270.00 discounted value
   $82,568.70 + $85,093.85 + $91,947.33 + $1,158,270.00 =
   $1,417,880 (rounded)

9. (c) $350,000 ÷ 0.7312 = $478,665.20

10. (b) $1,500 × 12 = $18,000 annual debt service
    $22,400 − $18,000 = $4,400
    $4,400 ÷ 0.12 = $36,666.67 or $36,667 (rounded)

CHAPTER

13

Prorations

In preparation for the closing of a real estate transaction, expenses directly related to the transaction involving the buyer and the seller must be considered. To *prorate* certain expenses of a real estate transaction is to divide the items *proportionally* between the seller and the buyer. We prorate to equitably divide the ongoing expenses of a property between the buyer and the seller. The seller gives money to the buyer for items that have not yet become due, such as taxes. The buyer gives money to the seller for items that the seller paid in advance but that have not been fully used, such as Homeowners' Association dues. Items that are typically prorated at the closing of a real estate transaction are

- ad valorem taxes,
- Homeowners' Association dues,
- loan interest, when there is an assumption of an existing loan,
- insurance premiums,
- rents,
- maintenance fees, and
- propane, fuel oil, coal, and so on.

Delinquent monthly payments, late charges, and security deposits are not prorated, but simply transferred from the seller to the buyer at closing or paid to the third parties to whom they are owed from the seller's proceeds. Prorated items appear on a closing statement as debits or charges to one of the parties and as credits to the other party. Any prorated charge or prorated debit to one party is always a credit to the other party. For example, a charge to the seller for the ad valorem taxes from January 1 through closing will show as a credit to the buyer.

Some of the items that get prorated are paid in advance, such as insurance premiums and maintenance fees, and some are paid in arrears, such as taxes and interest. Items paid in advance are paid before a party receives the benefit or incurs the expense. Items paid in arrears will be paid in full by the buyer at a later date.

It should also be noted that prorations may be done to or *through* the day of closing. The purchase agreement (sales contract) between the buyer and the seller might specify which party will pay for the actual day of closing. However, it is usually determined by someone other than the buyer and seller. It can be simply a matter of local practice or as directed by a lender. When an item is prorated to closing, the buyer pays for the day of closing. When an item is prorated *through* closing, the seller pays for the day of closing.

When calculating prorations, some areas of the country typically use a *banker's* or a *statutory* year.

1 year = 12 months of 30 days
1 year = 360 days

Other areas use a *calendar* year in the calculation of prorations.

1 year = 12 months of 28 to 31 days
1 year = 365 days in a regular calendar year
366 days in a leap year

On the real estate exam, salesperson and broker candidates may be asked to prorate to or through the day of closing, using either the banker's (statutory) or calendar year. Read the problems carefully for these details.

At the conclusion of your work in this chapter, you will be able to accurately calculate prorations for taxes, interest, insurance, and rents, using both the 360-day and the 365-day years.

For all proration problems, you must determine

- the annual cost (monthly cost for rent),
- the number of days to be charged,
- the amount to be credited or debited,
- the party to receive the credit, and
- the party to receive the debit.

Remember:

Calendar year = 365 days (366 days if a Leap Year)

Banker's (or statutory) year = 360 days, or 30 days/month

The following charts create timelines to show the period of time to be prorated for taxes, interest, insurance, rent, and maintenance fees. Figure 13.1 prorates through the day of closing, which means the seller pays the expense for closing day. Figure 13.2 prorates to the day of closing, which means the buyer pays the expense for closing day.

FIGURE 13.1

Prorations Through the Day of Closing

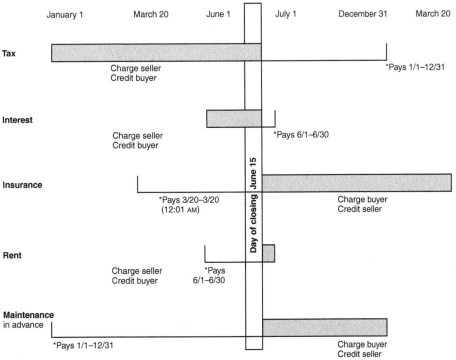

*Indicates when the item is typically paid.

FIGURE 13.2

Prorations to the Day of Closing

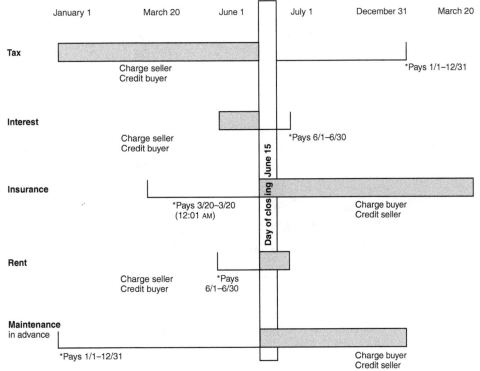

*Indicates when the item is typically paid.

PRORATING TAXES

When prorating ad valorem taxes, calculate the amount of money the seller will pay to the buyer for that portion of the year the seller owns the house. Taxes are usually paid in arrears and represent a charge to the seller and a credit to the buyer. Follow the following three steps:

Step 1. Determine the number of days to be charged to or through the closing date.

Step 2. Calculate the dollar amount per day.

$$\text{Annual tax} \div \text{Days in year} = \$ \text{ per day}$$

Step 3. Calculate the proration by multiplying the total from step 2 by the total from step 1.

$$\$ \text{ per day} \times \text{Days due} = \text{Proration}$$

CALCULATE
You may duplicate the following to help you calculate the ad valorem tax proration.

Step 1. Calculate the days due.

J   F   M   A   M   J   J   A   S   O   N   D = Days due

___ + ___ + ___ + ___ + ___ + ___ + ___ + ___ + ___ + ___ + ___ + ___ = _____

Step 2. Calculate the $ per day.
Annual tax ÷ Days in year = $ per day
(Do not clear your calculator; do not round; move on to step 3.)

Step 3. Calculate the proration.
Step 2   × Step 1   = Step 3
$ per day × Days due = Proration
$_____   × _____ = $_____

EXAMPLE: Using a banker's or statutory year, prorate the taxes for a June 18 closing. The annual tax bill is $1,440 and is to be prorated through the day of closing.

Step 1.

J   F   M   A   M   J
30 + 30 + 30 + 30 + 30 + 18 = 168 days due

Step 2.

Annual tax ÷ Days in year = $ per day
$1,440   ÷   360   = $ 4 per day

Step 3.

$\quad\quad$ \$ per day $\times$ Days due $\,=\,$ Proration

$\quad\quad\quad$ \$4 $\quad\times\quad$ 168 $\quad\quad=$ \$672 debit seller/credit buyer

Using a regular calendar year, it would look like this:

Step 1.

$\quad\quad$ J $\quad$ F $\quad$ M $\quad$ A $\quad$ M $\quad$ J

$\quad\quad$ 31 + 28 + 31 + 30 + 31 + 18 = 169 days due

Step 2.

$\quad\quad$ Annual tax $\,\div\,$ Days in year $\,=\,$ \$ per day

$\quad\quad\quad$ \$1,440 $\quad\div\quad$ 365 $\quad\quad=$ \$3.94521 per day

Step 3.

$\quad\quad$ \$ per day $\times$ Days due $\,=\,$ Proration

$\quad\quad$ \$3.94521 $\times\quad$ 169 $\quad\quad=$ \$666.74 debit seller/credit buyer (rounded)

In a leap year, it would look like this:

Step 1.

$\quad\quad$ J $\quad$ F $\quad$ M $\quad$ A $\quad$ M $\quad$ J

$\quad\quad$ 31 + 29 + 31 + 30 + 31 + 18 = 170 days due

Step 2.

$\quad\quad$ Annual tax $\,\div\,$ Days in year $\,=\,$ \$ per day

$\quad\quad\quad$ \$1,440 $\quad\div\quad$ 366 $\quad\quad=$ \$3.93443 per day

Step 3.

$\quad\quad$ \$ per day $\times$ Days due $\,=\,$ Proration

$\quad\quad$ \$3.93443 $\times\quad$ 170 $\quad\quad=$ \$668.85 debit seller/credit buyer (rounded)

Now you try one.

For a closing on August 28, what would you charge the seller if the annual tax bill is \$1,680 and the proration is calculated through the day of closing?

Banker's year:

Step 1.

$\quad\quad$ J $\quad$ F $\quad$ M $\quad$ A $\quad$ M $\quad$ J $\quad$ J $\quad$ A

$\quad\quad$ ___ + ___ + ___ + ___ + ___ + ___ + ___ + ___ = ___ days due

Step 2.

Annual tax ÷ Days in year = $ per day

$_____ ÷ _____ = $_____

Step 3.

$ per day × Days due = Proration

$_____ × _____ = $_____ debit seller/credit buyer

Calendar year (regular):

Step 1.

J   F   M   A   M   J   J   A

___ + ___ + ___ + ___ + ___ + ___ + ___ + ___ = ____ days due

Step 2.

Annual tax ÷ Days in year = $ per day

$_____ ÷ _____ = $_____

Step 3.

$ per day × Days due = Proration

$_____ × _____ = $_____ debit seller/credit buyer

Calendar year (leap year):

Step 1.

J   F   M   A   M   J   J   A

___ + ___ + ___ + ___ + ___ + ___ + ___ + ___ = _____ days due

Step 2.

Annual tax ÷ Days in year = $ per day

$_____ ÷ _____ = $_____

Step 3.

$ per day × Days due = Proration

$_____ × _____ = $_____ debit seller/credit buyer

Check your answers:

Banker's year:

Step 1.

J   F   M   A   M   J   J   A

<u>30</u> + <u>30</u> + <u>30</u> + <u>30</u> + <u>30</u> + <u>30</u> + <u>30</u> + <u>28</u> = <u>238</u> days due

Step 2.

> Annual tax ÷ Days in year = $ per day
>
> $ <u> 1,680 </u> ÷ <u>   360   </u> = $4.66667

Step 3.

> $ per day   × Days due = Proration
>
> $<u> 4.66667 </u> × <u>   238   </u> = $1,110.67 debit seller/credit buyer

Calendar year (regular):

Step 1.

> J   F   M   A   M   J   J   A
>
> <u>31</u> + <u>28</u> + <u>31</u> + <u>30</u> + <u>31</u> + <u>30</u> + <u>31</u> + <u>28</u> = <u> 240 </u> days due

Step 2.

> Annual tax ÷ Days in year = $ per day
>
> $ <u>   1,680   </u> ÷ <u>   365   </u> = $4.60274

Step 3.

> $ per day   × Days due   = Proration
>
> $<u> 4.60274 </u> × <u>   240   </u> = $1,104.66 debit seller/credit buyer

Calendar year (leap year):

Step 1.

> J   F   M   A   M   J   J   A
>
> <u>31</u> + <u>29</u> + <u>31</u> + <u>30</u> + <u>31</u> + <u>30</u> + <u>31</u> + <u>28</u> = <u> 241 </u> days due

Step 2.

> Annual tax ÷ Days in year = $ per day
>
> $ <u> 1,680 </u> ÷ <u>   366   </u> = $4.59016

Step 3.

> $ per day   × Days due   = Proration
>
> $ <u> 4.59016 </u> × <u>   241   </u> = $1,106.23 debit seller/credit buyer

If the purchase agreement (sales contract) or local custom calls for the taxes to be prorated to the day of closing, each of the above examples would cost the seller one day less.

The above examples and the problems that follow assume that taxes are paid in arrears. When taxes are paid before the closing date, count the days from closing (prorated to) or from the day after closing (prorated through) through the end of the period for which the taxes have been paid in advance. Divide the tax bill by the number of days in the year and multiply by the number of days to be charged. When taxes have been paid in advance, you will debit the buyer and credit the seller.

1. Using a regular calendar year, prorate the taxes for a closing on November 30 on a seller's home, which has an annual tax bill of $2,840. The purchase agreement calls for the seller to pay through the day of closing.

2. Carl is selling his home to Erica, who has agreed that all prorations will be calculated to the day of closing. If Carl's home is assessed at $189,400 and the combined tax rate is $3.34 per $100 valuation, what will he be charged at a May 23 closing? (Use a banker's year.)

PRORATING INTEREST ON LOANS BEING ASSUMED

Interest on loans is paid in arrears. Usually, the seller's loan payment is due on the first day of the month and includes the interest charge for the preceding month. For example, if you have a closing scheduled for March 23, you will charge the seller for 23 days of interest and credit it to the buyer. This is because the April 1 payment, which will be paid by the buyer when the loan is assumed, will include the interest charge for the entire month of March.

As with the proration of taxes, it is important to read the purchase agreement to see whether prorations are to be to or through the day of closing. In the examples that follow, the seller pays for the day of closing (through). If you were calculating to the day of closing, you would charge the seller for one day less.

You will again need to use three steps to prorate interest on loans being assumed:

Step 1. Determine the number of days to be charged to or through the closing date.

Step 2. Calculate the dollar amount per day.
Loan balance × Annual interest rate ÷ Days in year = $ per day

Step 3. Calculate the proration by multiplying the total from step 2 by the total from step 1.
$ per day × Days due = Proration, debit seller/credit buyer

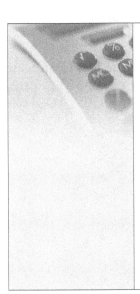

CALCULATE

You may duplicate the following to help you calculate the interest proration.

Step 1. Calculate the days due.
Count the days from the last payment to or through closing.

Step 2. Calculate the $ per day.
Loan balance × Annual interest rate ÷ Days in year = $ per day
(Do not clear your calculator; do not round; move on to step 3.)

Step 3. Calculate the proration.
Step 2   × Step 1   = Proration
$ per day × Days due = Proration
$ _____ × _____ = $

E X A M P L E :   Using a banker's year, calculate the proration of interest for an outstanding loan with a balance of $103,680 and an 8 percent annual interest rate. (Closing is scheduled for April 4 and the April 1 payment has been made.)

Step 1. April 4 = 4 days due

Step 2.

Loan balance × Annual interest rate ÷ Days in year = $ per day
$103,680   ×   0.08   ÷   360   = $23.04

Step 3.

$ per day × Days due = Proration
$23.04   ×   4   = $92.16 debit seller/credit buyer

Using a regular calendar year, the above would look like this:

Step 1. April 4 = 4 days due

Step 2.

Loan balance × Annual interest rate ÷ Days in year = $ per day
$103,680   ×   0.08   ÷   365   = $22.72438

Step 3.

$ per day × Days due = Proration
$22.72438 ×   4   = $90.90 debit seller/credit buyer

Now you try one.

For a closing on November 21, what credit would the buyer receive for interest on a loan being assumed if the loan balance is $68,374 and it carries an annual interest rate of 6.25 percent? (The purchase agreement calls for prorations to be calculated to the day of closing. Use a calendar year.)

Step 1. November 21 = _____ days due

Step 2.

Loan balance × Annual interest rate ÷ Days in year = $ per day

$_____ × _____ ÷ _____ = $_____

Step 3.

$ per day × Days due = Proration

$_____ × _____ = $_____ debit seller/credit buyer

Check your answers:

Step 1. November 21 = 21 – 1 day = 20 days due
The buyer pays for the day of closing.

Step 2.

Loan balance × Annual interest rate ÷ Days in year = $ per day

$___68,374___ × ___0.0625___ ÷ ___365___ = $11.70788

Step 3.

$ per day × Days due = Proration

$ 11.70788 × ___20___ = $ 234.16 debit seller/credit buyer

3. Ms. Murphy will assume a loan with an outstanding balance of $92,355 at an October 16 closing. The purchase agreement calls for the seller to pay through the day of closing. The annual interest rate on the loan is 6.875 percent. What amount will the seller be charged at closing, using a regular calendar year?

4. Prorate the interest using a banker's year for a March 17 closing if the loan balance is $43,560, the interest rate is 4.5 percent, and the purchase agreement calls for all prorations to be to the day of closing.

PRORATING INSURANCE

Insurance premiums are paid in advance of the period covered by the policy. When an insurance policy is assumed by a buyer at closing, you will need to calculate the unused number of days and charge the buyer to reimburse the seller for the unused part of the premium.

Again, we shall use a three-step process to determine the insurance proration. In our examples, the seller pays through the day of closing. If a purchase agreement called for prorations to be to the day of closing, you would add a day when you calculate the days due.

The three steps are as follows:

Step 1. Calculate the number of days from the closing to the day of expiration of the policy.

Step 2. Calculate the dollar amount per day.
Annual premium ÷ Days in year = $ per day

Step 3. Calculate the proration by multiplying the total from step 2 by the total from step 1.
$ per day × Days due = Proration

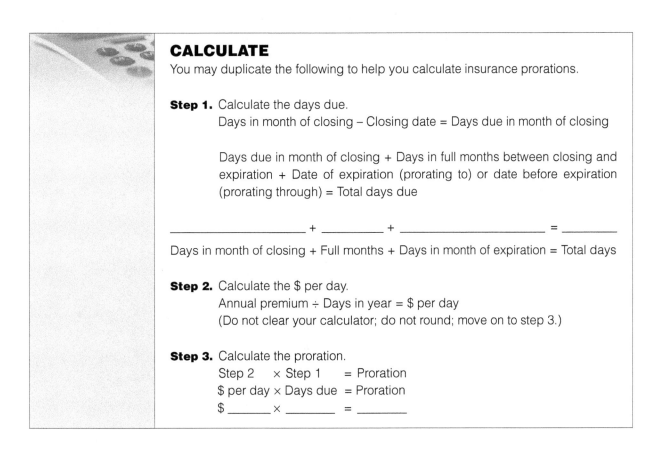

CALCULATE
You may duplicate the following to help you calculate insurance prorations.

Step 1. Calculate the days due.
Days in month of closing – Closing date = Days due in month of closing

Days due in month of closing + Days in full months between closing and expiration + Date of expiration (prorating to) or date before expiration (prorating through) = Total days due

_____ + _____ + _____ = _____
Days in month of closing + Full months + Days in month of expiration = Total days

Step 2. Calculate the $ per day.
Annual premium ÷ Days in year = $ per day
(Do not clear your calculator; do not round; move on to step 3.)

Step 3. Calculate the proration.
Step 2   × Step 1   = Proration
$ per day × Days due = Proration
$ _____ × _____ = _____

EXAMPLE: A buyer is assuming a one-year homeowner's policy that was taken out on May 27, for an annual premium of $456.25. What amount of money will the seller receive from the buyer at closing to reimburse him for the unused portion of the policy? (The closing will take place on October 5, and the sales agreement calls for prorations to be calculated through the day of closing.)

Calendar year (regular):

Step 1.   Days in month of closing
            – Closing date
             Days due in month of closing

        Oct. 31   N   D   J   F   M   A   M

        –   5

             26 + 30 + 31 + 31 + 28 + 31 + 30 + 26 = 233 days due

Had the sales agreement called for proration to the day of closing, you would add one additional day, for a total of 234 days.

Step 2.

        Annual premium ÷ Days in year = $ per day
           $456.25   ÷   365   = $1.25 per day

Step 3.

        $ per day × Days due = Proration
          $1.25   ×   233   = $291.25 debit buyer/credit seller

Banker's year:

Step 1.

        Oct. 30   N   D   J   F   M   A   M

        –   5

             25 + 30 + 30 + 30 + 30 + 30 + 30 + 26 = 231 days due

Step 2.

        Annual premium ÷ Days in year = $ per day
           $456.25   ÷   360   = $1.26736

Step 3.

        $ per day   × Days due = Proration
        $1.26736   ×   231   = $292.76 debit buyer/credit seller

Now you try two problems.

Using a banker's year, prorate a one-year insurance policy being assumed by the buyer that will expire on December 23. (The transaction will close on February 21. The annual premium paid by the seller was $874. Prorate through the day of closing.)

Step 1.

Feb. 30
–   21   M   A   M   J   J   A   S   O   N   D
___ + ___ + ___ + ___ + ___ + ___ + ___ + ___ + ___ + ___ + ___ = ____ days due

Step 2.

Annual premium ÷ Days in year = $ per day
$_____ ÷ _____ = $_____

Step 3.

$ per day × Days due = Proration
$_____ × _____ = $_____ debit buyer/credit seller

Check your answers:

Step 1.

Feb. 30
–   21   M   A   M   J   J   A   S   O   N   D
 9 + 30 + 30 + 30 + 30 + 30 + 30 + 30 + 30 + 30 + 22 = 301 days due

Step 2.

Annual premium ÷ Days in year = $ per day
$ 874   ÷   360   = $ 2.42778

Step 3.

$ per day × Days due = Proration
$ 2.42778 ×   301   = $ 730.76 debit buyer/credit seller

Using a calendar year, prorate an insurance policy that will be assumed at an August 28 closing. The policy was taken out on October 4 and will expire at 12:01 am on October 4. The earnest money contract calls for all items to be prorated through the day of closing. The premium paid was $456.25.

Step 1.

August. 31
–   28   S   O
___ + ___ + ___ = ____ days due

Step 2.

Annual premium ÷ Days in year = $ per day

$_____ ÷ _____ = $_____

Step 3.

$ per day × Days due = Proration

$_____ × _____ = $_____ debit buyer/credit seller

Check your answers:

Step 1.

August. 31

−   28   S   O

            _3_ + _30_ + _3_ = _36_ days due

Step 2.

Annual premium ÷ Days in year = $ per day

$___456.25___ ÷ ___365___ = $__1.25__

Step 3.

$ per day × Days due = Proration

$__1.25__ × ___36___ = $__45__ debit buyer/credit seller

5. Mary Hughes paid $684 for a policy taken out on April 5. The buyer will assume the policy. Calculate the proration through the day of closing on December 19. Calculate using a calendar year.

6. What is the charge to the buyer for an assumed insurance policy at an April 15 closing? The one-year policy was purchased on May 15 of the previous year and the purchase agreement calls for all prorations to be through the day of closing using a banker's year. The seller paid $650 for the annual premium.

PRORATING RENT

When a transaction involving rental units closes, only rents that have been paid before the closing day will be prorated. Usually, rents will be prorated through the day of closing. The seller will give the rent to the buyer for the days after closing through the end of the month. Any security deposit being held by the seller is not prorated and should be transferred to the buyer at closing. The buyer will be expected to refund it to the tenant at the end of the lease.

NOTE: Remember that rents are due on a monthly basis and are not subject to a daily amount calculation over an annual basis. For the sake of these calculations use a 30-day month (banker's year) and *through the day of closing* as the default.

There are three steps in prorating rent:

Step 1. The number of days owed by the seller to the buyer.
Total days in month (30) – Closing date = Days due

Step 2. Calculate the dollar amount per day.
Monthly rent ÷ Days in month (30) = $ per day

Step 3. Calculate the proration by multiplying the total from step 2 by the total from step 1.
$ per day × Days due = Proration

EXAMPLE: A duplex with a garage apartment is being sold and will close on September 16. All rents have been paid for September. Each side of the duplex rents for $500 per month, and the garage apartment rents for $350 per month. Each tenant has paid the equivalent of one month's rent as a security deposit. How much will the buyer be credited at closing using a banker's year?

Step 1. Days in month = 30 days
Closing   – 16
          14 days due

Step 2. $500 + 500 + 350 = $1,350 total monthly rent

Monthly rent ÷ Days in month = $ per day
    $1,350   ÷   30   = $45

Step 3.

    $ per day × Days due = Proration
      $45   ×   14   = $630 debit seller/credit buyer

The seller owes the buyer a total of $1,980 ($630 prorated rent + $1,350 security deposit).

Now you try one.

Prorate the rent for a four-plex that will close on May 23. Three units are occupied, with the seller holding a security deposit of $200 for each unit. The rent of $400 per month per unit has been paid for May. How much will the buyer be credited at closing?

Step 1. Days in month = _____ days

           Closing   – _____

                         _____ days due

Step 2.

        Monthly rent ÷ Days in month = $ per day

        $_____ ÷ _____ = $_____

Step 3.

        $ per day × Days due = Proration

        $_____ × _____ = $_____

                            + $_____ security deposit

                             $_____ debit seller/credit buyer

Check your answers:

Step 1.   May = __31__ days

          Closing – __23__

                  __8__ days due

Step 2.

        Monthly rent ÷ Days in month = $ per day

        $__1,200__ ÷ ____31____ = $ 38.70968

Step 3.

        $ per day   × Days due = Proration

        $ 38.70968 × ___8___ = $ 309.68

                            + $ 600.00 security deposit

                            $ 909.68 debit seller/credit buyer

7. Philip is purchasing a duplex. The closing date is August 11. What credit will he receive if both tenants have paid their rent on August 1? (The upper unit rents for $1,250 and the lower unit rents for $1,650.) Proration calculations are to include the day of closing.

8. Prorate the rent through the day of closing on a garage apartment for a February 16 closing in a leap year if the unit rents for $500 per month and the February rent has been paid.

PRORATING MAINTENANCE FEES

Homeowners' association dues and maintenance fees are typically paid in advance in January for the entire year. However, these charges may be assessed and collected monthly, quarterly, or annually. The problems in this section will illustrate annual fees. To prorate, use the following three steps:

Step 1. Calculate the number of days from closing through the last day of December.

Step 2. Calculate the dollar amount per day.
Annual fee ÷ Days in year = $ per day

Step 3. Calculate the proration by multiplying the total from step 2 by the total from step 1.
$ per day × Days due = Proration

EXAMPLE: The annual maintenance fee of $250 was paid on January 1. What would you credit the seller for a September 15 closing using a banker's year, with the seller paying through the day of closing?

Step 1. September = 30 days
         − 15   O   N   D
            15 + 30 + 30 + 30 = 105 days due

Step 2.

Annual fee ÷ Days in year = $ per day
   $250   ÷   360   = $0.69445

Step 3.

$ per day × Days due = Proration
$0.69445 ×   105   = $72.92 debit buyer/credit seller

Now you try one.

The annual homeowners' association dues of $360 were paid in January. How much will the buyer be charged for a July 28 closing using a regular calendar year if prorations are calculated through the day of closing?

Step 1. July = _____ days
       Closing – _____   A   S   O   N   D
       _____ + __ + __ + __ + __ + __ = _____ days due

Step 2.

    Annual fee ÷ Days in year = $ per day
    $_____ ÷ _____ = $_____

Step 3.

    $ per day × Days due = Proration
    $_____ × _____ = $_____ debit buyer/credit seller

Check your answers:

Step 1. July = __31__ days
       Closing – __28__   A   S   O   N   D
       __3__ + 31 + 30 + 31 + 30 + 31 = 156 days due

Step 2.

    Annual fee ÷ Days in year = $ per day
    $__360__ ÷ __365__ = $__0.98630__

Step 3.

    $ per day × Days due = Proration
    $0.98630 × __156__ = $153.86 debit buyer/credit seller

PRORATING MISCELLANEOUS ITEMS

For items such as propane gas or heating oil, calculate the value of the product remaining in the tank, then debit the buyer and credit the seller.

E X A M P L E : Thirty gallons of heating oil remain in the tank at closing. If the seller paid $1.10 per gallon when he filled the tank, the buyer would owe the seller 30 times $1.10 or $33 for the oil that he receives.

ADDITIONAL PRACTICE

Caution: In many state licensing exams, questions are designed to determine whether the examinee can carefully read and follow instructions. When reading a proration problem, be alert as to whether the calculation is to be to or through the day of closing and whether you are to base the calculation on a banker's or a calendar year. Practice in these matters will vary widely in different states. Your instructor may wish to assign only those problems that reflect local practice in your jurisdiction.

When you have finished these problems, check your answers at the end of the chapter. If you miss any of the problems, review this chapter before going on to Chapter 14.

1. A home with a market value of $175,000 was assessed at 82 percent of its value. The tax rate was $4.20 per $100. Figure the tax proration through the day of closing, using a banker's year for a closing on June 1.
   a. $2,426.84
   b. $2,486.54
   c. $2,493.36
   d. $2,527.99

2. The previous year's taxes on Steve's home were paid in full on December 31 and amounted to $2,753. Steve sold his home to Bill and closed the sale on May 4. What was the prorated tax amount, using a calendar year and prorating through the day of closing? Was the proration a credit to the buyer or the seller?
   a. $935.27 credit buyer
   b. $939.26 credit buyer
   c. $935.27 credit seller
   d. $939.26 credit seller

3. The annual taxes on a house are $1,837.50. For a closing date of May 21, what will be the prorated amount using a banker's year? (The seller will pay for the day of closing.)
   a. $713.82
   b. $718.56
   c. $719.69
   d. $720.29

4. Cheryl is purchasing a small studio which has been assessed at a value of $71,400 for tax purposes. If the tax rate is $2.17 per $100 and the sale will close on September 12 in a leap year, what will be the tax proration, using a calendar year and prorating to the day of closing?
   a. $1,078.17
   b. $1,079.49
   c. $1,082.44
   d. $1,097.48

5. Annual taxes for a property that is set to close on July 16 are as follows: $350 for school tax, $280 for city tax, and $177 for county tax. What is the tax proration, using a calendar year and prorating through the day of closing?
   a. $433.35
   b. $434.37
   c. $435.56
   d. $441.61

6. After the monthly payment due on January 1 was made, $66,600 is the unpaid balance of a seller's 6 percent assumable mortgage. The purchaser assumed the seller's mortgage and the closing was set for January 16. Find the amount of accrued interest, using a statutory year and prorating to the day of closing.
   a. $165.96
   b. $166.50
   c. $167
   d. $167.24

7. A buyer has agreed based on the favorable sales price to assume the seller's current interest of 8.5 percent on an outstanding mortgage balance of $102,743.50. Calculate the proration on an assumption with a closing date of June 21. The June 1 payment has been made and the principal reduction is reflected in the above balance. Use a regular calendar year to calculate the proration through the day of closing.

   a. $455.74
   b. $478.53
   c. $501.09
   d. $502.46

8. After an October 1 monthly payment of $765.42 was made, the seller's loan balance was $36,569.20. The mortgage has an interest rate of 5.5 percent. Compute the proration, using a regular calendar year, if the day of closing is October 18. (The seller will pay interest through the day of closing.)

   a. $98.19
   b. $98.99
   c. $99.19
   d. $99.99

9. After the August 1 payment was made, a homeowner's mortgage balance was $120,853. Her monthly payment of $1,160 includes principal and interest only on a 7¾ percent subprime loan. The sale of her home is to close on August 29. What will be the proration through closing, using a banker's year?

   a. $728.48
   b. $742.12
   c. $744.16
   d. $754.49

10. The premium of $673 was paid in full for a one-year insurance policy that expires on May 21 at 11:59 PM. The house sale is scheduled to close on February 1. Compute the proration through the day of closing, using a statutory year.

   a. $203.77 debit buyer/credit seller
   b. $203.77 debit seller/credit buyer
   c. $205.64 debit seller/credit buyer
   d. $205.64 debit buyer/credit seller

11. The total annual premium for a $40,000 fire insurance policy is $615. This premium was paid on January 5. What will be the proration, using a banker's year, if the policy is transferred to the buyer at closing on September 5 with proration calculated through the day of closing?

   a. $200.51
   b. $201.63
   c. $203.29
   d. $205

12. Frank purchased a one-year homeowner's policy on January 13 and paid the $730 premium in full. He sold the home and closed on October 23. How much was Frank's credit at closing, using a regular calendar year, if the buyer assumed the policy and the policy was prorated through the day of closing?

   a. $162
   b. $164.25
   c. $565.75
   d. $568

13. Ray paid the $844 insurance premium for a one-year policy on March 18. He will sell his home and close the sale on November 26. When the buyer assumes the policy, how much will the prorated amount be, using a regular calendar year, if Ray pays through the day of closing?

   a. $253.66
   b. $254.36
   c. $256.67
   d. $260.23

14. The sale of a home will close on September 28. Included in the sale is a garage apartment that is rented to a tenant for $525 per month. The tenant paid the security deposit of two months' rent when she leased the apartment and has paid the September rent. What is the rent proration?

   a. $35
   b. $52.50
   c. $1,085
   d. $1,090

15. An apartment complex contains 100 units, of which 50 units are one-bedroom and rent for $600 per month; 30 units are two-bedrooms and rent for $825 per month; 20 units are three-bedrooms and rent for $1,100 per month. Prorate the rent for a closing on February 18 using a banker's year and prorate through the day of closing, assuming all units are occupied and have paid the rent for February.
    a. $26,465.52
    b. $27,410.71
    c. $30,151.79
    d. $30,700

16. Nancy is selling her home, which has a garage apartment that rents for $465 per month. If the rent was paid on September 1, what amount will Nancy be charged through the day of closing for the rent proration? (The closing is on September 18.)
    a. $180
    b. $186
    c. $270
    d. $279

17. Erica is purchasing her first home. Taxes will be due by December 31 for the current year. The sales agreement calls for the seller to pay expenses through the day of closing. If the annual taxes are $3,212, what credit will Erica receive at closing on August 8, using a statutory year?
    a. $1,918.40
    b. $1,928.04
    c. $1,935.64
    d. $1,945.04

18. A retired person is selling her home. She made a monthly mortgage payment on July 1 that paid interest through June 30. Her principal balance is now $22,450.40; the interest rate is 5 percent. The closing is set for July 21. What amount of accrued interest will be charged to the seller at closing? (Prorate through the date of closing, using a regular calendar year)
    a. $64.40
    b. $64.58
    c. $67.59
    d. $67.68

19. Patsy has a one-year security company agreement that expires on December 13 at 11:59 PM. The annual agreement was purchased at a cost of $959. The buyer intends to continue with the security agreement. Calculate the security agreement proration that the buyer will owe the seller at the closing on June 18. (Prorate through the date of closing, using a banker's year.)
    a. $463.52
    b. $466.18
    c. $468.16
    d. $469.18

20. Taxes on a seller's home are $2.28 per $100 of assessed valuation. What amount would the seller be charged for an August 15 closing on the home, assessed at $187,650, using a calendar leap year and charging the seller to the day of closing?
    a. $2,653.56
    b. $2,660.83
    c. $2,665.25
    d. $2,687.78

SOLUTIONS: PROBLEMS IN CHAPTER 13

1.

J F M A M J J A S O N
31 + 28 + 31 + 30 + 31 + 30 + 31 + 31 + 30 + 31 + 30 = 334
$2,840 ÷ 365 = $7.78082
$7.78082 × 334 = $2,598.79388 debit seller/credit buyer

2. $189,400 ÷ 100 × $3.34 = $6,325.96

J F M A M
30 + 30 + 30 + 30 + 22 = 142
$6,325.96 ÷ 360 = $17.57211
$17.57211 × 142 = $2,495.23978 debit seller/credit buyer

3. $92,355 × 0.06875 ÷ 365 = $17.39563
$17.39563 × 16 = $278.33 debit seller/credit Murphy

4. $43,560 × 0.085 ÷ 360 = $10.285
$10.285 × 16 = $164.56 debit seller/credit buyer

5.

J F M A
December 31 − 19 = 12 + 31 + 28 + 31 + 4 = 106
$684 ÷ 366 = $1.86885
$1.86885 × 106 = $198.0981

6. April 30 − 15 = 15
15 + 14 = 29
$650 ÷ 360 = $1.80556
$1.80556 × 29 = $52.36124 debit buyer/credit seller

7. 30 days in rental month − 11 = 19 days
$1,250 + 1,650 = $2,900
$2,900 ÷ 30 = $96.66667
$96.66667 × 19 = $1,836.66673 credit Phillip

8. February 29 − 16 = 13
$500 ÷ 29 = $17.24138
$17.24138 × 13 = $224.14 debit seller/credit buyer

SOLUTIONS: ADDITIONAL PRACTICE

1. (d) $175,000 × 0.82 ÷ 100 × $4.20 = $6,027

   J F M A M J
   30 + 30 + 30 + 30 + 30 + 1 =151
   $6,027 ÷ 360 = $16.74167
   $16.74167 × 151 = $2,527.99 debit seller/credit buyer

2. (a)

   J F M A M
   31 + 28 + 31 + 30 + 4 =124
   $2,753 ÷ 365 = $7.54247
   $7.54247 × 124 = $935.27 debit seller/credit buyer

3. (c)

   J F M A M
   30 + 30 + 30 + 30 + 21 =141
   $1,837.50 ÷ 360 = $5.104667
   $5.104667 × 141 = $719.69 debit Williamson/credit buyer

4. (b) $71,400 ÷ 100 × $2.17 = $1,549.38

   J F M A M J J A S
   31 + 29 + 31 + 30 + 31 + 30 + 31 + 31 + 11 =255
   $1,549.38 ÷ 366 = $4.23328
   $4.23328 × 255 = $1,079.49 debit seller/credit Cheryl

5. (c) $350 + $280 + $177 = $807

   J F M A M J J
   31 + 28 + 31 + 30 + 31 + 30 + 16 =197
   $807 ÷ 365 × 197 = $435.56 debit seller/credit buyer

6. (b) $66,600 × 0.06 ÷ 360 = $11.10
   $11.10 × 15 = $166.50debit seller/credit buyer

7. (d) $102,743.50 × 0.085 ÷ 365 = $23.92657
   $23.92657 × 21 = $502.46 debit seller/credit buyer

8. (c) $36,569.20 \times 0.055 \div 365 = \$5.51043$
   $\$5.51043 \times 18 = \$99.19$

9. (d) $\$120,853 \times 0.0775 \div 360 = \$26.01697$
   $\$26.01697 \times 29 = \$754.49$

10. (d)   M   A   M
   February $30 - 1 = 29 + 30 + 30 + 21 = 110$
   $\$673 \div 360 = \$1.86944$
   $\$1.86944 \times 110 = \$205.64$ debit buyer/credit seller

11. (c)   O   N   D   J
   September $30 - 5 = 25 + 30 + 30 + 30 + 4 = 119$
   $\$615 \div 360 = \$1.70833$
   $\$1.70833 \times 119 = \$203.29$ debit buyer/credit seller

12. (a)   N   D   J
   October $31 - 23 = 8 + 30 + 31 + 12 = 81$
   $\$730 \div 365 = \$2$
   $\$2 \times 81 = \$162$ debit buyer/credit Fulton

13. (c)   D   J   F   M
   November $30 - 26 = 4 + 31 + 31 + 28 + 17 = 111$
   $\$844 \div 365 = \$2.31233$
   $\$2.31233 \times 111 = \$256.67$ debit buyer/credit Thomas

14. (a) 30 day rental month September $30 - 28 = 2$
   $\$525 \div 30 = \$17.50$
   $\$17.50 \times 2 = \$35$ debit Gaston/credit buyer

15. (d) $50 \times \quad \$600 = \$30,000$
   $30 \times \quad \$825 = \$24,750$
   $\underline{20} \times \$1,100 = \underline{\$22,000}$
   $100 \qquad\qquad \$76,750$
   30 day rental month $- 18 = 12$
   $\$76,750 \div 30 = \$2,558.33333$
   $\$2,558.33333 \times 12 = \$30,700$ debit seller/credit buyer

16. (b) 30 day rental month $- 18 = 12$
   $\$465 \div 30 = \$15.50$

$15.50 \times 12 = \$186$

17. (d) January – July = 7 months
$7 \times 30 = 210$
$210 + 8 = 218$
$\$3,212 \div 360 = \$8.922222 \times 218 = \$1,945.04$

18. (b) $\$22,450.40 \times 0.05 \div 365 = \$1,356.250192 \times 21 = \$64.58$

19. (b)   J   J   A   S   O   N   D
$30 - 18 = 12 + 30 + 30 + 30 + 30 + 30 + 13 = 175$
$\$959 \div 360 = \$2.66388889 \times 175 = \$466.18$

20. (a) $\$187,650 \div \$100 \times \$2.28 = \$4,278.42$

     J   F   M   A   M   J   J   A
$31 + 29 + 31 + 30 + 31 + 30 + 31 + 14 = 227$
$\$4,278.42 \div 366 = \$11.689672 \times 227 = \$2,653.56$

Closing Statements

The real estate professional can use the information in this chapter in two practical ways: (1) Closing statements are usually prepared by those who actually close the transaction, but the real estate broker or salesperson should always check the statements for accuracy before closing. (2) Real estate licensees routinely use aids called net sheets in every listing appointment, preparation of an offer from a buyer, and presentation of an offer to a seller. Prospective sellers are obviously very interested in the amount they will net from the proposed sale, and prospective buyers likewise are interested in their net due at closing. The generation of these figures involves the preparation of a document similar to a closing statement.

A closing statement is used in closing a real estate transaction. It is the document on which you will record the prorations that you learned to calculate in Chapter 13. It is, basically, a balance sheet on which debits and credits to the buyer and seller are recorded, and from the totals, the amount owed by the buyer is determined as well as the net amount that the seller will receive or must pay.

In this chapter, you will work with prorations and learn to enter them on a closing statement as well as the new federal HUD-1 form. The examples used are generalities because many of the expenses are negotiable and can be paid by either the buyer or the seller. Also, the methods of closing a real estate transaction vary greatly across the nation and even within states. For example, depending on the area, brokers, attorneys, title insurance companies, or escrow companies may routinely close real estate transactions. In this text, title or escrow companies will be considered to be the closers, and the examples and problems are treated accordingly, even though this may not be the practice in your area.

CLOSING STATEMENT FORMS

Every real estate transaction involving the transfer of property requires the preparation of a written form called a closing or settlement statement.

The closing statement is used to balance the books. It is a way of calculating how much money is owed or due, taking all factors into account. Instead of exchanging money for each part of the transaction, the amounts are entered separately on the closing statement. The entire statement is then balanced to determine the total amount owed. This way, there is only one exchange of money, and the closing statement serves as a summary of the receipts and disbursements of the transaction. For instance, if the sellers have 40 gallons of fuel left in their tank on the day of closing, they could either siphon it out or ask the buyer for its value in cash. Instead, the value is entered on the closing statement as a credit to the seller and as a debit or charge to the buyer, who owes the seller that amount.

A DEBIT takes money From.

A CREDIT gives money To.

The amounts charged to the buyer increase the buyer's acquisition cost for the property. Amounts that the seller owes the buyer are entered as credits to the buyer and reduce the seller's net from the sale. The overall equations for closing statements are as follows:

Buyer's charges – Buyer's credits = Cash buyer owes at closing
Seller's credits – Seller's charges = Cash seller will receive at closing

CREDITS

Let us consider who receives credit for certain items. Items credited to the *buyer* may include

- the earnest money deposit (treated as a partial payment);
- the existing loan balance, when assumed by the buyer;
- items—such as real estate taxes—that have accrued or are accruing, but are not yet due or paid and for which the seller is debited, or charged, at the closing (see Chapter 13);
- unearned revenues (revenues—such as rent—collected in advance, but not yet earned); and
- proceeds of a new loan to be taken out by the buyer.

Items credited to the *seller* may include

- the sales price, and
- prepaid items (items paid in advance—such as Homeowners' Association dues paid for a term that has not fully expired or fuel on hand).

NOTE: Accrued items are credits to the buyer, and prepaid items are credits to the seller.

The following chart indicates charges that would normally be credited to the buyer and those that would normally be credited to the seller. See explanation notes below the chart.

	Credit to Buyer	Credit to Seller
a. Sales price of property ($100,000)		X
b. Balance of existing loan, assumed by the buyer ($40,500)	X	
c. Mortgage interest accrued, but not yet due on the loan assumed by the buyer ($300)	X	
d. Property tax reserve account ($600)		X
e. Accrued portion of real estate tax ($450)	X	
f. Prepaid security service ($175)		X
g. Fuel oil in tank on closing day ($150)		X
h. Water bill proration earned, but not yet due ($100)	X	
i. Rents collected, but unearned ($805)	X	
j. Tenants' security deposit ($2,000)	X	

a. The seller receives credit for the total selling price of the property, which the buyer has agreed to pay.

b. The buyer receives credit for assuming the seller's existing loan. The balance due on the assumed note is an offset to the selling price.

c. The buyer receives credit for the interest incurred to date by the seller, which the buyer must pay at the next mortgage payment date.

d. When the buyer assumes the seller's mortgage, the seller receives credit for any money held in a tax reserve account with the mortgage lender that will be transferred to the buyer.

e. The buyer receives a credit for the seller's share of the accrued real estate tax up to the closing date because the buyer must pay the total tax when it becomes due.

f. The seller receives credit for money paid in advance for services that will benefit the buyer after the closing.

g. The seller receives credit for fuel on hand that has already been paid for but that the buyer will use.

h. The buyer receives credit for the water that the seller has used before closing because the buyer will have to pay for the total billing period when the bill becomes due.

i. The buyer receives credit for rent collected in advance by the seller, which represents rent for that part of the month during which the buyer will own the building.

j. The buyer receives credit for each security deposit held by the seller but that the buyer, as the new landlord, must return if a tenant decides not to renew a lease.

For each of these credits, there must be a debit, or charge, to the other party, who must pay for the items. For example, the selling price is a credit to the seller and must be a debit to the buyer.

1. Balance the following chart by entering the amount of each debit in the debit column of the buyer or seller.

		Buyer		Seller	
		Debit	**Credit**	**Debit**	**Credit**
a.	Sales price				$100,000
b.	Assumed loan balance		$40,500		
c.	Accrued interest on assumed loan		300		
d.	Tax reserve account				600
e.	Accrued portion of real estate tax		450		
f.	Prepaid security service				175
g.	Fuel oil in tank				150
h.	Prorated accrued water bill		100		
i.	Unearned rents collected		805		
j.	Tenants' security deposits		2,000		

ENTRY OF FIGURES

Definite rules govern the entry of the figures in a four-column closing statement. In problem 2, you followed Rule 1:

Rule 1. The sales price and all the prorations of accrued and prepaid items between buyer and seller are each entered as a debit to one party and a credit to the other party.

Three kinds of items are entered only once. These are debits or credits to one party without offsetting second entries. Such items are covered by Rule 2:

Rule 2.

- Earnest money—a credit to the buyer. This money is deposited by the buyer and is usually held by the title company in an escrow account until the closing, when it is applied toward the purchase price. This money is not directly credited to the seller, but becomes part of the balance due the seller at closing.

- Seller's expenses—debits to the seller. These are personal expenses of the seller—such as broker's commission, transfer tax stamps, and so on that do not involve the buyer.

- Buyer's expenses—debits to the buyer. These are third-party expenses of the buyer—such as the fee for recording the seller's deed and the lender's fee for the buyer's assumption of the seller's loan balance—that do not affect the seller.

The following chart indicates which items are entered once and which are entered twice. It also shows how items are entered.

	Entered Once	Entered Twice	How Entered			
		Debit and Credit	Credit Seller	Debit Seller	Credit Buyer	Debit Buyer
Sales price		X	X			X
Earnest money deposit	X				X	
Assumed loan balance		X		X	X	
Interest on assumed loan		X		X	X	
Real estate tax proration*		X		X	X	
Fuel oil in tank		X	X			X
Recording fee for seller's deed	X					X
Seller's commission to broker	X			X		
Buyer's title examination cost	X					X

*Taxes have not been paid as of the closing date.

Types of Entries

The following list shows all entries included in the preparation of a closing statement, grouped by type of entry and how each is typically debited or credited. Local practices may differ.

1. *Purchase price*—debited to the buyer and credited to the seller.
2. *Earnest money*—credited only to the buyer.
3. *Balance of assumed loan and accrued interest*—debited to the seller and credited to the buyer. (The proceeds of a new mortgage obtained by the buyer, however, are credited to the buyer without a corresponding debit to the seller because the buyer receives this money from the lender. The seller's existing mortgage must then be paid off by a debit to the seller.)
4. *Purchase-money loan*—credited to the buyer, who assumes an obligation for future payments; also debited to the seller, who accepts the note in lieu of cash.
5. *Prorations*—debited to one party and credited to the other.

Items debited to buyer and credited to seller:

- Prepaid real estate taxes, when applicable
- Insurance and tax reserve impound account balance
- Coal or fuel oil on hand
- Prepaid utilities
- Personal property purchased by buyer
- Prepaid homeowners' association or maintenance fees

Items debited to seller and credited to buyer:

- Principal of loan assumed by buyer
- Accrued interest on existing assumed loan not yet payable
- Accrued portion of real estate tax not yet due
- Unearned portion of rent collected in advance
- Accrued salaries of personnel (such as janitor or manager)
- Tenants' security deposits

Other items may be included, depending on the customs of your area.

6. Expenses charged (debited) to seller or buyer—to be disbursed by the closer.
    Debits to seller:

- Broker's commission
- Legal fee for drawing the deed
- Title expenses required by the sales contract
- Loan discount points
- Repairs (as required by the sales contract)
- Loan payoff fees
- Filing fee for release of lien
- Loan discount fees (if negotiated in the sales contract)

Debits to buyer:

- Assumption or transfer fee (when buyer assumes an existing loan)
- Survey (if required by lender)
- Recording fees for deed and mortgage
- Loan origination fee
- Loan discount points
- Loan discount fees (if required by lender)
- Certified copies of deed restrictions
- Credit report
- Photos of property
- Prepaid taxes, insurance, and interest
- Mortgage insurance premium (PMI or MIP, when required by lender)
- Flood insurance premium/homeowner's insurance premium
- Appraisal fee
- Termite, structural, mechanical, and environmental inspections (Termite inspection is a charge to the seller in transactions with a VA-guaranteed loan.)

Debits to party responsible or shared by seller and buyer:

- Transfer tax
- Cost of title insurance or title examination
- Legal fees
- Escrow fee
- Inspection fees

Other items may be included, depending on the customs of your area and the provisions of the sales contract.

The preparation of the closing statement is similar to the preparation of separate closing statements for the seller and buyer. These statements consist of debits and credits. A debit is a charge—a debit or an amount that the party being debited owes and must pay out of the closing proceeds. A credit is an amount entered in a party's favor, which the party being credited has already paid or promises to pay, in the form of a note for a loan, or for which the party must be reimbursed. When the buyer's debits have been entered and totaled, the buyer's credits are totaled and subtracted from the debits. This will determine the net amount of cash the buyer must pay to close the purchase. The difference between the seller's total credits and debits represents the amount due to the seller or owed by the seller at the closing.

Examine the following situation, then enter the items on the form provided and determine (1) the amount the buyer will owe at closing, and (2) the amount the seller will receive at closing.

2. A house has been sold for $240,000 and the buyer has placed an earnest money deposit of $20,000 with the seller's real estate broker. The seller has agreed to pay the broker a 7 percent commission on the sales price.

	Buyer		Seller	
	Debit	Credit	Debit	Credit
Sales price				
Earnest money				
Broker's commission				
Subtotals				
Due from buyer at closing				
Due to seller at closing				
Totals				

A typical Settlement Statement Worksheet, which is used by an escrow officer or closing agent to record debit and credit computations for buyers and sellers in the closing of a real estate transaction, is shown below. Remember that in most cases data is actually entered directly into a software program designed for and used by escrow officers and their assistants in a title company.

SETTLEMENT STATEMENT WORKSHEET

Settlement date _____	Buyer's Statement		Seller's Statement	
	Debit	Credit	Debit	Credit
Purchase price				
Earnest money				
Assumed loan balance				
Interest on assumed loan				
Real estate taxes through date				
Tax reserve				
Insurance premium proration				
Buyer's expenses:				
Assumption fee				
Recording fee				
Seller's expenses				
Title search				
Broker's commission				
Transfer tax				
Subtotals				
Due from buyer				
Due to seller				
Totals				

RECONCILIATION

The closing statement yields complete and accurate figures of the net amounts that the buyer must pay after deducting the buyer's credits and that the seller will receive or owe after paying the broker's commission and all other seller's expenses.

For the escrow officer (closer) to be sure that all entries on the statement are properly handled and that more funds are not paid out than are received, a cash reconciliation or recapitulation will always be prepared. The forms used by escrow officers or the individual conducting the actual closing will vary.

CLOSER'S RECONCILIATION STATEMENT

Items	Receipts	Disbursements
Earnest money	$6,000.00	
Due from buyer at closing		
Seller's expenses paid:		$ 9,160.00
Buyer's expenses paid:		900.00
Amount paid to seller at closing		
Totals		

For instructional purposes, we have used simple forms in this chapter; in actual practice, each person or title company performing a closing will use the settlement statement developed by the Department of Housing and Urban Development (HUD). This is a result of legislation known as the Real Estate Settlement Procedures Act (RESPA). A copy of this three-page form is shown in Figure 14.1. Page 2 of the HUD form must be completed first because page 1 summarizes the detailed items there. Also, the term *debit* is not used; the RESPA form merely says "paid from borrower's/seller's funds." In this chapter, you learned that in real estate settlement language, *debit* means *charged to* or a *cost to* the buyer or the seller.

FEDERALLY REQUIRED CLOSING FORMS

The HUD-1, as it is known throughout the real estate industry, is shown in Figure 14.1. This version became federally mandated in January of 2010 and is directly tied through comparison figures to the new Good Faith Estimate (Figure 14.2) which also became required as of 2010.

FIGURE 14.1

Settlement Statement (HUD-1)

OMB Approval No. 2502-0265

A. **Settlement Statement (HUD-1)**

B. Type of Loan

1. ☐ FHA	2. ☐ RHS	3. ☐ Conv. Unins.	6. File Number:	7. Loan Number:	8. Mortgage Insurance Case Number:
4. ☐ VA	5. ☐ Conv. Ins.				

C. Note: This form is furnished to give you a statement of actual settlement costs. Amounts paid to and by the settlement agent are shown. Items marked "(p.o.c.)" were paid outside the closing; they are shown here for informational purposes and are not included in the totals.

D. Name & Address of Borrower:	E. Name & Address of Seller:	F. Name & Address of Lender:
G. Property Location:	H. Settlement Agent:	I. Settlement Date:
	Place of Settlement:	

J. Summary of Borrower's Transaction		K. Summary of Seller's Transaction	
100. Gross Amount Due from Borrower		**400. Gross Amount Due to Seller**	
101. Contract sales price		401. Contract sales price	
102. Personal property		402. Personal property	
103. Settlement charges to borrower (line 1400)		403.	
104.		404.	
105.		405.	
Adjustment for items paid by seller in advance		**Adjustment for items paid by seller in advance**	
106. City/town taxes to		406. City/town taxes to	
107. County taxes to		407. County taxes to	
108. Assessments to		408. Assessments to	
109.		409.	
110.		410.	
111.		411.	
112.		412.	
120. Gross Amount Due from Borrower		**420. Gross Amount Due to Seller**	
200. Amount Paid by or in Behalf of Borrower		**500. Reductions In Amount Due to seller**	
201. Deposit or earnest money		501. Excess deposit (see instructions)	
202. Principal amount of new loan(s)		502. Settlement charges to seller (line 1400)	
203. Existing loan(s) taken subject to		503. Existing loan(s) taken subject to	
204.		504. Payoff of first mortgage loan	
205.		505. Payoff of second mortgage loan	
206.		506.	
207.		507.	
208.		508.	
209.		509.	
Adjustments for items unpaid by seller		**Adjustments for items unpaid by seller**	
210. City/town taxes to		510. City/town taxes to	
211. County taxes to		511. County taxes to	
212. Assessments to		512. Assessments to	
213.		513.	
214.		514.	
215.		515.	
216.		516.	
217.		517.	
218.		518.	
219.		519.	
220. Total Paid by/for Borrower		**520. Total Reduction Amount Due Seller**	
300. Cash at Settlement from/to Borrower		**600. Cash at Settlement to/from Seller**	
301. Gross amount due from borrower (line 120)		601. Gross amount due to seller (line 420)	
302. Less amounts paid by/for borrower (line 220)	( )	602. Less reductions in amounts due seller (line 520)	( )
303. Cash ☐ From ☐ To Borrower		**603. Cash** ☐ To ☐ From Seller	

The Public Reporting Burden for this collection of information is estimated at 35 minutes per response for collecting, reviewing, and reporting the data. This agency may not collect this information, and you are not required to complete this form, unless it displays a currently valid OMB control number. No confidentiality is assured; this disclosure is mandatory. This is designed to provide the parties to a RESPA covered transaction with information during the settlement process.

Previous edition are obsolete — Page 1 of 3 — HUD-1

L. Settlement Charges

700. Total Real Estate Broker Fees		Paid From Borrower's Funds at Settlement	Paid From Seller's Funds at Settlement
Division of commission (line 700) as follows :			
701. $ to			
702. $ to			
703. Commission paid at settlement			
704.			

800. Items Payable in Connection with Loan			
801. Our origination charge	$ (from GFE #1)		
802. Your credit or charge (points) for the specific interest rate chosen	$ (from GFE #2)		
803. Your adjusted origination charges	(from GFE #A)		
804. Appraisal fee to	(from GFE #3)		
805. Credit report to	(from GFE #3)		
806. Tax service to	(from GFE #3)		
807. Flood certification to	(from GFE #3)		
808.			
809.			
810.			
811.			

900. Items Required by Lender to be Paid in Advance			
901. Daily interest charges from to @ $ /day	(from GFE #10)		
902. Mortgage insurance premium for months to	(from GFE #3)		
903. Homeowner's insurance for years to	(from GFE #11)		
904.			

1000. Reserves Deposited with Lender			
1001. Initial deposit for your escrow account	(from GFE #9)		
1002. Homeowner's insurance months @ $ per month $			
1003. Mortgage insurance months @ $ per month $			
1004. Property Taxes months @ $ per month $			
1005. months @ $ per month $			
1006. months @ $ per month $			
1007. Aggregate Adjustment -$			

1100. Title Charges			
1101. Title services and lender's title insurance	(from GFE #4)		
1102. Settlement or closing fee	$		
1103. Owner's title insurance	(from GFE #5)		
1104. Lender's title insurance	$		
1105. Lender's title policy limit $			
1106. Owner's title policy limit $			
1107. Agent's portion of the total title insurance premium to	$		
1108. Underwriter's portion of the total title insurance premium to	$		
1109.			
1110.			
1111.			

1200. Government Recording and Transfer Charges			
1201. Government recording charges	(from GFE #7)		
1202. Deed $ Mortgage $ Release $			
1203. Transfer taxes	(from GFE #8)		
1204. City/County tax/stamps Deed $ Mortgage $			
1205. State tax/stamps Deed $ Mortgage $			
1206.			

1300. Additional Settlement Charges			
1301. Required services that you can shop for	(from GFE #6)		
1302.	$		
1303.	$		
1304.			
1305.			

1400. Total Settlement Charges (enter on lines 103, Section J and 502, Section K)			

Comparison of Good Faith Estimate (GFE) and HUD-1 Charrges		Good Faith Estimate	HUD-1
Charges That Cannot Increase	**HUD-1 Line Number**		
Our origination charge	# 801		
Your credit or charge (points) for the specific interest rate chosen	# 802		
Your adjusted origination charges	# 803		
Transfer taxes	# 1203		

Charges That In Total Cannot Increase More Than 10%		Good Faith Estimate	HUD-1
Government recording charges	# 1201		
	#		
	#		
	#		
	#		
	#		
	#		
	Total		
Increase between GFE and HUD-1 Charges		$ or	%

Charges That Can Change		Good Faith Estimate	HUD-1
Initial deposit for your escrow account	# 1001		
Daily interest charges $ /day	# 901		
Homeowner's insurance	# 903		
	#		
	#		
	#		

Loan Terms

Your initial loan amount is	$
Your loan term is	years
Your initial interest rate is	%
Your initial monthly amount owed for principal, interest, and any mortgage insurance is	$ includes ☐ Principal ☐ Interest ☐ Mortgage Insurance
Can your interest rate rise?	☐ No ☐ Yes, it can rise to a maximum of %. The first change will be on and can change again every after . Every change date, your interest rate can increase or decrease by %. Over the life of the loan, your interest rate is guaranteed to never be **lower** than % or **higher** than %.
Even if you make payments on time, can your loan balance rise?	☐ No ☐ Yes, it can rise to a maximum of $
Even if you make payments on time, can your monthly amount owed for principal, interest, and mortgage insurance rise?	☐ No ☐ Yes, the first increase can be on and the monthly amount owed can rise to $. The maximum it can ever rise to is $.
Does your loan have a prepayment penalty?	☐ No ☐ Yes, your maximum prepayment penalty is $
Does your loan have a balloon payment?	☐ No ☐ Yes, you have a balloon payment of $ due in years on .
Total monthly amount owed including escrow account payments	☐ You do not have a monthly escrow payment for items, such as property taxes and homeowner's insurance. You must pay these items directly yourself. ☐ You have an additional monthly escrow payment of $ that results in a total initial monthly amount owed of $. This includes principal, interest, any mortgage insurance and any items checked below: ☐ Property taxes ☐ Homeowner's insurance ☐ Flood insurance ☐ ☐ ☐

Note: If you have any questions about the Settlement Charges and Loan Terms listed on this form, please contact your lender.

FIGURE 14.2

Good Faith Estimate

OMB Approval No. 2502-0265

Good Faith Estimate (GFE)

Name of Originator	Borrower
Originator Address	Property Address
Originator Phone Number	
Originator Email	Date of GFE

Purpose

This GFE gives you an estimate of your settlement charges and loan terms if you are approved for this loan. For more information, see HUD's *Special Information Booklet* on settlement charges, your *Truth-in-Lending Disclosures*, and other consumer information at www.hud.gov/respa. If you decide you would like to proceed with this loan, contact us.

Shopping for your loan

Only you can shop for the best loan for you. Compare this GFE with other loan offers, so you can find the best loan. Use the shopping chart on page 3 to compare all the offers you receive.

Important dates

1. The interest rate for this GFE is available through _____. After this time, the interest rate, some of your loan Origination Charges, and the monthly payment shown below can change until you lock your interest rate.

2. This estimate for all other settlement charges is available through _____.

3. After you lock your interest rate, you must go to settlement within ___ days (your rate lock period) to receive the locked interest rate.

4. You must lock the interest rate at least ___ days before settlement.

Summary of your loan

Your initial loan amount is	$
Your loan term is	years
Your initial interest rate is	%
Your initial monthly amount owed for principal, interest, and any mortgage insurance is	$ per month
Can your interest rate rise?	☐ No ☐ Yes, it can rise to a maximum of %. The first change will be in .
Even if you make payments on time, can your loan balance rise?	☐ No ☐ Yes, it can rise to a maximum of $
Even if you make payments on time, can your monthly amount owed for principal, interest, and any mortgage insurance rise?	☐ No ☐ Yes, the first increase can be in and the monthly amount owed can rise to $. The maximum it can ever rise to is $.
Does your loan have a prepayment penalty?	☐ No ☐ Yes, your maximum prepayment penalty is $.
Does your loan have a balloon payment?	☐ No ☐ Yes, you have a balloon payment of $ due in years.

Escrow account information

Some lenders require an escrow account to hold funds for paying property taxes or other property-related charges in addition to your monthly amount owed of $ _____ .
Do we require you to have an escrow account for your loan?
☐ No, you do not have an escrow account. You must pay these charges directly when due.
☐ Yes, you have an escrow account. It may or may not cover all of these charges. Ask us.

Summary of your settlement charges

A	Your Adjusted Origination Charges *(See page 2.)*	$
B	Your Charges for All Other Settlement Services *(See page 2.)*	$
A + B	Total Estimated Settlement Charges	$

Good Faith Estimate (HUD-GFE) 1

Understanding your estimated settlement charges

Some of these charges can change at settlement. See the top of page 3 for more information.

Your Adjusted Origination Charges

1. Our origination charge
This charge is for getting this loan for you.

2. Your credit or charge (points) for the specific interest rate chosen

☐ The credit or charge for the interest rate of ☐ % is included in "Our origination charge." (See item 1 above.)

☐ You receive a credit of $ ☐ for this interest rate of ☐ %. This credit **reduces** your settlement charges.

☐ You pay a charge of $ ☐ for this interest rate of ☐ %. This charge (points) **increases** your total settlement charges.

The tradeoff table on page 3 shows that you can change your total settlement charges by choosing a different interest rate for this loan.

| **A** | Your Adjusted Origination Charges | $ |

Your Charges for All Other Settlement Services

3. Required services that we select
These charges are for services we require to complete your settlement. We will choose the providers of these services.

Service	Charge

4. Title services and lender's title insurance
This charge includes the services of a title or settlement agent, for example, and title insurance to protect the lender, if required.

5. Owner's title insurance
You may purchase an owner's title insurance policy to protect your interest in the property.

6. Required services that you can shop for
These charges are for other services that are required to complete your settlement. We can identify providers of these services or you can shop for them yourself. Our estimates for providing these services are below.

Service	Charge

7. Government recording charges
These charges are for state and local fees to record your loan and title documents.

8. Transfer taxes
These charges are for state and local fees on mortgages and home sales.

9. Initial deposit for your escrow account
This charge is held in an escrow account to pay future recurring charges on your property and includes ☐ all property taxes, ☐ all insurance, and ☐ other ☐

10. Daily interest charges
This charge is for the daily interest on your loan from the day of your settlement until the first day of the next month or the first day of your normal mortgage payment cycle. This amount is $ ☐ per day for ☐ days (if your settlement is ☐).

11. Homeowner's insurance
This charge is for the insurance you must buy for the property to protect from a loss, such as fire.

Policy	Charge

| **B** | Your Charges for All Other Settlement Services | $ |

| **A** + **B** | Total Estimated Settlement Charges | $ |

 Good Faith Estimate (HUD-GFE) 2

Instructions

Understanding which charges can change at settlement

This GFE estimates your settlement charges. At your settlement, you will receive a HUD-1, a form that lists your actual costs. Compare the charges on the HUD-1 with the charges on this GFE. Charges can change if you select your own provider and do not use the companies we identify. (See below for details.)

These charges **cannot increase** at settlement:	The total of these charges **can increase up to 10%** at settlement:	These charges **can change** at settlement:
■ Our origination charge ■ Your credit or charge (points) for the specific interest rate chosen (after you lock in your interest rate) ■ Your adjusted origination charges (after you lock in your interest rate) ■ Transfer taxes	■ Required services that we select ■ Title services and lender's title insurance (if we select them or you use companies we identify) ■ Owner's title insurance (if you use companies we identify) ■ Required services that you can shop for (if you use companies we identify) ■ Government recording charges	■ Required services that you can shop for (if you do not use companies we identify) ■ Title services and lender's title insurance (if you do not use companies we identify) ■ Owner's title insurance (if you do not use companies we identify) ■ Initial deposit for your escrow account ■ Daily interest charges ■ Homeowner's insurance

Using the tradeoff table

In this GFE, we offered you this loan with a particular interest rate and estimated settlement charges. However:

■ If you want to choose this same loan with **lower settlement charges,** then you will have a **higher interest rate.**
■ If you want to choose this same loan with a **lower interest rate,** then you will have **higher settlement charges.**

If you would like to choose an available option, you must ask us for a new GFE.

Loan originators have the option to complete this table. Please ask for additional information if the table is not completed.

	The loan in this GFE	The same loan with lower settlement charges	The same loan with a lower interest rate
Your initial loan amount	$	$	$
Your initial interest rate¹	%	%	%
Your initial monthly amount owed	$	$	$
Change in the monthly amount owed from this GFE	No change	You will pay $ **more** every month	You will pay $ **less** every month
Change in the amount you will pay at settlement with this interest rate	No change	Your settlement charges will be **reduced** by $	Your settlement charges will **increase** by $
How much your total estimated settlement charges will be	$	$	$

¹ *For an adjustable rate loan, the comparisons above are for the initial interest rate before adjustments are made.*

Using the shopping chart

Use this chart to compare GFEs from different loan originators. Fill in the information by using a different column for each GFE you receive. By comparing loan offers, you can shop for the best loan.

	This loan	Loan 2	Loan 3	Loan 4
Loan originator name				
Initial loan amount				
Loan term				
Initial interest rate				
Initial monthly amount owed				
Rate lock period				
Can interest rate rise?				
Can loan balance rise?				
Can monthly amount owed rise?				
Prepayment penalty?				
Balloon payment?				
Total Estimated Settlement Charges				

If your loan is sold in the future

Some lenders may sell your loan after settlement. Any fees lenders receive in the future cannot change the loan you receive or the charges you paid at settlement.

 Good Faith Estimate (HUD-GFE) 3

The HUD-1

Figure 14.3 (*see below*) illustrates a correct usage of the HUD-1 for the following scenario:

An owner has agreed to sell his property to a buyer for $357,000. The owner will pay the listing company 5 percent of this amount. The buyer paid $15,000 in earnest money with the contract. During contract negotiations, the seller agreed to contribute $3,000 toward the buyer's closing costs.

The buyer succeeded in obtaining conventional financing for $321,300 at 4.5 percent annual interest. The lender will not require mortgage insurance since the loan amount is only 90 percent of the value. The lender will require the buyer to pay interest at closing on the new loan for the 15 days from May 17 through the May 31. The buyer will purchase a homeowners insurance policy from Nationwide for $2,668.00 annually. The lender will collect money from the buyer to pay future real estate tax and insurance bills. These collected monies will be placed in an escrow account.

The closing date is May 17, 2011. The seller has to be out of town in May so he assigned a limited power of attorney to his sister to conclude the sale. The seller will owe real estate taxes at the closing; the $4,773 paid in early January was for 2010 (taxes are paid in arrears). Since the seller has already paid $225 to the Homeowners' Association for 2011, the buyer will reimburse the seller for the days remaining in 2011 after closing. The seller's existing mortgage loan will be paid in full at closing. The amount due includes unpaid principal plus accrued interest.

As you review the completed HUD-1 in Figure 14.3, locate each of the facts described in the above scenario. This should lead to a more complete understanding of this form.

FIGURE 14.3

Completed HUD-1 for the Closing Scenario

OMB Approval No. 2502-0265

 A. **Settlement Statement (HUD-1)**

B. Type of Loan		
1. ☐ FHA 2. ☐ RHS 3. ☒ Conv. Unins.	6. File Number:	7. Loan Number:	8. Mortgage Insurance Case Number:
4. ☐ VA 5. ☐ Conv. Ins.			

C. Note: This form is furnished to give you a statement of actual settlement costs. Amounts paid to and by the settlement agent are shown. Items marked "(p.o.c.)" were paid outside the closing; they are shown here for informational purposes and are not included in the totals.

D. Name & Address of Borrower:	E. Name & Address of Seller:	F. Name & Address of Lender:

G. Property Location:	H. Settlement Agent:	I. Settlement Date:
Dorchester County, South Carolina	H.L. Smith Title Co.	May 17, 2011
	Place of Settlement: Summerville, SC 29483	

J. Summary of Borrower's Transaction		K. Summary of Seller's Transaction	
100. Gross Amount Due from Borrower		**400. Gross Amount Due to Seller**	
101. Contract sales price	$357,000.00	401. Contract sales price	$357,000.00
102. Personal property		402. Personal property	
103. Settlement charges to borrower (line 1400)	$11,067.10	403.	
104.		404.	
105.		405.	
Adjustment for items paid by seller in advance		**Adjustment for items paid by seller in advance**	
106. City/town taxes to		406. City/town taxes to	
107. County taxes to		407. County taxes to	
108. Assessments to		408. Assessments to	
109. HOA $225/year; 5/18/2011 to 12/31/2011	$140.55	409. HOA $225/year; 5/18/2011 to 12/31/2011	$140.55
110.		410.	
111.		411.	
112.		412.	
120. Gross Amount Due from Borrower	$368,207.65	**420. Gross Amount Due to Seller**	$357,140.55
200. Amount Paid by or in Behalf of Borrower		**500. Reductions In Amount Due to seller**	
201. Deposit or earnest money	$15,000.00	501. Excess deposit (see instructions)	
202. Principal amount of new loan(s)	$321,300.00	502. Settlement charges to seller (line 1400)	$19,200.90
203. Existing loan(s) taken subject to		503. Existing loan(s) taken subject to	
204.		504. Payoff of first mortgage loan to Wells Fargo	$224,328.17
205.		505. Payoff of second mortgage loan	
206.		506.	
207.		507.	
208.		508.	
209. Closing cost paid by seller	$3,000.00	509. Closing cost paid by seller	$3,000.00
Adjustments for items unpaid by seller		**Adjustments for items unpaid by seller**	
210. City/town taxes to		510. City/town taxes to	
211. County taxes 1/1/2011 to 5/17/2011	$1,791.51	511. County taxes 1/1/2011 to 5/17/2011	$1,791.51
212. Assessments to		512. Assessments to	
213.		513.	
214.		514.	
215.		515.	
216.		516.	
217.		517.	
218.		518.	
219.		519.	
220. Total Paid by/for Borrower	$341,091.51	**520. Total Reduction Amount Due Seller**	$248,320.58
300. Cash at Settlement from/to Borrower		**600. Cash at Settlement to/from Seller**	
301. Gross amount due from borrower (line 120)	$368,207.65	601. Gross amount due to seller (line 420)	$357,140.55
302. Less amounts paid by/for borrower (line 220)	($341,091.51)	602. Less reductions in amounts due seller (line 520)	($248,320.58)
303. Cash ☒ From ☐ To Borrower	$27,116.14	603. Cash ☒ To ☐ From Seller	$108,819.97

The Public Reporting Burden for this collection of information is estimated at 35 minutes per response for collecting, reviewing, and reporting the data. This agency may not collect this information, and you are not required to complete this form, unless it displays a currently valid OMB control number. No confidentiality is assured; this disclosure is mandatory. This is designed to provide the parties to a RESPA covered transaction with information during the settlement process.

L. Settlement Charges

700. Total Real Estate Broker Fees

	Paid From Borrower's Funds at Settlement	Paid From Seller's Funds at Settlement
Division of commission (line 700) as follows :		
701. $ to		
702. $ to		
703. Commission paid at settlement to Laurel Smith Realty		$17,850.00
704.		

800. Items Payable in Connection with Loan

			Paid From Borrower's Funds at Settlement	Paid From Seller's Funds at Settlement
801. Our origination charge	$ 3,213.00	(from GFE #1)		
802. Your credit or charge (points) for the specific interest rate chosen	$	(from GFE #2)		
803. Your adjusted origination charges		(from GFE #A)	$3,213.00	
804. Appraisal fee to LAC Appraisers LLC	POC $375.00	(from GFE #3)		
805. Credit report to		(from GFE #3)		
806. Tax service to		(from GFE #3)		
807. Flood certification to		(from GFE #3)		
808.				
809.				
810.				
811.				

900. Items Required by Lender to be Paid in Advance

			Paid From Borrower's Funds at Settlement	Paid From Seller's Funds at Settlement
901. Daily interest charges from 5/17/11 to 5/31/11 @ $ 39.61 /day		(from GFE #10)	$594.18	
902. Mortgage insurance premium for months to		(from GFE #3)		
903. Homeowner's insurance for 1.0 years to Nationwide		(from GFE #11)	$2,668.00	
904.				

1000. Reserves Deposited with Lender

				Paid From Borrower's Funds at Settlement	Paid From Seller's Funds at Settlement
1001. Initial deposit for your escrow account			(from GFE #9)	$2,731.07	
1002. Homeowner's insurance	4	months @ $ 222.33	per month $ 889.32		
1003. Mortgage insurance		months @ $	per month $		
1004. Property Taxes	9	months @ $ 397.75	per month $ 3,579.75		
1005.		months @ $	per month $		
1006.		months @ $	per month $		
1007. Aggregate Adjustment		-$ 1,738.00			

1100. Title Charges

			Paid From Borrower's Funds at Settlement	Paid From Seller's Funds at Settlement
1101. Title services and lender's title insurance		(from GFE #4)	$885.00	
1102. Settlement or closing fee to H.L. Smith Title Co.	$ 350.00			
1103. Owner's title insurance AAA Title Insurance Inc.		(from GFE #5)	$935.85	
1104. Lender's title insurance AAA Title Insurance Inc.	$ 100.00			
1105. Lender's title policy limit $ 321,300.00				
1106. Owner's title policy limit $ 357,000.00				
1107. Agent's portion of the total title insurance premium to H.L. Smith Title Co.	$ 621.51			
1108. Underwriter's portion of the total title insurance premium to AAA Title Insurance Inc.	$ 414.34			
1109.				
1110.				
1111.				

1200. Government Recording and Transfer Charges

			Paid From Borrower's Funds at Settlement	Paid From Seller's Funds at Settlement
1201. Government recording charges to Recorder's Office		(from GFE #7)	$40.00	
1202. Deed $ 10.00 Mortgage $ 30.00 Release $				
1203. Transfer taxes		(from GFE #8)		
1204. City/County tax/stamps Deed $ 1,320.90 Mortgage $				$1,320.90
1205. State tax/stamps Deed $ Mortgage $				
1206. Record POA to Recorder's Office				$30.00

1300. Additional Settlement Charges

			Paid From Borrower's Funds at Settlement	Paid From Seller's Funds at Settlement
1301. Required services that you can shop for POC $105.00		(from GFE #6)		
1302. Termite Report (CL-100) to Hardy Pest Control	POC: $ 150.00			
1303.	$			
1304.				
1305.				

1400. Total Settlement Charges (enter on lines 103, Section J and 502, Section K)

	Paid From Borrower's Funds at Settlement	Paid From Seller's Funds at Settlement
1400. Total Settlement Charges (enter on lines 103, Section J and 502, Section K)	$11,067.10	$19,200.90

Comparison of Good Faith Estimate (GFE) and HUD-1 Charrges		Good Faith Estimate	HUD-1
Charges That Cannot Increase	**HUD-1 Line Number**		
Our origination charge	# 801	$3,300.00	$3,213.00
Your credit or charge (points) for the specific interest rate chosen	# 802		
Your adjusted origination charges	# 803	$3,300.00	$3,213.00
Transfer taxes	# 1203	$1,713.56	

Charges That In Total Cannot Increase More Than 10%		Good Faith Estimate	HUD-1
Government recording charges	# 1201	$43.00	$40.00
Appraisal Fee	# 804	$400.00	$375.00
	#		
	#		
	#		
	#		
	#		
	#		
Total		$443.00	$415.00
Increase between GFE and HUD-1 Charges		$ -28 or	-6.32 %

Charges That Can Change		Good Faith Estimate	HUD-1
Initial deposit for your escrow account	# 1001	$2,851.16	$2,731.07
Daily interest charges $ 39.61 /day	# 901	$396.12	$594.18
Homeowner's insurance	# 903	$2,500.00	$2,668.00
Title Services and Lender's Title Ins.	# 1101	$1,470.85	$885.00
Owner's Title Insurance	# 1103	$700.00	$935.85
Termite Report (CL-100)	# 1302	$125.00	$150.00

Loan Terms

Your initial loan amount is	$ 321,300.00
Your loan term is	30 years
Your initial interest rate is	4.5 %
Your initial monthly amount owed for principal, interest, and any mortgage insurance is	$ 1628.99 includes [X] Principal [X] Interest [ ] Mortgage Insurance
Can your interest rate rise?	[X] No [ ] Yes, it can rise to a maximum of %. The first change will be on and can change again every after . Every change date, your interest rate can increase or decrease by %. Over the life of the loan, your interest rate is guaranteed to never be **lower** than % or **higher** than %.
Even if you make payments on time, can your loan balance rise?	[X] No [ ] Yes, it can rise to a maximum of $
Even if you make payments on time, can your monthly amount owed for principal, interest, and mortgage insurance rise?	[X] No [ ] Yes, the first increase can be on and the monthly amount owed can rise to $. The maximum it can ever rise to is $.
Does your loan have a prepayment penalty?	[X] No [ ] Yes, your maximum prepayment penalty is $
Does your loan have a balloon payment?	[X] No [ ] Yes, you have a balloon payment of $ due in years on .
Total monthly amount owed including escrow account payments	[ ] You do not have a monthly escrow payment for items, such as property taxes and homeowner's insurance. You must pay these items directly yourself. [X] You have an additional monthly escrow payment of $ 620.08 that results in a total initial monthly amount owed of $ 2249.07 . This includes principal, interest, any mortgage insurance and any items checked below: [X] Property taxes [X] Homeowner's insurance [ ] Flood insurance [ ] [ ] [ ]

Note: If you have any questions about the Settlement Charges and Loan Terms listed on this form, please contact your lender.

NOTE: The prorations shown in Figure 14.3 are consistent with what was discussed in Chapter 13. Notice that taxes (lines 211 and 511) and Home Owners' Association dues (lines 109 and 409) were prorated. Can you determine whether the escrow officer used to or *through* the day of closing?

ADDITIONAL PRACTICE

The Uniform Settlement Statement is the HUD-1. It will be used at most, if not all, of the sale or loan closings which agents attend. The following questions and exercises are designed to familiarize the learner with this form. Use Figure 14.1 to complete these problems.

1. Identify each subgroup of section L (page 2). For example, the 700 subgroup covers Total Real Estate Broker Fees.

   a. 700.   Total Real Estate Broker Fees
   b. 800.   _____
   c. 900.   _____
   d. 1000. _____
   e. 1100. _____
   f. 1200. _____
   g. 1300. _____

2. Find Section J, Summary of the Borrower's Transaction, on page 1. Which of the following is/are *TRUE?*

   a. Section 100 is credits, 200 is debits, and 300 has credits minus debits.
   b. Section 100 is debits, 200 is credits, and 300 has debits minus credits.
   c. The borrower's debits minus credits equals amount due from/to the buyer.
   d. The borrower's credits minus debits equals amount due from/to the buyer.

3. Find Section K, Summary of the Seller's Transaction, on page 1. Which of the following is/are *TRUE?*

   a. Section 400 is credits, 500 is debits, and 600 has credits minus debits.
   b. Section 400 is debits, 500 is credits, and 600 has debits minus credits.
   c. The seller's debits minus credits equals amount due to/from the seller.
   d. The seller's credits minus debits equals amount due to/from the seller.

4. Compare adjacent subgroups (100s to 400s, 200s to 500s) in section J to those in section K. Which of the following is(are) *TRUE?*

   a. Where credits are entered in J, debits are entered in K.
   b. Where credits are entered in J, credits are entered in K.
   c. There is no set pattern or relationship.
   d. The top subgroup minus the second subgroup equals line 303/603.

5. Compare adjacent line items in sections J and K. Identify the nine line items that would have the same amount of money entered in Sections J and K. For example, line 101 debits the buyer for the sales price; then, on line 401, the seller is credited for the same amount of money.

   a. __101__ and __401__
   b. _____ and _____
   c. _____ and _____
   d. _____ and _____
   e. _____ and _____
   f. _____ and _____
   g. _____ and _____
   h. _____ and _____
   i. _____ and _____

SOLUTIONS: PROBLEMS IN CHAPTER 14

1.

		Buyer		Seller	
		Debit	**Credit**	**Debit**	**Credit**
a.	Sales price	$100,000			$100,000
b.	Assumed loan balance		$40,500	$40,500	
c.	Accrued interest on assumed loan		300	300	
d.	Tax reserve account	600			600
e.	Accrued portion of real estate tax		450	450	
f.	Prepaid security service	175			175
g.	Fuel oil in tank	150			150
h.	Prorated accrued water bill		100	100	
i.	Unearned rents collected		805	805	
j.	Tenants' security deposits		2,000	2,000	

2.

	Buyer		Seller	
	Debit	**Credit**	**Debit**	**Credit**
Sales price	$240,000			$240,000
Earnest money		$ 20,000		
Broker's commission			$ 16,800	
Subtotals	$240,000	20,000	16,800	$240,000
Due from buyer at closing		220,000		
Due to seller at closing			223,200	
Totals	**$240,000**	**$240,000**	**$240,000**	**$240,000**

SOLUTIONS: ADDITIONAL PRACTICE

1. 700: Total Real Estate Broker Fees
    800: Items Payable in Association with Loan
    900: Items Required by Lender to Be Paid in Advance
    1000: Reserves Deposited with Lender
    1100: Title Charges
    1200: Government Recording and Transfer Charges
    1300: Additional Settlement Charges

2. b and c

3. a and d

4. a and d

5. 101 and 401
    102 and 402
    106 and 406
    107 and 407
    108 and 408
    203 and 503
    210 and 510
    211 and 511
    212 and 512

Lease Calculations

Commercial leases generally run for three or more years and contain clauses that permit periodic increases of rent. Such leases can be quite complex and usually involve the assistance of an attorney.

Retail leases may call for a base rental amount plus a percentage of gross sales in excess of an amount established in the lease. Leases for office space may call for rental escalations based on increases in one of the U.S. government consumer price indexes (CPIs) for a given geographic area. Other commercial and industrial leases may pass through some or all of the operating expenses to the tenant.

At the conclusion of your work in this chapter, you will be able to calculate

- the rent for a given number of square feet when rent is expressed as gross rent per square foot,

- the total rent due under a percentage lease, and

- a rental increase called for in a lease with a CPI escalation clause.

RENT PER SQUARE FOOT

Commercial rent is usually stated as being so many dollars per square foot on an annual or monthly basis.

E X A M P L E :   The rental rate in a new office building is $12.10 per square foot. What is the *monthly* rent for a space having 1,800 square feet?

First find the total annual rent:

$$1,800 \text{ square feet} \times \$12.10 \text{ per square foot} = \$21,780$$

Then convert the annual rent to monthly rent:

$$\$21,780 \text{ annual rent} \div 12 \text{ months} = \$1,815$$

Or the rent might be stated on a monthly basis and then converted to an annual rate per square foot for comparison. If the monthly rent is $2,000 for a 2,220-square-foot space, what is the annual rate per square foot?

First find the total annual rent:

$$\$2,000 \times 12 \text{ months} = \$24,000$$

Then find the rent per square foot:

$$\$24,000 \text{ annual rent} \div 2,200 \text{ square feet} = \$10.91 \text{ per square foot (rounded)}$$

PERCENTAGE LEASE

Under a percentage lease, the annual rent is a percentage of the gross sales, usually subject to a minimum monthly payment. The tenant generally pays a minimum monthly rent plus a percentage of gross sales income if it exceeds the stipulated minimum amount. Some leases may provide for a minimum (base) rent plus a percentage of all gross sales income. This type of lease is usually associated with retail properties.

E X A M P L E :   A percentage lease calls for a minimum monthly rental fee of $500, plus 6 percent of gross annual sales in excess of $100,000 per year. Based on gross annual sales of $250,000, compute the total rent for the year.

Remember:
The lease rate quoted per square foot is on an annual basis. Divide by 12 to get a monthly rate.

Residential leases are paid on a monthly basis.

First, find the minimum annual rent:

$$\$500 \text{ per month} \times 12 \text{ months} = \$6,000$$

Then, find the percentage of gross sales to add to the minimum:

$250,000   actual gross sales
$-100,000   sales covered by minimum rent
$150,000   sales subject to percentage rent

$$\$150,000 \times 0.06 = \$9,000 \text{ additional rent due}$$

The total annual rent is the minimum plus the additional rent due:

$$\$6,000 + \$9,000 = \$15,000$$

Minimum or Base Rent

EXAMPLE: Mr. Muncie pays 2 percent of his total gross sales for rent, with a minimum base rental of $1,000 per month. In the past year, his sales volume was $400,000. How much rent did he pay? At what sales volume will Mr. Muncie effectively begin to pay percentage rent?

$1,000 base monthly rental × 12 months = $12,000 minimum annual rent
$400,000 sales volume × 0.02 = $8,000 percentage rent

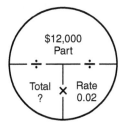

Mr. Muncie paid the minimum rent, $12,000, because it was greater than the percentage rent.

$12,000 ÷ 0.02 = $600,000 total gross sales to reach minimum rent

When Mr. Muncie exceeds $600,000 in total gross sales, his percentage rent will be greater than the minimum rent and he will pay that rather than the minimum rent.

1. If a percentage lease requires a tenant to pay $400 monthly minimum rent plus 4 percent of gross annual sales in excess of $120,000, what was the total rent paid for a year in which gross sales amounted to $360,000?

2. A lease provides for the tenant to pay $450 monthly minimum rent plus 4 percent of gross sales in excess of $135,000 per year. What were the gross sales last year if the lessee paid a total rent of $12,420?

3. A business owner has operated a flower shop for several years in a highly desirable, active shopping center. The company has a lease requiring a $500-per-month base rental plus a percentage of gross sales in excess of $275,000 per year. If gross sales for the year totaled $341,250 and rent paid amounted to $11,300, what percentage rate was contained in the lease?

4. A delicatessen pays a monthly rental of $330 plus 4 percent of annual gross sales exceeding $99,000. Last year, the gross sales were $300,000. What is the current monthly rent for the delicatessen?

5. The Ski Shop had a three-year lease that required a $600-per-month rental minimum plus an escalating percentage of annual gross sales in excess of $180,000. Complete the schedule that follows by determining how much rent was paid each year:

Year	Percentage of Gross Sales	Actual Gross Sales	Annual Rent
1	4	$200,000	
2	4.5	$160,000	
3	5	$250,000	

6. ABC Property Management collects rent from four stores in a small shopping center. Last year, ABC collected $12,500 from tenant A, $14,000 from tenant B, and $9,000 from Tenant C. Rent is also collected from tenant D, a long-standing tenant, who pays 5 percent of all gross sales above $60,000 along with a minimum payment of $375 per month. His gross sales last year were $59,990. How much annual rent did ABC Property Management collect from tenant D last year?

INDEX (VARIABLE) LEASE CALCULATIONS

Every month, the U.S. government, through the Bureau of Labor Statistics, publishes data that reflect the costs of goods and services. These costs are shown as percentages of change over the past year and the past month. The percentages are then used to adjust the CPI. In general, index numbers indicate the change in the size of something over time, by comparison with its size at some specified time. Specifically, the CPI compares the number of dollars needed to buy a certain bundle of goods each year with the number of dollars needed to buy those goods in 1967. Thus, 1967 is the base year for the CPI. The CPI for 1967 is 100. In a later year, when the CPI was 303, the bundle of goods that would have cost $100 in 1967 would now cost $303.

A landlord can use the CPI to help decide on the size of annual rent adjustments. By tying the adjustments to this index, the landlord is better able to offset the effects of inflation on property management expenses. Other indexes are used for lease adjustments; however, for simplicity of illustration, only the CPI will be used in this book. The math for using another index is the same as the math involved in using the CPI.

First, divide the current index by the previous year's index to obtain the adjustment factor:

$$\frac{308 \ (1997 \ \text{index})}{299 \ (1996 \ \text{index})} = 1.030 \ (\text{rounded})$$

Then, multiply the rent by the adjustment factor to calculate the adjusted rent:

$$\$600 \ (\text{for example}) \times 1.03 = \$618$$

Remember:

When computing leases using the change in the CPI index, multiply the current index by the original lease amount and divide by the original index. This will give you the new lease amount.

7. When a new office space was initially leased for $4,000 per month, the CPI stood at 300. What will the adjusted rent be in each of the next three years if the indexes at each adjustment time are 305, 309, and 315, respectively?

ADDITIONAL PRACTICE

When you have finished these problems, check your answers at the end of the chapter. If you miss any of the problems, review this chapter.

1. A small business owner pays a monthly minimum rent of $300 plus 4.5 percent of gross sales in excess of $180,000 per year. If gross sales last year were $225,000, how much monthly rent does the business owner pay?
   a. $168.75
   b. $313.50
   c. $468.75
   d. $472.85

2. If the lease on a 1,750-square-foot office is $14.50 per square foot, what is the monthly rent (rounded)?
   a. $2,022.44
   b. $2,114.58
   c. $2,212.51
   d. $25,375

3. A craft shop pays $600 monthly minimum rent plus a percentage of gross sales in excess of $144,000 per year. Last year, gross sales totaled $350,000 and the total rent paid amounted to $17,500. What percentage of gross sales is required by this lease?
   a. 0.02 or 2 percent
   b. 0.05 or 5 percent
   c. 0.0528 or 5.28 percent
   d. 0.055 or 5.5 percent

4. A nail salon lease provides for the tenant to pay a minimum monthly rental of $420 plus 6 percent of gross annual sales exceeding $100,000. What were gross annual sales last year if the tenant paid a total of $8,640 in rent?
   a. $100,000
   b. $130,334
   c. $158,769
   d. $160,000

5. A small flower shop's lease requires a minimum monthly rental of $600 plus a percentage of gross annual sales in excess of $180,000. If gross sales for last year were $264,000 and the tenant's total rent was $13,080, what is the percentage rate stated in the lease?
   a. 6 percent
   b. 6.5 percent
   c. 7 percent
   d. 7.5 percent

6. A tenant's lease requires a payment of $2,000 per month. If the lease provides for an adjustment based on the CPI, which was 300 a year ago and is now 306, what will the new monthly payment be?
   a. $2,040
   b. $2,120
   c. $2,200
   d. $2,250

7. A store tenant's lease called for $600 per month guaranteed rental plus 4.5 percent of gross annual sales exceeding $180,000. When gross annual sales were $164,000, what was the amount of the tenant's total annual rent?
   a. $7,200
   b. $7,380
   c. $7,500
   d. $8,100

8. An accounting business is leasing office space for which it is paying annual rent of $18 per rentable square foot. What number of square feet is the business leasing if the monthly rent payment is $4,500?
   a. 2,750 square feet
   b. 3,000 square feet
   c. 3,200 square feet
   d. 3,350 square feet

9. A store lease provides for minimum monthly rental payments of $425 plus 8 percent of gross annual sales exceeding $160,000. Last year, when gross annual sales were $229,500, what was the tenant's total gross rent bill for the year?

    a. $10,660
    b. $13,787
    c. $14,100
    d. $14,659

10. Mr. Jones's lease requires that he pay a monthly minimum rent of $250 plus 5 percent of gross sales exceeding $60,000. Mr. Jones paid $10,500 in rent last year. What were his gross sales?

    a. $60,000
    b. $160,000
    c. $210,000
    d. $215,000

11. A small salon has a lease that provides for the tenant to pay a minimum monthly rent of $375 plus 4.5 percent of gross sales in excess of $100,000 per year. The gross sales last year were $250,000. What was annual rent?

    a. $4,500
    b. $6,750
    c. $10,500
    d. $11,250

12. Two years ago, the Salon's rent came to $8,100 (see problem 11). What were the gross sales for that year?

    a. $175,000
    b. $179,500
    c. $179,880
    d. $180,000

13. Your office rent last year was $2,460 per month. Your lease calls for you to pay increased rent based on the prior year's upturns in the CPI tracked by the U.S. government. What will your rent be in the coming year if the CPI stood at 332 when you signed your lease and has increased by 50 points last year?

    a. $2,149.26
    b. $2,380.48
    c. $2,684.14
    d. $2,830.48

14. What is the monthly rent for a 3,680-square-foot space if the annual rent being charged is $18.50 per square foot?

    a. $4,836.24
    b. $5,673.33
    c. $6,808
    d. $6,880

15. A lease calls for base rent of $12,000 per year plus 4 percent of gross sales in excess of $100,000. What is your total rent in a year in which your business generates $86,000 in gross sales?

    a. $11,500
    b. $12,000
    c. $13,500
    d. $14,200

SOLUTIONS: PROBLEMS IN CHAPTER 15

1. $360,000 – $120,000 = $240,000
   $240,000 × 0.04 = $9,600
   $400 × 12 = $4,800
   $4,800 + $9,600 = $14,400

2. $450 × 12 = $5,400
   $12,420 – $5,400 = $7,020
   $7,020 ÷ 0.04 = $175,500
   $175,500 + $135,000 = $310,500

3. $500 × 12 = $6,000
   $11,300 – $6,000 = $5,300
   $341,250 – $275,000 = $66,250
   $5,300 ÷ $66,250 = 0.08 or 8%

4. $300,000 – $99,000 = $201,000
   $201,000 × 0.04 = $8,040
   $8,040 ÷ 12 = $670
   $670 + $330 = $1,000

5. 1. $600 × 12 = $7,200
      $200,000 – $180,000 = $20,000
      $20,000 × 0.04 = $800
      $800 + $7,200 = $8,000
   2. Because $160,000 is less than $180,000, only base rent of $7,200 is due.
   3. $250,000 – $180,000 = $70,000
      $70,000 × 0.05 = $3,500
      $3,500 + $7,200 = $10,700

6. $375 × 12 = $4,500

7. 1. 305 ÷ 300 × $4,000 = $4,066.67 (rounded)
   2. 309 ÷ 300 × $4,000 = $4,120
   3. 315 ÷ 300 × $4,000 = $4,200

SOLUTIONS: ADDITIONAL PRACTICE

1. (c) $225,000 – $180,000 = $45,000
   4.5% = 0.045
   $45,000 × 0.045 ÷ 12 = $168.75
   $168.75 + $300 = $468.75

2. (b) 1,750 square feet × $14.50 = $25,375
   $25,375 ÷ 12 = $2,114.58 (rounded)

3. (b) $350,000 – $144,000 = $206,000
   $600 x 12 = $7,200
   $17,500 – $7,200 = $10,300
   $10,300 ÷ $206,000 = 0.05 or 5%

4. (d) $420 × 12 = $5,040
   $8,640 – $5,040 = $3,600
   $3,600 ÷ 0.06 = $60,000
   $60,000 + $100,000 = $160,000

5. (c) $264,000 – $180,000 = $84,000
   $600 × 12 = $7,200
   $13,080 – $7,200 = $5,880
   $5,880 ÷ $84,000 = 0.07 or 7%

6. (a) 306 ÷ 300 × $2,000 = $2,040

7. (a) $600 × 12 = $7,200

8. (b) $4,500 × 12 ÷ $18 = 3,000 square feet

9. (a) $425 × 12 = $5,100
   $229,500 – $160,000 = $69,500
   $69,500 × 0.08 = $5,560
   $5,560 + $5,100 = $10,660

10. (c) $250 \times 12 = \$3,000$
  $\$10,500 - \$3,000 = \$7,500$
  $\$7,500 \div 0.05 = \$150,000$
  $\$150,000 + \$60,000 = \$210,000$

11. (d) $\$250,000 - \$100,000 = \$150,000$
  $4.5\% = 0.045$
  $\$150,000 \times 0.045 = \$6,750$
  $\$375 \times 12 = \$4,500$
  $\$4,500 + \$6,750 = \$11,250$

12. (d) $\$8,100 - \$4,500 = \$3,600$
  $\$3,600 \div 0.045 = \$80,000$
  $\$80,000 + \$100,000 = \$180,000$

13. (d) $332 + 50 = 382$
  $382 \div 332 = 1.15060$
  $1.15060 \times \$2,460 = \$2,830.48$ (rounded)

14. (b) 3,680 square feet $\times \$18.50 \div 12 = \$5,673.33$ (rounded)

15. (b) $12,000

PRACTICE MAKES PERFECT

PART 3

COMPREHENSIVE REVIEW EXAM

Work the 50 questions that follow in preparation for the Final Exam in this course and as a review of math topics prior to taking your state licensing examination. As a suggestion, work the problems that seem the easiest first, followed by the ones that are more challenging for you, and finally, the ones that on first read seem the most complicated and/or time consuming. This approach will tend to minimize any stress that you might feel. You will discover that you know more than you think by following this approach. You should have ample time to work a few challenging problems. As always, check your answers and go back into the specific chapter for further review if you are having difficulty with certain problems.

1. If a property is purchased for $300,000 and later sold for $345,000, what percentage of profit is earned?
   a. 14 percent
   b. 15 percent
   c. 110 percent
   d. 115 percent

2. A bank-owned property was listed at $200,000 and after 6 months on the market sold for 60 percent of the list price. For how much did it sell?
   a. $120,000
   b. $170,000
   c. $180,000
   d. $250,000

3. A seller listed her home at $100,000 and later sold it for 90 percent of the list price. The buyer sold the property six months later for $100,000. What percentage of profit did the buyer realize?
   a. 10 percent
   b. 11.1 percent
   c. 12 percent
   d. 15 percent

4. The assessed value of a home is $132,500, which is 53 percent of market value. What is the market value of this home?
   a. $202,725
   b. $205,000
   c. $250,000
   d. $250,725

5. A listing broker charged Andrea 6 percent of the sales price to sell her home. The broker split the fee giving 40 percent of the total fee to a selling broker, who split the fee equally with the salesperson who sold the property. What sales price was paid if the salesperson received a commission check for $1,200?
   a. $40,000
   b. $80,000
   c. $92,500
   d. $100,000

6. If a seller is charged 6 percent commission on the first $100,000 of the sales price, 5 percent on the second $100,000, and 3.5 percent on the balance of the sales price, what will the seller pay in commission if his home sells for $486,500?
   a. $6,000
   b. $10,027.50
   c. $21,027.50
   d. $29,190

7. The sales associate received a commission check for $18,000 for selling a property. If he received 60 percent of the total commission and the house sold for $300,000, what rate of commission was charged?
   a. 5 percent
   b. 6 percent
   c. 7 percent
   d. 10 percent

8. A property is listed for $1.4 million and sells for $1.2 million. If the broker charges an 8 percent commission, gives the listing salesperson 10 percent of the total commission, and splits the balance equally with the selling salesperson, what would the salesperson earn for both listing and selling this property?
   a. $52,800
   b. $60,000
   c. $72,000
   d. $120,000

9. A seller received $156,000 after paying her broker a negotiated 4 percent brokerage fee. What was the selling price of her home?
   a. $156,400
   b. $159,784
   c. $162,240
   d. $162,500

10. You purchase a lot measuring 75 feet by 125 feet for $4.80 per square foot. During your ownership, the street is paved and a paving lien of $2.50 per front foot is placed against the property. What must the property's sales price be if you wish to realize a 15 percent net profit after you pay off the paving lien, pay $1,860 in closing costs, and pay your broker a 7 percent brokerage fee?
   a. $51,750
   b. $53,797.50
   c. $57,563.33
   d. $57,846.77

11. If you purchased a bank owned property for $80,000 and sold it for $96,000, what percentage of profit would you realize?
   a. 10 percent
   b. 18 percent
   c. 20 percent
   d. 25 percent

12. A property sold for $240,000, which was 80 percent of the list price. What was the list price?
   a. $282,353
   b. $288,000
   c. $295,000
   d. $300,000

13. If you purchased a property for the list price less 20 percent and sold it for the list price plus 10 percent, what percentage of profit would you realize?
   a. 20 percent
   b. 25 percent
   c. 37.5 percent
   d. 80 percent

14. The area of a rectangle 75 feet by 150 feet is
   a. 416.67 square yards.
   b. 600 linear feet.
   c. 1,250 square yards.
   d. 9,375 square feet.

15. You have purchased a tract of land that measures 800 feet by 545 feet. You plan to develop it into building lots measuring 60 feet by 100 feet. If you set aside a strip of land 800 feet by 20 feet for a road, how many building lots can you create?
   a. 60.5 lots
   b. 65 lots
   c. 70 lots
   d. 72.67 lots

16. What will it cost to purchase three-fifths of a six-acre tract at $2.25 per square foot?
   a. $156,816
   b. $261,360
   c. $294,030
   d. $352,836

17. Calculate the cost to build a 3-inch-thick patio measuring 48 feet by 18 feet if concrete will cost $70 per cubic yard and the workers will charge $5 per square foot for finish work.
   a. $3,240
   b. $4,680
   c. $4,880
   d. $5,160

18. You purchase a property for $185,000, of which 25 percent is land value. What is the annual depreciation of the improvement if depreciated over 40 years?
    a. $1,156.25
    b. $3,468.75
    c. $4,625
    d. $5,550

19. A property was purchased for $235,000. At the time of purchase, the land was worth 22 percent of the total property value. The purchaser held the property for seven years, during which time the land appreciated 6 percent per year straight-line and the building depreciated 2.5 percent per year straight-line. What is the value of the property at the end of the seven years?
    a. $224,636.50
    b. $232,081.46
    c. $233,623.29
    d. $243,225

20. If $50,000 in cash is paid down on a $250,000 property having land value of $60,000, how much can be depreciated over the useful life of the property?
    a. $60,000
    b. $190,000
    c. $200,000
    d. $250,000

21. The four units in a fourplex rent at $250 each per month. If the property generates $7,200 in annual operating expenses and maintains an occupancy rate of 95 percent, what is the property's indicated value to an investor seeking a 9 percent annual rate of return?
    a. $43,200
    b. $46,666.67
    c. $53,333.33
    d. $58,967.43

22. Using the cost approach, calculate the indicated value of a property with a 2,300 square-foot building sitting on an $18,000 plot of land if construction costs in this area are $74 per square foot. (The building's effective age is eight years, and it appears to have a remaining useful life of 42 years.)
    a. $142,968
    b. $155,781
    c. $160,968
    d. $188,200

23. ABC Bank collected $8,400 in principal and interest at the end of six months on a term loan of $8,000. What rate of interest did the borrower pay?
    a. 10 percent
    b. 12 percent
    c. 15 percent
    d. 20 percent

24. How long will it take for $15,000 to yield $2,250 at 5 percent annual simple interest?
    a. 9 months
    b. 12 months
    c. 36 months
    d. 4 years

25. If an interest payment of $300 is made every three months on a $10,000 loan, what annual rate of interest is being charged?
    a. 10 percent
    b. 12 percent
    c. 15 percent
    d. 18 percent

26. Bob and Judy want to purchase a home for $270,000 with a 90 percent conventional loan. If the lender uses qualifying ratios of 28/36, how much verifiable income must they show to qualify for a 30-year loan that requires monthly principal and interest payments of $6 per $1,000? (The annual taxes are $3,600 and the annual insurance premium will be $1,800.)
   a. $6,600.67
   b. $6,729.89
   c. $6,789.24
   d. $6,814,29

27. If you are required to pay 1.5 discount points, a 1-point loan origination fee, a 0.75 point private mortgage insurance premium, and $3,800 for other closing costs and prepaids, how much cash will you need to close the 90 percent conventional loan on your new $148,500 home? (You have previously deposited $8,000 in earnest money with the escrow officer.)
   a. $8,143.63
   b. $13,943.63
   c. $14,993.63
   d. $18,143.63

28. A buyer can obtain a 95 percent conventional loan on a home selling for $337,600. Her required down payment will be
   a. $13,380.
   b. $16,875.
   c. $18,440.
   d. $18,480.

29. Javier can obtain a 30-year, 90 percent conventional loan at 4.5 percent interest that will require monthly principal and interest payments of $5.07 per $1,000. If his annual gross income is $62,500 and the lender will permit him to devote 25 percent of his gross monthly income to his monthly principal and interest payment, how much loan can he obtain?
   a. $255,675.34
   b. $256,820.51
   c. $256,900.21
   d. $256,998.78

30. A property has a market value of $348,000 in an area where a 53 percent assessment ratio is used. What is the annual tax bill if taxes are charged at $4.25 per $100 of assessed value?
   a. $783.87
   b. $1,479
   c. $7,838.70
   d. $14,790

31. A property is assessed at $175,000. If the tax rate is 23 mills, what is the amount of the annual tax bill?
   a. $230
   b. $402.50
   c. $3,450
   d. $4,025

32. A home is valued at $150,000 and assessed for 60 percent of its value. If the tax bill is $2,700, what is the tax rate per $100 of valuation?
   a. $3
   b. $6
   c. $8
   d. $27

33. Your new home has a market value of $152,000. The taxes in the area are levied on 66 percent of market value at a rate of $2.50 per $100 of assessed value. What will be the amount of your first annual tax bill?
   a. $1,003
   b. $1,672
   c. $2,508
   d. $3,800

34. The Johnsons are selling their home to the Cain family for $108,000. The Cains will assume the present loan balance of $28,000, the Johnsons will carry back a second loan for $40,000, and the Cains will pay the difference in cash. What will be the amount of the transfer tax if the state requires $0.50 per $500 or fraction thereof and exempts assumed loans?
   a. $80
   b. $104
   c. $120
   d. $160

35. How many acres are in the N¼ of the SW¼ of the NE¼ of section 32?
    a. 7.5
    b. 10
    c. 60
    d. 480

36. John sold the N½ of the SW¼ of the NW¼ of section 10 and all of section 9 to James for $1,200 per acre. How much did Mr. Johns pay Mr. James for this land?
    a. $768,000
    b. $780,000
    c. $792,000
    d. $840,000

37. Prorate the annual taxes of $3,600 for an August 28 closing using a statutory year through the day of closing. (Taxes are paid in arrears.)
    a. $2,347.40 debit seller
    b. $2,347.40 credit buyer
    c. $2,370 debit seller
    d. $2,370 debit buyer

38. A loan with an outstanding balance of $148,600 is being assumed. The loan was taken at 9 percent annual interest back in 1991 and is current in its payments as of June 1. What credit will the buyer receive from the seller at closing on June 16 for interest if the proration is calculated using a regular calendar year through the day of closing?
    a. $512.98
    b. $520.10
    c. $586.26
    d. $594.40

39. Peter is purchasing a fourplex and closing on February 16 of a leap year. Each unit rents for $680, with unit 3 vacant as of February 1. Using a proration, how much rent will be credited to the buyer at closing?
    a. $914.48
    b. $1,165.71
    c. $1,262.86
    d. $1,500.69

40. Using a banker's year, prorate the insurance premium for a policy that was purchased on October 16 at a cost of $450. (The closing will take place August 20, and the contract calls for all prorations to be calculated through the day of closing.)
    a. $70 charge buyer/credit seller
    b. $70 credit buyer/charge seller
    c. $380 charge buyer/credit seller
    d. $380 credit buyer/charge seller

In problems 41 through 44, identify how each would be entered on a closing statement in the most typical transaction.

41. Earnest money
    a. Credit to the seller only
    b. Credit to the buyer/debit to the seller
    c. Credit to the buyer only
    d. Debit to the buyer/credit to the seller

42. Tax proration for closing in June of a given year, when taxes are paid in arrears
    a. Debit to the seller only
    b. Debit to the seller/credit to the tax collector
    c. Credit to the seller/debit to the buyer
    d. Credit to the buyer/debit to the seller

43. Loan balance being assumed
    a. Credit to the buyer/debit to the seller
    b. Debit to the buyer/credit to the seller
    c. Debit to the buyer only
    d. Credit to the buyer only

44. Proceeds of a new loan
    a. Debit to the buyer only
    b. Credit to the buyer only
    c. Debit to the buyer/credit to the seller
    d. Credit to the seller only

45. Another name for HUD Form 1 is the
    a. Transaction Balance Sheet.
    b. Standardized Closing Form.
    c. RESPA Disbursement Form.
    d. Uniform Settlement Statement.

46. Hilda's Hair Salon pays minimum rent of $650 per month plus 5 percent of annual gross sales in excess of $125,000. What monthly rent total will Hilda pay in a year in which her gross sales are $155,000?

   a. $125
   b. $645.83
   c. $775
   d. $1,295.83

47. Another tenant in the center where Hilda's salon is located (see problem 46) has a lease that requires a minimum monthly rental of $1,200 plus a percentage of gross annual sales in excess of $360,000. If gross sales were $528,000 and the tenant paid a total of $26,160 in rent, what percentage is stated in the lease?

   a. 6 percent
   b. 6.5 percent
   c. 7 percent
   d. 7.5 percent

48. Joan earns $78,000 annually. While she has several credit issues, a lender will permit her to devote 24 percent of her gross monthly income to a principal and interest payment. How much can she spend each month for this payment if she can get a 15-year, 95 percent conventional loan that requires monthly payments of $784? (The loan is offered with 4.875 percent annual interest.)

   a. $1,487
   b. $1,537
   c. $1,547
   d. $1,560

49. Prorate the taxes for an April 4 closing using a regular calendar year and prorating through the day of closing. If the tax rate is $3.80 per $100 of valuation on a home with an assessed value of $203,000, the credit to the buyer is

   a. $1,965.48.
   b. $1,986.62.
   c. $1,992.78.
   d. $2,014.21.

50. What is the down payment on a home that sells for $398,000 if the buyer gets a 90 percent conventional loan for 30 years at 4.5 percent interest? (The transaction will close on December 6. The appraiser estimates the market value of the home to be $388,000.)

   a. $38,800
   b. $39,800
   c. $47,900
   d. $79,600

SOLUTIONS: REVIEW EXAM

1. (b) $345,000 - $300,000 = $45,000
   $45,000 ÷ $300,000 = 0.15 or 15%

2. (a) $200,000 × 0.6 = $120,000

3. (b) $100,000 × 0.9 = $90,000
   $100,000 - $90,000 = $10,000
   $10,000 ÷ $90,000 = 0.111 (rounded)
   or 11.1%

4. (c) $132,500 ÷ 0.53 = $250,000

5. (d) $1,200 ÷ 0.5 = $2,400
   $2,400 ÷ 0.4 = $6,000
   $6,000 ÷ 0.06 = $100,000

6. (c) $100,000 × 0.06 = $6,000
   $100,000 × 0.05 = $5,000
   $486,500 - $200,000 = $286,500
   $286,500 × 0.035 = $10,027.50
   $10,027.50 + $6,000 + $5,000 = $21,027.50

7. (d) $18,000 ÷ 0.6 = $30,000
   $30,000 ÷ $300,000 = 0.1 or 10%

8. (a) 100% - 10% = 90%
   90% × 0.5 = 45%
   10% + 45% = 55%
   $1,200,000 × 0.08 = $96,000
   $96,000 × 0.55 = $52,800

9. (d) 100% - 4% = 96%
   $156,000 ÷ 0.96 = $162,500

10. (d) 75' × 125' = 9,375 square feet
9,375 square feet × $4.80 = $45,000
75' × $2.50 = $187.50
$45,000 × 1.15 = $51,750
$51,750 + $187.50 + $1,860 = $53,797.50
$53,797.50 = 93% of sales price
$53,797.50 ÷ 0.93 = $57,846.77 (rounded)

11. (c) $96,000 – $80,000 = $16,000
$16,000 ÷ $80,000 = 0.2 or 20%

12. (d) $240,000 ÷ 0.8 = $300,000

13. (c) 100% – 20% = 80%
100% × 1.1 = 110%
110% ÷ 80% = 1.375
1.375 – 1 = 0.375 or 37.5%

14. (c) 75' × 150' = 11,250 square feet
11,250 square feet ÷ 9 = 1,250 square yards

15. (c) 800 × 545 = 436,000 square feet
800' × 20 = 16,000 square feet
436,000 square feet – 16,000 square feet = 420,000 square feet
60 × 100 = 6,000 square feet
420,000 square feet ÷ 6,000 square feet = 70

16. (d) 6 acres × 43,560 square feet = 261,360 square feet = 0.6
0.6 × 261,360 square feet = 156,816 square feet
156,816 square × $2.25 = $352,836

17. (c) 48 × 18 × 0.25 = 216 cubic feet
216 cubic feet ÷ 27 = 8 cubic yards
8 cubic yards × $70 = $560
48' × 18' = 864 square feet
864 square feet × $5 = $4,320
$4,320 + $560= $4,880

18. (b) $185,000 × 0.75 = $138,750
$138,750 ÷ 40 = $3,468.75

19. (a) $235,000 × 0.22 = $51,700
    $235,000 – $51,700 = $183,000
    7 × 6% = 42%
    100% + 42% = 142%
    7 × 2.5% = 17.5%
    100% – 17.5% = 82.5%
    $51,700 × 1.42 = $73,414
    $183,300 × 0.825 = $151,222.50
    $151,222.50 + $73,414 = $224,636.50

20. (b) $250,000 – $60,000 = $190,000

21. (b) $250 × 4 × 12 = $12,000
    $12,000 × 0.95 = $11,400
    $11,400 – $7,200 = $4,200
    $4,200 ÷ 0.09 = $46,666.67

22. (c) 2,300 square feet × $74 = $170,200
    8 + 42 = 50
    $170,200 ÷ 50 × 42 = $142,968
    $142,968 + $18,000 = $160,968

23. (a) $8,400 – $8,000 = $400
    $400 ÷ 6 × 12 = $800 (rounded)
    $800 ÷ $8,000 = 0.1 or 10%

24. (c) $15,000 × 0.05= $750
    $750 ÷ 12 = $62.50
    $2,250 ÷ $62.50 = 36 months

25. (b) $300 ÷ 3 × 12 = $1,200
    $1,200 ÷ $10,000 = 0.12 or 12%

26. (d) $270,000 × 0.9 = $243,000
$243,000 ÷ $1,000 × $6 = $1,458
$3,600 + $1,800 = $5,400
$5,400 ÷ 12 = $450
$450 + $1,458 = $1,908
$1,908 ÷ 0.28 = $6,814.29

27. (c) $148,500 × 0.9 = $133,650
$148,500 × 0.1 = $14,850
1.5 + 1 + 0.75 = 3.25
0.0325 × $133,650 = $4,343.63 (rounded)
$4,343.63 + $3,800 = $8,143.63
$8,143.63 + $14,850 − $8,000 = $14,993.63

28. (b) 100% − 95% = 5%
5% = 0.05
$337,500 × 0.05 = $16,875

29. (b) $62,500 ÷ 12 × 0.25 = $1,302.08 (rounded)
$1,302.08 ÷ $5.07 × $1,000 = $256,820.51

30. (c) $348,000 × 0.53 = $184,440
$184,440 ÷ 100 × $4.25 = $7,838.70

31. (d) 23 ÷ 1,000 = 0.023
$175,000 × 0.023 = $4,025

32. (a) $150,000 × 0.60 = $90,000
$90,000 ÷ $100 = 900
$2,700 ÷ 900 = $3

33. (c) $152,000 × 0.66 = $100,320
$100,320 ÷ $100 × $2.50 = $2,508

34. (a) $108,000 − $28,000 = $80,000
$80,000 ÷ $500 × $0.50 = $80

35. (b) $640 \times 0.25 \times 0.25 \times 0.25 = 10$ acres

36. (c) $640 \times 0.5 \times 0.25 \times 0.25 = 20$ acres
   20 acres + 640 acres = 660 acres
   660 acres $\times$ \$1,200 = \$792,000

37. (c) January – July = 7 months $\times$ 30 days = 210 days + 27 days = 237
   \$3,600 $\div$ 360 $\times$ 237 days due = \$2,370 debit seller

38. (c) \$148,600 $\times$ 0.09 $\div$ 365 $\times$ 16 = \$586.26 (rounded)

39. (a) $29 - 16 = 13$
   \$680 $\times$ 3 = \$2,040
   \$2,040 $\div$ 29 $\times$ 13 = \$914.48 (rounded)

40. (a) Closing: Aug. 20; Expires: Oct. 16
   $30 - 20 = 10$ (days in August)
   $10 + 30 + 16 = 56$ days
   \$450 $\div$ 360 $\times$ 56 = \$70 charge buyer/credit seller

41. (c) Credit to the buyer only

42. (d) Credit to the buyer/debit to the seller

43. (a) Credit to the buyer/debit to the seller

44. (b) Credit to the buyer only

45. (d) Uniform Settlement Statement

46. (c) \$155,000 – \$125,000 = \$30,000
   \$30,000 $\times$ 0.05 = \$1,500
   \$1,500 $\div$ 12 = \$125
   \$650 + \$125 = \$775

47. (c) \$1,200 $\times$ 12 = \$14,400
   \$528,000 – \$360,000 = \$168,000
   \$26,160 – \$14,400 = \$11,760
   \$11,760 (part) $\div$ \$168,000 (total) = 0.07 or 7% (rate)

48. (d) $78,000 \div 12 \times 0.24 = \$1,560$

49. (b) $\$203,000 \div \$100 \times \$3.80 = \$7,714$

    J   F   M   A

    31 + 28 + 31 + 4 = 94

    $\$7,714 \div 365 \times 94 = \$1,986.62$ (rounded)

50. (a) $\$388,000 \times 0.9 = \$349,200$

    $\$388,000 - \$349,200 = \$38,800$

Measurements and Formulas

TABLES OF MEASURE

Measure of Length

1 foot (ft) = 12 inches (in)

1 yard (yd) = 3 feet (ft)

1 rod (rd) = 5.5 yards

1 rod = 16.5 feet

1 mile (mi) = 5,280 ft

1 mile = 320 rods (rd)

1 chain = 66 feet

1 chain = 4 rods

4 rods = 100 links

1 link = 7.92 inches

1 vara = 33.333 inches (Texas)

Measures of Surface (Square Measure)

1 square foot (sq ft) = 144 square inches (sq in)

1 square yard (sq yd) = 9 square feet (sq ft)

1 square rod (sq rd) = 30.25 square yards (sq yd)

1 township = 36 sections, or 36 square miles

1 township = 23,040 acres

1 section = 1 square mile (sq mi)

1 square mile = 640 acres

1 acre = 43,560 square feet

Circular Measure

Area = 3.14 × radius × radius

360 degrees (°) = 1 circle

90 degrees (°) = ¼ circle

1 degree (°) = 60 minutes (')

1 minute (') = 60 seconds (")

FORMULAS

Part—Total—Rate **(The "T" formula)**	Total = Part ÷ Rate Rate = Part ÷ Total Part = Total × Rate
Area and Volume	Area of a rectangle = Length × Width Area of a triangle = ½ (Base × Height) Volume of a rectangular prism = Length × Width × Height Volume of a triangular prism = ½ (Base × Height × Width)
Simple Interest	Principal × Rate × Time = Annual interest PRT = I I ÷ PT = R I ÷ RT = P I ÷ PR = T
Income Approach to Appraising	Net income ÷ Rate of return = Value I ÷ R = V I ÷ V = R V × R = I

Cost Approach Method of Appraising

Building replacement cost – Depreciation + Land value = Estimated property value

Straight-Line Method of Computing Depreciation

Replacement cost ÷ Years of useful life = Annual depreciation change

100% ÷ Years of useful life = Depreciation rate

Percentage of depreciation × Building replacement cost = Total depreciation

Amortized Principal and Interest Payment

Loan amount/1,000 × Money factor = Monthly P&I

Annual Property Taxes

Assessed value/$100 × Tax rate = Annual taxes

Glossary

Accrued depreciation   Straight-line (same amount each year) depreciation accumulating over time; for example, five years' accrued depreciation at $1,000 per year equals $5,000.

Accrued interest   Accumulated interest, simple or compound, that has not yet been paid.

Acre   A tract or parcel of land containing 43,560 square feet.

Actual age   The chronological age of a structure.

Add-on-interest   Interest that is calculated on the entire principal balance for the term of the loan before dividing the sum of the principal and interest into equal monthly installments. Example: 36 months, 6 percent loan on $10,000. $10,000 × 6% = $600 × 3 years + $10,000 = $11,800 ÷ 36 = $327.78 monthly payment.

Adjustable rate mortgage loan   A loan that may have periodic adjustments made to the interest rate and/or terms over the life of the loan. The adjustments may be made monthly, quarterly, or annually and may or may not be capped.

Adjusted basis   The acquisition cost of a property plus capital improvements less benefits derived from the property.

Ad valorem   In proportion to or according to value.

Altitude   The height of something above a defined base or plane.

Amortization   Liquidation of a debt through regular, periodic payments of principal and accrued interest.

Angle   A measure of the figure formed by two intersecting lines, expressed in degrees, minutes, and seconds.

Annual   Occurring once each year.

Annual percentage rate (APR)   A uniform measure of the cost of credit expressed as an annual rate of simple interest.

Apportionment   The process in determining annual ad valorem tax that distributes or allocates the tax burden over the properties subject to taxation; establishes the tax rate to be charged.

Appraisal   An opinion or estimate of a defined value of adequately described property as of a specific date.

Appreciation   An increase in property value.

Area   The measure in square inches, feet, yards, or miles of a surface defined by a length and a width; L × W = Area.

Arrears   Something paid after the fact, such as ad valorem taxes that are paid at the end of the year for which they are assessed.

Assessed value   Value established by local authorities for the purpose of assessing and collecting ad valorem taxes.

Balloon payment   A final payment on an amortized loan that is significantly larger than the previous payments.

Base   The beginning or foundation.

Base line   A line running east and west that intersects a principal meridian in the government (rectangular) survey system.

Basis   The purchase price plus the acquisition costs used to determine the cost recovery deduction for investment property.

Biannual   Occurring twice a year at regular intervals; semiannual.

Bimonthly   Once every two months or twice a month (semimonthly is the preferred term for occurring twice a month).

Building line   A line established in zoning ordinances or deed restrictions (restrictive covenants) beyond which no building or improvement may project. Also called setback.

Buydown   An upfront premium paid by a borrower to obtain a lower interest rate on an amortized-loan, usually expressed in points.

Capital gain   Profit realized when a capital asset is sold at a realized selling price higher than the acquisition cost paid by the owner.

Capitalization   Conversion of an income stream into an indication of value, used by an appraiser in the income approach to an appraisal.

Capitalization rate   The annual rate of return used to capitalize or convert the annual net operating income into an indication of value.

Cash flow   Net spendable income produced by an investment property after paying all operating expenses and any debt service.

Cash-on-cash A return expressed as the relationship between an investor's annual cash flow and the total equity position plus acquisition costs that the investor has put into the property.

Certificate of reasonable value The document that reports the estimated market value when a VA-guaranteed loan is being used to purchase the property.

Circle A single curved line connecting points on a plane equally distant from the center.

Circumference The distance around the perimeter of a circle.

Commission The percentage of the sales price of a property paid to an agent as compensation for brokerage services provided.

Comparables Recently sold properties, similar in features to the subject property, used to apply the sales comparison approach in the appraisal process.

Compound interest Interest calculated on the principal plus accrued interest not yet paid, as opposed to simple interest that is calculated only on the outstanding principal balance.

Conventional loan A loan that is neither insured nor guaranteed by an agency of government.

Correction lines Every fourth township line, which is adjusted to compensate for the curvature of the earth's surface.

Cost approach One of the three approaches used in the appraisal process; cost of improvements less accrued depreciation is added to the estimated market value of the land to arrive at an estimate of the value of the property.

Cost recovery The U.S. Tax Code name for allowable depreciation deductions on investment real estate and personal property used in the production of income.

Credit Money given to a party on a closing (settlement) statement for a real estate transaction.

Cube A three-dimensional figure made up of six sides meeting each other at 90-degree angles.

Debenture A voucher or certificate acknowledging that a debt is owed; a bond.

Debit Money charged to or taken from a party on a closing (settlement) statement.

Debt Something owed by one individual or legal entity to another.

Debt service The monthly or annual amount of an amortized loan payment that is made up of principal and interest.

Delinquent tax A tax obligation not remitted in a timely manner.

Denominator The bottom number of a fraction that identifies the number of equal parts into which something is divided.

Depreciation A loss of value over time experienced by the owner of a capital asset.

Diameter A straight line that divides a circle into two exactly equal parts when it passes through the center of the circle.

Difference The number obtained when a smaller number is subtracted from a larger number.

Discount point One percent of the loan amount, charged by a lender upfront to increase the yield to the lender.

Discount rate The rate that is charged to member banks when they borrow money from the Federal Reserve Bank.

Discounting A mathematical process used by investors to reduce expected future cash flows (income) to a present value using a selected annual rate of interest for a specified period of time.

Dividend The number being divided by another number.

Divisor The number by which another number is divided.

Economic life In appraisal, the period of time over which a property improvement will generate sufficient income to justify its continued existence.

Economic rent A synonym for market rent; the rent a property will generate when employed to its highest efficiency.

Effective age Based on observed condition by the appraiser, the age that the improvements appear to be rather than the chronological age of the improvements.

Equalization The adjusting, that is, raising or lowering, of assessed values in one taxing authority to make them equal to assessed values in other taxing authorities.

Equalization factor The number or factor by which an estimated value is multiplied to adjust and bring the value in line with other properties for the assessment and collection of ad valorem taxes.

Equity An investor's cash position in a property; the difference between current market-value of a particular property and the outstanding indebtedness secured by the property.

Escrow account   A trust account established to hold funds belonging to others.

Fannie Mae   A corporation that buys and sells closed mortgage loans in the secondary market to facilitate the movement of loanable funds from one area to another.

Federal Reserve System   The United States' central bank that establishes and oversees the nation's monetary policies.

Freddie Mac   A government-sponsored enterprise established to purchase primarily conventional mortgage loans in the secondary mortgage market.

FHA-insured loan   A loan insured by the federal government to enable persons with limited financial resources to be able to acquire and enjoy home ownership.

Front feet   The linear measurement on the street side of a lot; the dimension stated first when the dimensions of a lot are given.

Government survey system   Another name for the rectangular survey system.

Graduated-payment loan (mortgage)   Fixed-rate amortized loan that begins with payments at a lower level in the early year(s) that will increase to predetermined higher levels later in the life of the loan repayment schedule.

Gross income (rent) multiplier   A number that will multiply annual or monthly gross rent into an indication of value.

Gross lease   A lease that obligates the tenant to pay a flat rental rate each period with the landlord being responsible for all property operating expenses, repairs, and so on, with no ability to pass unexpected costs through to the tenant; most commonly used for the rental of residential property.

Gross rent multiplier   See gross income multiplier.

Ground lease   A lease of the land only, on which the tenant is permitted to build improvements that remain the property of the tenant; usually long-term leases.

Height   The vertical distance measured from a point on the base of a figure to the figure's highest point.

Home equity loan   A loan secured by a portion of the equity that an owner has in a residence.

Improper fraction   A fraction that has a numerator larger than the denominator; a fraction that represents parts that exceed the whole.

Income approach   A step in the appraisal process that looks at the property's ability to produce a net operating income (NOI) and capitalizes it into an indication of value; NOI ÷ Capitalization rate = Value.

Index lease   A lease, usually a long-term commercial lease, that calls for rental increases at predetermined intervals, such increases being based on movements in an identified economic/financial index over which the landlord has no control. Rental increases are usually tied to a selected CPI (consumer price index) published by the government.

Interest   Rent charged for the use of another's money.

Interest rate   The annual rate charged by a lender for another to use that lender's money for an identified period of time.

Lease   A contract that grants possessory rights to a tenant by the owner of the fee estate in a property.

Legal description   A land description that is of such certainty and accuracy that one can locate the property; a description of property acceptable as defined by a statute of frauds.

Levy   To assess real property and establish the tax rate and amount of ad valorem tax due.

Linear foot   Twelve inches measured along a straight line.

Liquidity   The ability to convert the equity portion of an asset into cash.

Loan origination fee   A fee charged by a lender to reimburse the lender for the expenses incurred in originating a loan, usually expressed in points.

Loan service fee   The fee charged by a loan servicer to the owner of the loan for collecting payments from the borrower, seeing that the borrower does not slip into default, and forwarding funds to the owner of the loan per the servicing agreement.

Loan-to-value ratio   The mathematical relationship between the amount of the loan and the purchase price or appraised value, whichever is less.

Loss   The dollar amount by which the expenses exceed the income of an investment property.

Lot-and-block   A land description system that references the location of a parcel of land within a subdivision by reference to a plat that has been recorded at the county courthouse.

Market value   The most probable price at which a property will sell given an informed, willing buyer and seller and adequate marketing time for an adequately described piece of property.

Metes-and-bounds   A legal land description that begins and ends at a well-defined monument (point of beginning) and describes the connecting lines that create a parcel's boundaries.

Mile   A distance of 5,280 linear feet.

Mill   One-tenth of 1 percent (0.001); a means of expressing the tax rate in some jurisdictions.

Mixed number   A number containing a whole number and a proper fraction, as opposed to an improper fraction.

Monetary policy   Control of the amount of currency in circulation, as established by the Federal Reserve System.

Monthly   Occurring on an established date in each of the 12 months of a calendar year.

Mortgage   The pledge of collateral (property) to secure repayment of a loan.

Mortgagee   The lender in whose favor the property is pledged.

Mortgagor   The borrower who pledges the collateral.

Multiplier   A number by which a second number is multiplied.

Net lease   A lease that requires that the tenant pay defined operating expenses, such as taxes, maintenance, and insurance, in addition to an established base rent.

Net operating income (NOI)   Income that remains after an investor pays all fixed and variable operating expenses but before any debt service is paid.

Note   Evidence of a debt obligation and the promise to repay that obligation.

Numerator   The top number of a fraction; the number that is divided by the denominator, the bottom number of a fraction.

Parallel   Lines that always remain an exact distance apart.

Parallelogram   A plane figure with four sides, having the opposite sides equal and parallel.

Participation loan   A loan in which more than one lender owns an interest.

Participation mortgage   A pledged loan arrangement in which the mortgagor promises to pay part of the cash flow to the lender in addition to the principal and interest payment.

Payment cap   The maximum amount a monthly payment may be increased at any one adjustment period on an adjustable rate mortgage.

Percentage   An expression of parts of 100.

Percentage lease   A lease that requires rental payments as a percentage of the tenant's gross sales.

Perimeter   The total distance or sum of the measures of the sides or outer boundaries of a figure.

Pi   The ratio of the circumference of a circle to its diameter.

Point   One percent of the principal amount of the loan.

Prepaid items   Items appearing on a closing statement that must be paid by the borrower in advance.

Prepayment penalty   A penalty charged the borrower, usually a percentage of the loan amount, when a loan is paid in full in advance of the maturity date.

Principal meridian   Lines running north and south in the government survey system of land description.

Private mortgage insurance (PMI)   Insurance that protects the lender against financial loss in the event a borrower with a high loan-to-value ratio defaults on the loan.

Product   The result when two numbers are multiplied.

Profit   The benefit realized when something is sold for more than its owner paid for it.

Promissory note   The loan document that promises to pay and sets forth the repayment terms of the loan, including the amount of rent (interest) to be paid for the use of the money.

Proportion   Two fractions, percentages, or ratios that are equal, for example, $3/4 = 6/8$.

Prorate   To equitably divide the ongoing expenses of the property between the buyer and the seller to or through the day of closing (settlement).

Purchase-money mortgage   A loan, secured by pledged collateral, used for the acquisition of a property.

Radius   One-half of the diameter of a circle; a straight line from the center of a circle to its circumference.

Rate   A percentage; for example, the percentage of the principal to be charged as interest.

Ratio   Relation of one number to another; the result of dividing one number by another.

Real estate settlement   The final event in a real estate transaction when the seller delivers title and the buyer delivers money; also called the closing.

Real Estate Settlement Procedures Act (RESPA)   A federal law that regulates the closing procedures on residential loans that are related to the federal government, such as FHA-insured, VA-guaranteed, and conventional loans made by a federally chartered or insured depository institution.

Rectangle   A four-sided plane or figure with sides that meet at 90-degree angles.

Rectangular survey system   Another name for the government survey or U.S. lands survey system.

Regulation Z   A federal regulation that requires that lenders disclose the actual cost of credit expressed as a uniform measure known as the APR (annual percentage rate).

Remaining economic life   The difference between the anticipated total useful life of an improvement and its current effective age.

Replacement cost   The cost to build an improvement with the same utility as the subject using today's construction techniques and materials.

Reproduction cost   Today's cost to build an exact duplicate of the subject improvements.

Return of investment   Recapture of invested capital over time.

Return on investment   Profit received after recapturing the invested capital.

Reverse-annuity mortgage (RAM)   A loan arrangement that provides an owner payments over time against the owner's equity in the home.

Revenue cash flow   A loss, sometimes called negative cash flow.

Right angle   Two intersecting lines that meet to form a 90-degree angle.

Sales comparison approach   An appraisal approach that compares a subject property with three or more similar properties that have sold recently; dollar adjustments are made to the comparables' sale prices to make them more identical to the subject property and arrive at an estimate of the subject property's value.

Section   One square mile of land; 640 acres.

Security deposit   An amount of money collected at the beginning of a lease to offset monetary loss to the landlord in the event of default by the tenant.

Semiannual   Occurring every six months.

Setback   See building line.

Shared-appreciation loan   A loan arrangement that pays the lender a percentage of the profit when the property is sold; a form of participation mortgage.

Square   A rectangle with four equal sides.

Square-foot method   A method of computing replacement cost that multiplies the number of square feet of an improvement by the estimated construction cost per square foot.

Straight loan   A term loan; a loan that calls for payment of interest only until the maturity date, when the full principal amount of the loan is due and payable.

Tax credit   A direct deduction from the amount of tax due and payable.

Tax deduction   A reduction in the amount of adjusted gross income on which the tax is calculated.

Term loan   See straight loan.

Time value of money   A recognition that, over time, money in hand is capable of growing and becoming more valuable; money to be delivered in the future is presently worth less than its future value.

Township   36 square miles (sections) of land.

Transfer tax   A tax that is assessed in some jurisdictions when ownership of property is transferred from the grantor to the grantee and the transfer is registered with the state or local government.

Trapezoid   A four-sided figure that has only two parallel sides.

Usury   Charging an interest rate in excess of limits established by state law.

VA-guaranteed loan   A loan backed by the Department of Veterans Affairs to make home ownership more accessible to eligible veterans with limited cash resources.

Volume   Measured in cubic units; the space contained within a three-dimensional object.

Whole number   A nonfractional number; a number that is used in counting.

Index